Scratch
An Actor

NED SHERRIN

SINCLAIR-STEVENSON

First published in Great Britain in 1996
by Sinclair-Stevenson
an imprint of Reed International Books Ltd
Michelin House, 81 Fulham Road, London sw3 6rb
and Auckland, Melbourne, Singapore and Toronto

A CIP catalogue record for this book
is available at the British Library

isbn 1 85619 321 7
Phototypeset in 11.5 on 14.5 point Sabon
by Intype London Ltd
Printed and bound in
by Clays Ltd, St Ives plc

Scratch An Actor
A novel

'Scratch an actor and you'll find an actress'

Dorothy Parker

Cast

The Family

SIR MARTYN MILMAN	Actor, composer, dramatist, director
MAUDE HYDE (Lady Milman)	His wife, actress
DARCY MILMAN	Oldest son, actor
LYSANDER MILMAN	Second son, actor
IMOGEN MILMAN	Daughter, drama student
MAX MILMAN	Martyn's father, actor
AMANDA BOLLINGTON	Max's ex-wife, actress

The Milmans' Inner Circle

TONY	Butler, chauffeur
GRACE	Cook, housekeeper
VIOLA REDDING	Publicist
HANNA PAXMANN	Emigré actress
KURT KORNFELD	Medical student, Hanna's son
HARRY HARMON	Producer
BILLY LITTLE	Agent
ADELA SKELTON	Contralto
FREDA AUGUST	Musical secretary
DYMPHNA OATES	Casting director
CEDRIC BISHOP	Designer
TOMMY TANQUERAY	Designer
CARL SHELTON	Musical director

America

ZELDA FANE	Hollywood musical star
BRADEN JEFFERSON	Actor
KEATE WATERSHED	Western movie star
GOTTFRIED SAXON	Director
LOUIS ARMBRUSTER	Choreographer

Fleet street

CHAUNCEY MARTIN — Journalist

Australia

VICTOR INGRAMS	Solicitor
MAE MADELY	Librarian
MRS TUSSOCH	Landlady
MADGE PARSONS	Amateur actress
MAISIE MARY HANNIGAN	Mae's grandmother
NANCY LOLA HANNIGAN	Mae's great-grandmother
ROMANY FRENCH	Actress-manager
RALPH DONALDSON	Impresario
DOROTHY DONALDSON	Ralph's sister
NELLY O'KEEFE	Hostess
BEN TEAL	Director
MARIE DE BRAY	Brothel-keeper
FIFI DE BRAY	Marie's daughter
RAY COMSTOCK	Actor
JOSS BIMROSE	Gold prospector
JOHN FLYNN	Padre
ESME NAPIER	Farmer's widow
GREGAN MCMAHON	Director
BEAUMONT COOPER	Producer
LOTTIE LOVELY	Beaumont's wife, actress
VIVIAN VAN DAWN	Film director
FRED L CURTIS	Reporter
'BLUEY'	Assistant director
HORATIO LIGHTBEAM	Medium
MRS LIGHTBEAM	Horatio's Wife
PINKERTON FROND	Psychic investigator

Bristol

SIMON COLDSTREAM	Prefect
REVEREND BLAKISTON	Housemaster
AUNTIE	Proprietor of a gay bar
COLIN	Informer
BISHOP	Soldier
MCNAB	Soldier
WELLS	Solicitor
KHAKI ROBERTS	QC
BLYTHELEY-CHAPLIN	Prosecuting counsel
RONALD	Stage doorman
REG	Production manager

ROBERT CASWELL   Stage manager
MR JUSTICE ORMSKIRK   Judge

On board Orsova

EVADNE RIVERS   Actress
AUBREY DESBOROUGH   Actor-manager
HERMIONE DESBOROUGH   Aubrey's wife, actress
GERALD   Juvenile
ARCHIE DURRANT   Passenger

Small Roles

Lance Baverstock, BBC radio drama producer;
Bobby, waiter;
Adrian Arbuthnot, actor;
Fanny Forsyth, touring actress;
Fairfax, doctor;
Wendy Baldpate, choreographer's assistant;
Masterson, producer.

Cameos

Sir Godfrey Teale, George Edwardes,
Oscar Wilde, Olga Nethersole,
Mercedes de Acosta, Marlene Dietrich,
Greta Garbo, Somerset Maugham,
Dorothy Gish, Fanny Brice,
Ina Claire, Durakhova,
Sir John Nott Bower, Sir Theobald Mathew,
Mary Ellis, Elisabeth Welch,
Evelyn Laye, Pat Kirkwood,
Noel Coward, Michael Redgrave,
Rex Harrison.

Extras

Actors, stagehands,
waiters, goldminers,
farmers, dancers.

Overture

Sir Martyn Milman announced his coronation musical as soon after the king's death as his press agent thought proper.

Martyn had been lingering over the score and cherishing it for months, but for all that time it had remained his secret.

The young queen had been advised to wait some seventeen months for her big day. Martyn reckoned that the first week of the New Year was the right time to tell the world about his big night.

Pacing the shiny pine boards in front of the high windows of his first-floor drawing-room in St Leonard's Terrace, Martyn congratulated himself on the economy of his press release. 'Sir Martyn Milman has completed a musical play, *In Society!*, based on Oscar Wilde's *An Ideal Husband*, which he is offering as his contribution to the coronation festivities. Sir Martyn has, as usual, written book, music and lyrics. Sir Martyn will direct and take the leading role.'

Martyn smoothed the ends of the neat moustache he had decided to grow for the role of Sir Robert Chiltern. He turned back from the Chelsea view he loved, winter sun brightening the playing-fields in front of the Royal Hospital, to check in the Chippendale looking-glass how his new acquisition was coming on. The adoring eyes of Viola Redding, his personal publicist, followed the casual movement. 'You haven't had a moustache since *April in Provence*,' she said. 'It makes you look even more distinguished.'

Martyn pulled in his stomach and turned his tall, slim figure sideways to see what the moustache did to his famous profile. He was pleased with the effect until he spotted a piece of fluff on the shoulder of his dove-grey suit. 'I thought I'd base him on Anthony Eden,' he said, flicking away the imperfection.

'You could be Anthony Eden,' said Vi loyally. 'But younger, of course,' she added hastily. Ever since his fortieth birthday her employer had fretted about his age. 'And stronger.'

Martyn was satisfied with both his appearance and his strategy. Having lit the blue touch-paper, all he now had to do was stand well away and watch the fireworks.

'I suppose we sit back and wait for the Pensioners to ring, Vi,' he sighed.

Sir Martyn was strong in his loyalty to his old colleagues, affectionately known as the 'Pensioners'. Few of them worked regularly for other managers.

'Have you found something for all of them, dear?' Vi asked. 'Any problems for me? Any naughty boys?'

Vi was not the very best person for grabbing headlines but she was tireless in scotching scandals. An indiscretion in a public place by an actor on tour and 'under creative strain' was meat and drink to Vi. She seemed to have a hot-line to a whole network of chief constables. The theatre is special, Vi used to tell herself, all those hot-house plants – so beautiful, so forced, so frail. And it wasn't only 'her naughty boys'. She remembered the unfortunate Dulcie Monat's wrists tentatively slashed in the Randolph at Oxford when her second act number was taken away – not a moment too soon. Nutcombe Hawkins's lovely young head languishing in a gas oven in Greenwich Village during Martyn's last pre-war Broadway season. That was personal desperation, of course. Nutcombe had still been giving an impeccable perform-ance on stage. The one Vi had been unable to help was Vincent Nolan. It wasn't really her responsibility. He took the pills on New Year's Eve less than a year after his lover's death. Vincent was forty; Dominick, a choreographer who had often worked for Martyn, over seventy. Everyone thought Vincent had 'been in it only for the money'. Death was Vincent's drastic way of publicly contradicting them.

'I'm not sure about the Pensioners this time, Vi,' Martyn warned her. 'They may have to pocket their pride and make up a sort of glorified chorus. You see I've had an idea. What's called a "gimmick".' He flourished the word.

Viola Redding knew better than to second-guess the gimmick which was making her employer look so extraordinarily pleased with himself. It was past noon and for a few moments Martyn kept his secret smugly to himself.

He poured a generous glass of dry sherry and handed Vi the darker, sweeter one she preferred. They touched glasses in celebration of the morning's work.

'The Play!' Vi toasted.

'The Family!' said Martyn.

'The *family*?'

'That's my gimmick! I'm going to cast my entire bloody family!'

Lady Milman, tall, blonde, pale and gracious, had long grown used to her husband's impatience with her imperfections. Now she was at Broadcasting House recording a radio play for the BBC. The initial stratagem of the producer, Lance Baverstock, had been to persuade Sir Martyn to play Morell in Shaw's *Candida*, using her, Maude, as a bait. Unfortunately he was not the first to try that ploy and while Maude agreed enthusiastically, her husband had temporised, equivocated and finally declined, leaving Baverstock the embarrassing task of persuading Godfrey Tearle to play the role at the eleventh hour. It turned out to be his last performance. He was to die six days after the coronation.

Maude was enjoying herself. They were two days into rehearsals, and the attractive young actor who was playing Marchbanks was flirting with her in a very satisfactory manner. She wondered if there was anything for him in Martyn's new musical. He would certainly cheer her up on tour.

'Maude will play Lady Chiltern, of course,' Sir Martyn confided to Vi.

Maude Hyde and Martyn Milman had met in a repertory production of *The Vortex* in Liverpool. He was playing the Noel Coward role; she, an unrewarding flapper. It was one of those odd romances. Decorous, lightly played, innocent, exploratory. Martyn was twenty-one; Maude just eighteen. Martyn, tall, handsome, fair, had only recently realised the inevitability of becoming an actor. Slowly he was beginning to harness his bag of dilettante talents to an ambitious professionalism and was following the pattern of his peers by sliding into a romance for which he was not entirely ready. On the other hand, in the climate of the time getting married was expected and Maude was enchanting. He had lost his virginity to an actress friend of his mother's; explored and experimented delightfully with a couple of provincial leading ladies; and convinced himself that it was love at last with Maude when he found himself carrying her bags from Lime Street station.

They were assembling for rehearsals at the start of the new season – her first, his second. They exchanged histories. His tall, confident stride and the impressive list of parts he had been allotted for the season dazzled her. She was new to the profession. Her father, a retired soldier, had not been keen but her mother, a life-long Lewis Waller fan who had never dared to confide in her parents her own urge to act, was all enthusiasm. And what a stroke of luck, Maude told Martyn, that the local vicar, the Reverend Mr Phelps, knew a woman who had been running a drama school under the eaves of the Albert Hall since 1906. Maude told Martyn all about Elsie Fogerty whose Central School of Speech and Drama lent a little educational propriety to the not entirely respectable adventure of acting. Voice was Miss Fogerty's speciality and in 1913 the Bishop of London, dismayed by the noises some of his young clerics were making in the pulpit, had sent her a batch of them to learn to project. The Reverend Mr Phelps was one of the curates found wanting and now he in his turn recommended that Maude should benefit from the same discipline.

Martyn was impressed. He had slipped into acting when school and Oxford left him uncertain of what to do next. It was too late to go back to drama school but he was amused as Maude prattled on about Miss Fogerty, a dumpy but imperious old lady decked out in billowing robes, studded with unsuitable costume jewellery, her forceful baritone trumpeting from under a massive plumed hat. Her pupils were inclined to mock her obsession with the 'Voice Beautiful' but she drove them onwards. Miss Fogerty concentrated on elocution and voice production, backing them

4

up with physical training, dance classes and fencing. Occasionally she could be observed conducting an elaborate breathing exercise with one hand while waving a cheese sandwich in the other. The Reverend Mr Phelps made the initial overtures and after some scepticism from Miss Fogerty – 'Young woman, why aren't you at school?' – Maude was taken on. 'And,' she pointed out proudly to Martyn, 'of the fifty or so girls who were there only two of us went on the stage. The others were all debs waiting to get married.' She sniffed them away. 'Deportment was all they cared about.'

Maude had been determined. As her second year was ending she wrote several letters to provincial producers who did not bother to reply and one, enclosing a photograph, to Mr William Armstrong at the Liverpool Playhouse. Mr Armstrong was good enough to interview her in an office off Leicester Square the next time he was in London. He saw that her pretty face matched the photograph and, with half an ear, for he had more important things to ponder, heard her speak a little Shakespeare in Miss Fogerty's 'Most Beautiful Voice'. When he realised that she had finished, he engaged her on the spot.

Martyn and Maude were married at the end of the season and made their London débuts in *Pride and Prejudice* – a huge success for Martyn and an appropriately modest one for Maude, who conceived Darcy while playing the least interesting of the five Miss Bennetts and had to leave the run to give birth in 1932. Lysander followed a year later and Imogen in 1935. The Milman family's acting tradition was turning into a dynasty.

Unaware that his father was telling his press representative that his older son would be playing Lord Goring in *In Society!*, Darcy Milman was waking up in someone else's bed in Fulham. It was a large bed and in those uncertain waking moments he stretched out a leg to see if it touched another. It did not. However, he was pretty sure that there had recently been someone beside him. He concentrated, partly to reassure himself that he did not have a hangover – he didn't – and partly to remember whether he had been behaving badly the previous evening – he had. It all came back. He had sung the couple of songs and performed the handful of sketches that had brought him good reviews in the show at the Boltons, a tiny theatre off the Fulham Road. He had said a hasty good-night to the communal dressing-room and hastened away. It was a short show and there was time to get to the Queen's Head for a couple of drinks and the promise of new acquaintances. At first it looked as though the clientele offered only old acquaintances, which he was not anxious to revive, or plain acquaintances, which he was not keen to cultivate. Just before that desperate moment when he knew he must decide between second best, going home alone or taking a chance on the streets, he caught a pair of dark eyes which held his with a similar curiosity. Above the eyes was an attractive mop of black curly hair, below the thin nose and thin lips a thin, neatly clipped beard. Darcy looked away for a moment to ask the barman to refill his glass but the 'Time, Gentlemen' rush was on and there were a lot of gentlemen to be served. In the corner a man with a kilt was pounding show tunes on an ancient piano. When Darcy looked again the dark eyes had disappeared. He made another attempt to attract the barman – and was again unsuccessful. As he was about to give up the dark eyes appeared at his side. The bearded man was shorter than Darcy and a few years older, wearing a black leather jacket and jeans.

The jeans surprised Darcy. In 1953 a man wearing jeans was usually your plumber. 'What are you drinking?' the man, who was American, said, without attempting to introduce himself.

'Half of bitter,' Darcy replied.

'Cheap date,' said the American and, before Darcy could take offence, called out, 'Bartender!'

The barman turned immediately and Darcy recognised a pattern of authority in his new acquaintance which carried into their subsequent conversation. Louis Armbruster was a choreographer supervising one of the stockpile of American musicals which were dominating the London theatre. With hardly an invitation – more an assumption that it was mutually agreed – he walked Darcy briskly through the chilly night to his comfortable rented flat in Hollywood Road. As they got into bed he turned to Darcy. 'If you were thinking of running your hand through my hair,' he told him, 'it's a rug.'

Down in the kitchen at St Leonard's Terrace the other two Milman children, Lysander and Imogen, were clutching coffee cups.

Some of Martyn's Pensioners had penetrated his household. His dresser, Tony, doubled as butler and chauffeur between engagements, and Grace, a former dresser of Maude's, had given up the theatre long ago to run the house, nanny the children, act as Maude's companion during Martyn's absences and generally make herself indispensable. The third Pensioner, sitting in cosy conference with Lysander and Imogen, was Hanna, a refugee actress who had fled Germany in the thirties with a small son and a reputation based on her appearance in Brecht-Weill shows. Sadly it was a reputation which was not quite grand enough to hurl the English theatre at her feet. Her one break had been with the Milmans when Martyn revived *The Beggar's Opera* and thought it would be amusing to cast the Jenny Diver from Brecht's first *Threepenny Opera* in the same role in Gay's original. Most critics admired her singing but puzzled over a Viennese accent in one of Macheath's Marylebone whores. The engagement did not prove to be Hanna's passport to regular work but it did lead to a friendship with Maude, who discovered that Hanna was a miracle worker with a needle. Maude found a steady stream of little sewing jobs for her which provided a life-line during her moments of despair.

Hanna had gathered from Maude that Sir Martyn was hatching a new show and knew there was nothing in it for her. In this, she was ahead of Lysander and Imogen who were unaware of their father's plans.

Sipping her coffee and smiling indulgently at Lysander and Imogen, who were still easing the sleep from their eyes, Hanna contemplated her own day so far. While the young were going to bed at five she had got up to finish her work on Maude's frock. At eight she had gone to bathe and dress a curmudgeonly old bat for whom she performed this thankless service on the nurse's day off. At ten she went on to another of her regulars, a sweet old gentleman whose shirts she ironed once a week. Here she was given a cup of coffee and a biscuit and was ritually chased around

7

her ironing board by the aged satyr who always seemed relieved when she escaped.

'You were late in, Imogen,' said Grace with no hint of reproach.

'Yes. A lovely little dance at a house in Cathcart Road.' Imogen remembered it happily. 'One of the girls from school. There was a band and lots of boys.'

'The pimple brigade?' Lysander suggested.

'Certainly not. I danced with at least three men who were over twenty-five.'

'Those are the ones to watch, dear,' said Grace.

'They were all awfully sweet. One of them walked me home. We had a smashing breakfast on the stairs, eggs and bacon and sausages and then he walked me through the silent streets . . .'

'They weren't silent for long,' Lysander complained. 'I could hear you bawling "Singing in the Rain" – which it wasn't – all the way down Royal Avenue at about four o'clock.'

'An hour at which good little boys should be asleep,' countered his sister, 'and besides, he has a nice voice so we tried a few duets.'

'You'll be asking Dad to put him in his new show next.'

'I wonder if there's anything in it for us?'

'You're still at drama school.'

'But I've only got one term to go at RADA – he could easily get me out. It's not as though I'm going to win the Bancroft Medal.'

'When is he going to tell the papers about it?' asked Hanna.

'Vi's up there this morning,' said Grace. 'That usually means something's brewing.'

'I thought Vi's job was to hush things up, not to make a splash,' said Lysander. 'Still, I suppose even Vi can issue a simple press release. She's been doing it for long enough.'

'It'll be in *The Times* and the *Telegraph* tomorrow,' Vi said. 'When are you going to tell the family?'

'Maude knows, of course. But I don't think the others have an inkling. Imogen has a sweet voice. She'll be a lovely Mabel. According to Wilde she's my sister. I'm changing that to my niece

8

and ward. Lysander can't really carry a note at all; but the French attaché has only one point number so that's no problem.'

'There's nobody in the family who can play Mrs Cheveley, is there?'

'Ah, another coup! Zelda Fane!'

'Martyn, is that wise?'

'Nonsense, Vi!' Sir Martyn pooh-poohed. 'I telephoned Zelda last night. She's thrilled. She can sing, she can dance and she'll be terrific box-office. All that stuff's in the past. I've sworn her to secrecy.'

At that moment his telephone rang.

'It's for you, Vi, your secretary.' He handed her the phone.

Vi listened for a moment and then snapped, 'Deny it.'

She put down the instrument and turned to her employer.

'So much for secrecy,' she said. 'That nasty little man on the *Daily News* in New York has heard that Zelda Fane is coming to London to star in Sir Martyn Milman's new musical. He wants to know if Lady Milman approves.'

'Silly cow!' said Martyn.

Maude denied herself the pleasure of a drink with her Marchbanks as she left Broadcasting House and took a taxi to Sloane Square. It was an easy walk to St Leonard's Terrace and she wanted to breathe some air after a day cooped up in the basement studio. She loved the village atmosphere of the King's Road, the butchers, greengrocers and drapers whose small shops dotted the street along with old-fashioned dining-rooms, corner chemists and the odd jeweller and watchmaker. To get home most directly she should have turned down Cheltenham Terrace or, at the latest, Smith Street; but she wanted to buy some flowers and so far none of the shops into which she peered had blooms to please her. Post-war London was still drab and grey, and a splash of colour – even from winter flowers – always cheered her. She got as far as the Chelsea Palace before she gave up the chase. She paused for a moment outside the theatre to study the variety bill. Donald Peers, The Cavalier of Song, was top. Joan Turner, billed as The Wacky Warbler, was listed prominently on his right. She smiled as her eyes fell on Gillie Potter, The Squire of Hogsnorton. She and Martyn mixed little with variety people but she had met Mr Potter at the BBC and he had fascinated her with tales of Lewis Waller – his first London appearance had been walking on as a cowboy with Mr Waller in *The White Man* at the Lyric. She wondered if the children would like to come out to see him in the second house. His opening patter on the wireless, 'This is Gillie Potter speaking to you in English', was a family joke ever since Lysander had shone at English in his school certificate results – and not much else. Further down the bill two young comics, Morecombe and Wise, were listed in very small print.

Still flowerless, she walked back past the Pheasantry which looked decidedly the worse for wear and turned down Smith Street. She arrived to find that her husband had called a family conference. The children were all in the drawing-room on the first floor and so, to ram home the epoch-making seriousness of the occasion, was Martyn's mother.

Amanda Bollington, formidable in her mid-sixties, had never become one of her son's Pensioners. Her career had run along smooth, unsensational lines since the big hiccup some forty years before. Character roles had long been her lot – a dowager here, a severe nanny there, cosy nurse in *Romeo and Juliet*. She had been comfortably left by her second husband and chose her roles for congenial company, attractive dates and minimum exertion.

Maude embraced Amanda. She was not a difficult mother-in-law – indeed she showed very little interest in the Milman family of either generation. She enjoyed her independence. She had not been close to Martyn since his early childhood, had never acted in one of his companies and, sitting regally in a large armchair by the fireside, was frankly wondering why she had been summoned to what was obviously a family affair.

Grace was busying herself around the room with a large pot of tea and a plate of cakes – determined to keep her performance going until she could learn exactly what was going on. Martyn, who liked to be as theatrical at home as he was in the theatre, was waiting until the room was full to make his entrance. He was lounging in his dressing-room talking to Tony who, in his turn, was keeping an eye on the drawing-room door and checking the arrivals.

'Your mother's here, Martyn,' he said.

He always dropped the 'Sir' when they were alone and was punctilious about reinstating it in public.

'What's she wearing?'

'Purple.'

'That means she hasn't made up her mind what mood she's in. It's black when she's defensive; pastel when she's pleased; purple or lilac when she's being non-committal. She's probably intrigued by the summons but will be guarded until she finds out what it's all about.'

'Is she going to like the idea?'

'Don't fish, Tony.'

'Ready to make your entrance?'

'I don't think Darcy's in yet, is he?'

Darcy was at that moment turning the corner of St Leonard's Terrace and rushing towards the front door. He flung himself through it and took the stairs two at a time. He had only just extricated himself from Louis Armbruster's flat, indeed from his arms. Louis had insisted on a matinée before his departure.

Martyn paused at the door, smiled as he surveyed the full house and moved across to his mother, bending to kiss her lightly on the forehead.

'So kind of you to turn out, Mother.'

Tony who had slipped through the door immediately behind Martyn silently closed it and melted unobtrusively into the bookcase. Martyn took up a heavy paternal stance on the hearth rug and surveyed his audience.

'I think you know I've been working on a new show for nearly a year now. Well, I've finished it and I am going to offer it to the young queen as my coronation gift.'

'Does that mean you're giving her a share of your royalties?'

'Don't be silly, Lysander. It means I'm going to open it in coronation month.'

'When London will be crowded with tourists with nothing to do in the evening,' Amanda chipped in. 'I hope she doesn't come down with appendicitis like poor old Edward VII in 1901,' she added. 'That cast a blight on the whole season. Theatres were empty all summer.'

'The last time I had the privilege of attending on Her Majesty,' Martyn said pompously, 'she seemed particularly healthy – radiant indeed. I very nearly remarked on it.'

Darcy, who had thought that he might drift into sleep, pulled himself together. This could be his West End début. 'What's the show, Dad?'

'I'm glad one of the family – apart from you, Maude, of course – is interested in my work. I have completed my first post-war musical.'

'That lets me out,' Lysander interrupted again, 'I can't sing.'

'Nonsense. I have devised roles for the entire family. The show is called *In Society!*. I've based it on Oscar Wilde's *An Ideal Husband*. You will be playing the young French attaché, the Vicomte de Nanjac. You only have one point number. It's about the delights of the English language. It's extremely funny.'

'You can rely on Lysander to ruin it.'

Lysander hit his sister playfully. 'And Imo gets Mabel Chiltern, I suppose,' he said.

'Yes, I've made her my niece and ward instead of my sister. Your mother and I will play Sir Robert and Lady Chiltern.'

'What do I get?' Darcy did not know the play.

'Lord Goring,' his father told him. 'It's a very good role – lots of epigrams and you get to marry Imo in the end.'

'Who's playing Mrs Cheveley?'

It was the first question Maude had asked.

There was a pause.

'Zelda Fane. I'm bringing Zelda Fane over from Hollywood.'

'I heard her movie career was on the slide,' said Maude, as she studied the ceiling.

Partly to break the tense atmosphere and partly out of curiosity, Amanda intervened.

'I suppose you want me to play old Lady Markby?'

'Exactly, Mother.'

'And who is playing the Earl of Caversham?'

'Father.'

'Never!' said Amanda and, sweeping from the room, she left the house.

Max

Max Milman swigged at the second cold bottle of Toohey's beer in the bag of six that he had brought with him and considered his return to England after some forty years of self-imposed exile. God, Sydney had changed! What must have happened to London in the same time? Not that he'd seen much of London in the old days – or rather, not that London had seen much of him. Hoxton was as near as he had got to playing in the West End – though he knew the main railway stations nearly as well as he knew Crewe, the touring hub. But at least he had played leads during his peregrinations around the provinces, not ponced about downstage to some stuck-up London star.

He was musing in the parkland at the tip of Bradley's Head on the north shore of Sydney Harbour. Away before him stood a white naked steel mast, the celebrated fighting top of His Majesty's ship *Sydney*, which had sunk the German sea-raider *Emden* in 1914.

At seventy-three he was tall, straight-backed, bronzed and muscular. His shirt was open to his waist, his trunk-like, walnut legs were topped by baggy shorts. It was Sunday and looking out towards the south shore he could see past the Doric column which stood proud in the water proclaiming the beginning of a measured nautical mile. Once it had been part of the portico of the Sydney General Post Office.

Since arriving in Australia he had always enjoyed looking at the harbour, especially on Sundays. Never sea-minded at home, no matter how many times he had played Pompey, Plymouth, Liverpool, Chatham and the other naval dates, here he relished the flurry of little boats and the changing cast of larger vessels.

His adoption of Australia had coincided with the amiable separation of the Royal Australian Navy from its British parent. Sydney was the main base. When he first came there he was impressed by the solid grey conservative battleships which would sail to fight in the First War. Then, a few years later, came the nifty three-funnelled cruisers which elegantly patrolled the Pacific from their home base in the thirties. The Second War brought the spectacle of the huge carriers, some from America, some from the Old Country. Fashion was changing again and now destroyers entrailed with electronics were beginning to dominate the harbour.

Around them gambolled the fleet of pleasure yachts. Some, more sedate, glided through and, if he had bothered to put in his money and pick up a telescope, he would have seen plush Sydney sybarites slaking their thirst, scoffing cold food, burning their bodies and saluting one another as they crossed and recrossed the recreational water. A ferry plodded up the river to Parramatta; across its bows another plied to Manly, too far away for Max to hear the deck musicians serenading passengers as they sailed towards the choppy, unprotected water just inside the Heads.

Max drained his second bottle and opened a third. Many times he had taken girls to the early pleasure beaches of Manly and through the years he had absorbed the folklore of the ferries. When he first came to Sydney there was no Harbour Bridge and Sydney-siders hopped habitually on to the tall-funnelled craft at the Milson's Point ferry wharf and sped like flying fishes across the harbour.

Max saw himself as a bit of a writer. He had dashed off the occasional bush melodrama in his time (good roles for himself) and, from the moment he met Banjo Patterson, he had developed a facility for writing verse monologues which he would recite as curtain raisers or encores. One of his favourites celebrated an early ferryman, a Sydney character from the early 1800s, Billy Blue.

> Billy Blue was a blackamoor chappie,
> None knew of the place whence he came.
> In Sydney he lived long and happy,
> And that is the name of the game.

Max sighed. The fashion for recitation had long gone.

Across the harbour he could see the range of south shore buildings, from Woolloomooloo to Watson's Bay, a backdrop behind the skimming, scudding, tacking, racing yachts – eighteen-footers from the Sydney Flying Squadron. He could not pick out, but recalled, a Woolloomooloo eating place called Harry's Café on Wheels and a local speciality known as a Pie Floater – a meat pie floating in pea soup. He wondered if the food had changed much in England. In Oz it tended to be an approximation to the provincial food he'd known at home. Would there still be fish and chips as greasy as they were here in Sydney? Would there be cockles? And roasts? And Yorkshire? He opened another bottle and washed them down in happy anticipation.

He had come to the Head to take stock. He had never been a thoughtful chap. He saw himself as a sport. One who had some-how survived. Liked a jar. Stood his round. Sometimes a fool to himself. He had never felt homesick. Was he now feeling a little excited? God, no! It was a good life here even though he'd had his ups and downs.

Max speculated on what his ex-wife looked like now. Up to a point he knew. He'd seen her in a couple of cameos in British films which came to Australia. He hadn't looked out for her – just spotted a thickened version of someone he once knew. With his son it was different. He was a star. You couldn't go to a Martyn Milman picture unaware of what you were getting. They'd had no contact since the boy was barely three. He sup-posed that was due to Ruby. She had been Ruby Bollington when he met her. She became Amanda when she returned to England. He supposed she thought it sounded more West End. Or had she been trying to sever another link with him? He had gone the other way with his name. Maximilian Milman was a mouthful in Australia – so Max it became.

Why was he going back to England where he had always made a mess of things? The short answer was that there was nothing happening for him where he was; and the oily little creep who had arrived as Martyn's ambassador just after Christmas made it sound like a good idea.

Max was lying low in a boarding-house behind King's Cross. There wasn't much work. His I-just-happened-to-be-passing visits to his agents were beginning to irritate; his phone calls were getting past the front desk increasingly infrequently.

'When I was trying to track you down I told your agent it wasn't business,' Victor Ingrams said as he handed Max a card which announced that he was a solicitor. Max wondered what he might be served with or sued for, but the man with the briefcase and the pressed light-weight suit and stiff collar did not seem to be the bearer of bad tidings.

'It occurred to me,' he said, 'that as this proposition suggests a whole new start for you in London you might not want to be beholden to your Australian agent.'

'I'd be a better judge of that if you told me what it's all about,' said Max.

'Of course. Of course. How precipitate of me, Mr Milman. I am acting for your son's solicitors. Sir Martyn has a scheme in which he is extremely anxious to interest you.'

'I haven't seen the little bastard for forty years – except at the pictures.'

'Precisely. It is my job to break the ice. As you know the queen's coronation will take place in London this summer. Sir Martyn is planning a spectacular musical play. He wants you to take a part in it.'

'Bloody hell! He's never seen me act.'

'Perhaps your ex-wife suggested you?'

'She'd be more likely to suggest Florence fucking Nightingale! We haven't seen each other since she left me, and that wasn't on the best of terms.'

'Some months ago I was asked to go over the back numbers of the Australian papers to see if there were any reviews of your recent performances. I can't say I found many . . .'

'There haven't been many.'

' . . . but those I found were quite good.'

Max was disconcerted. The last review he had received was for a paid appearance with the Beacon Hill Players, a group of highly ambitious and desperately serious amateur women just outside Sydney. He had felt a fool giving his blind Tiresias in

Oedipus. Madge Parsons, the most serious of the serious women, played Jocasta and her bank manager husband was her son. They had not been able to cast Tiresias until they remembered Max and hired him. The only thing he had enjoyed, apart from the modest amount of money he earned, had been his make-up. 'If they want blind,' he said, 'I'll give the buggers blind!' He chopped up a table-tennis ball and painted it in vivid colours, made a pinprick in each hemisphere so that he could just about see and stuck them over his eyes. The local paper was impressed. 'Veteran actor Max Milman, a master of make-up, was outstanding as blind Tiresias . . .' He thanked God at the time that they had not mentioned his occasional lapses of memory – difficult stuff, that Greek rubbish. The Beacon Hill Players had boarded him on a mature post-mistress who was a fan and fed him like a prince. He persuaded her to relax the strict rules of celibacy which she had imposed on herself since her husband's death. It had been a pleasant interlude. The locals he met at the hotel bar were friendly and impressed. 'Glad you can see this morning,' said the jovial grocer, 'you had me worried when you nearly fell off the stage last night. Not much of a play, is it?' he offered. 'But old Madge was a great Joe Caster.'

'What sort of a show is the boy doing?' Max asked Ingrams.

'It's a musical version of *An Ideal Husband* – Oscar Wilde.'

'Rum bugger,' snorted Max. 'I was fifteen when they got the bastard. I was a call-boy at the Vaudeville – *The Strange Adventures of Miss Brown*, with Weedon Grossmith. Stupid piece but it ran over two hundred and fifty performances. *Ideal Husband* was at the Haymarket. 1895. George Alexander took Wilde's name off the bills. It opened about this time of the year. The first scandal was Wilde insisting the cast met to rehearse on Christmas Day. Old Charlie Brookfield wasn't at all happy. He didn't want to be in it in the first place. Took the smallest part, My Lord's Servant. It was all over the West End. He said to Wilde, "Don't you celebrate Christmas, Wilde?" "No," said Wilde. "Only Septuagesima. Do you celebrate Septuagesima, Brookfield?" "Not since I was a boy," snaps Brookfield. "Be a boy again," says Wilde. "Not if you're around," says Brookfield under his breath.' Max chuckled. He had not had a chance to tell this story for a long time. 'I was screwing Julia Neilson's maid at the time,' he added. 'That's who I got it from. What does he want me to play?'

'I don't know the play myself. I understand the role is the Earl of Caversham.'

'Don't know it either. I got out of calling soon after. Went into a stock company. We didn't do that drawing-room nonsense.'

'Apparently Sir Martyn is going to feature his entire family – including your ex-wife, Miss Bollington.'

'Christ!' said Max. 'I need a drink. There's a bar on the corner.'

They adjourned to the Antipodes bar where Max ordered himself a stiff scotch.

Ingrams sipped a beer. He drew a long letter from his briefcase. 'Sir Martyn thought it might take a little time to clear your affairs here . . .'

'Bloody Ruby!' Max muttered to himself.

'I understand there is no Mrs Milman to be transported to England?'

'Got shot of three after Ruby left me . . . and one before I married her.'

'Sir Martyn thought if you sailed towards the end of the month that would give you plenty of time to become acclimatised before rehearsals start.'

Max saw possibilities and rattled his glass on the bar.

'Same again, Max?' the barman enquired.

'Up to my mate here,' said Max. 'He's in the chair.'

'Same again,' Ingrams conceded. 'For Mr Milman,' he qualified.

'You do much theatrical business?' Max asked him. 'You seem to understand actors.'

'A thirsty breed, I am led to believe.'

'Any chance of an advance? I got a few things to settle up.'

'Sir Martyn thought there might be some outstanding obligations. I am empowered to make a small immediate payment.'

Ingrams handed him twenty pounds. Max slapped his knee. 'The next round's mine.'

'Not for me, thank you, Mr Milman, I must be getting back to the office. Here's my card. I'll let Sir Martyn know how pleased you are. He will be delighted. I shall cable him today.'

Max watched the neat little man make his prim exit and then

turned to the barman for another top up. 'Christ, it's hot,' he said.

'Come into funds, Max?' asked the barman.

'I'm going to England. I suppose you could say I was going home – only it doesn't feel like it.'

'I didn't know you came from England, Max.'

'How old are you, son?'

'Forty-two.'

'I could be your father.' Max did some laborious mental arithmetic. 'I'd been here a year before you were born.'

'Maybe you are,' said the barman. 'I never knew the bastard. Have one on me, Dad.'

By late afternoon Max was feeling sentimental; by early evening he was maudlin and by the six o'clock exit he was legless. The blowsy, middle-aged woman who had materialised to keep him company was wondering how much more he was good for. Smoothing her black sateen down over plump hips, moistening her heavily shadowed eyelids and primping her black hair which she had piled up high because some fool had once, long ago, told her as she sat astride him that when she let it fall around her face she was beautiful, she manoeuvred Max to his feet and piloted him out of the bar.

'Where d'you live, Max?'

'Follow me, my dear.' Max tried a courtly bow but keeled over and would have capsized had she not caught him.

'I can't follow. I'm bloody holding you up.'

Max stretched out an unencumbered arm and pointed shakily down the little hill which he had climbed so jauntily that morning. The woman, interpreting the gesture as a direction, supported him past a bottle shop, a pharmacy and a delicatessen. Suddenly Max stopped at an apartment building. Its front doors were flanked by two crumbling pillars. The roughcast which covered them was cracked and peeling. Some wounds were deeper than others. Perhaps a runaway truck had ricocheted off the sad structure. Max looked at the façade with loathing.

'A poor thing but my home – for the nonce.'

With an effort he made a little bow and motioned her forwards.

To her surprise he not only felt for, but found his keys. He let her in, climbed the stairs with only the bannisters for assistance and unlocked the door. There was a bed, a chair and a greasy stove.

'Shall it be chops?' asked Max. 'Or would Madame prefer me to fry her an egg?'

Having issued the invitation he passed out on the bed. She closed the door and straightened him on the stained and torn coverlet. Deftly she removed his coat and bundled it up to make an extra pillow under his head, but not before she had examined the pockets and found ten pounds which he had not yet blown. She also found a card. Because it looked legal and she was afraid it might connect her with the theft she was about to commit, she thought she had better take it with her. It read 'Victor Ingrams, Solicitor'. The name of the firm, Wyburd, Hunter and Wyburd meant nothing to her. She tucked it inside her black sateen breast along with the ten pounds and reckoned she'd give the bar behind the Cross a miss for a few weeks and go and stay with her sister Ena in Borowra.

Max opened his eyes painfully. Or had he opened them? Yes, it was dark and his head hurt and the angry red pharmacy light across the road fixed him with a glare. It shamed him into trying to remember. He recalled the woman first. With no enthusiasm. Indeed some distaste. Old fool. He stretched out a half-hearted arm but he knew she would not be beside him. Then it began to come back, to rewind. Swiftly and agonisingly alert, he felt for his coat. He couldn't find it. He lunged across to the bamboo bedside table and switched on the light. He surveyed the room. There was no sign of the coat. He turned over to bury his head in his pillow in despair and found that he was staring at his coat, roughly bundled up. He grabbed it and shook it down so that he could put his hand inside his breast pocket. Nothing. He tried the other. Bitch!

Max peered at his watch. It was midnight. He couldn't sleep. Staggering along the passage to the lavatory gave him much pain and then some relief. He remembered a chop that he had abandoned the night before and found it surrounded by yellowing grease in the primitive gas oven. It stared up at him like a giant reproachful eye. Perversely it reminded him of Ruby. He withdrew the pan, placed it on the top of the stove and lit the gas. Was this wise, he wondered? To hell with it, he'd feel better for a bite. He had eaten nothing all day and so he cracked an egg beside the chop to keep it company. And there was a crust of bread to mop up the fat when the egg had sizzled to completion.

As he sat on the edge of the bed, the enamel plate on his knees, and contemplated past, present and immediate future, Max could not decide whether to laugh the laugh of a man on the comeback trail, weep the tears of a foolish old drunk who had just thrown away his last ten pounds on a tart for whom he could not have performed, or, most soberingly, to wonder what his ex-wife was doing.

He stretched to get his coat and retrieve Ingrams's card. That was missing too. He cursed silently and cleaned the rim of the plate with the last piece of bread. He did not know how to run Ingrams down without his card. He dimly remembered other names but he knew that Ingrams did not have billing. He was an also-ran. Max decided to wait until morning. Ingrams had to find him sooner or later. But how was he going to manage for cash in the meantime? He couldn't touch the agents – especially as he was about to do a runner. He thought he might try Mrs Tussoch, the landlady. She would be glad to see the back of him so, if he could convince her that he really was going to leave, fully paid-up, he might spin a fiver out of her.

In a way Max was glad he'd passed out – even at the cost of a tenner. He might have got maudlin. Wept over the silly cow and explained that he was going home to his son whom he hadn't seen for nearly forty years. Who was now a Knight of the Realm and, possibly – he'd heard from a chap on a film set – a part-time poofteroo into the bargain. It could be lies of course. Max knew he had a wife. Lady Milman! Five Mrs Milmans were all he'd achieved, thank you very much. And there were probably kids. His grandchildren. How many? How old? Grandfathers brought presents, didn't they? Something Australian, that'd be the ticket. A couple of boomerangs and a pair of fluffy koala bears. That should cover all ages and both sexes. And he'd better get a copy of the bloody play. See what it was all about. That depended on how soon Ingrams showed of course. He wasn't going to spend Mrs Tussoch's fiver on Oscar Wilde. He hoped to Christ he didn't have love scenes with Ruby – Amanda. He'd better get used to saying 'Amanda'. On the other hand if it wasn't love scenes then it would have to be comedy. He didn't fancy playing comedy with Amanda. She had never had a sense of humour. She couldn't do it . . . he drifted off to sleep with one stinging thought about his ex-wife in his mind. 'Hm . . .' he muttered, 'she couldn't get a laugh if she pulled a platypus out of her pants.'

Then he slept.

Amanda

Amanda Bollington had not thought of Maximilian for thirty years. She had not thought kindly of him for forty.

The flat in Kinnerton Street to which she had moved when Archie died was the perfect setting for her self-contained life. The little street off Knightsbridge had enough theatre people to satisfy her occasional desire to gossip but it was equally easy for her to close her door and lead a life which approximated to the decorous pattern it had followed during her second marriage. Archie had been older, well-off, indulgent and only sufficiently interested in the theatre to applaud her successes and enjoy her company when she was between engagements. When he died she was playing in a long run and was grateful for the old show-must-go-on cliché which enabled her to disrupt her life as little as possible, mourn privately and move smoothly from the large, rather gloomy house in Roland Gardens.

Amanda arrived home in a state of shock. She was not a keen drinker but she slammed the door and before she could tear off her coat flew to the sideboard to pour herself a stiff brandy. She had seethed in the taxi she hailed in the King's Road, snapped at the young driver when he didn't know Kinnerton Street and now, as she swept into her kitchen, she swore uncharacteristically when she saw that her housekeeper had left her supper to be warmed up. If Ella had been in for the evening she could have moaned at her and it would have gone no further. If she raised a telephone to anyone the ghastly news would be all over London in five minutes. She could already hear the giggles behind the hands of those few who were still alive to remember her humiliation at Max's desertion and the sniggers of those whom she had sub-

23

sequently crossed when they grasped the ironies of Martyn's ludicrous scheme and Maximilian's resurrection.

Amanda had been a pretty *ingénue* – otherwise Maximilian would never have married her. Now, as she sat on her cream sofa in her cream drawing-room, her purple clad figure bulged considerably. Her neck, also thicker, flushed red and her face had set into a sternness which her current mood did nothing to soften. She stamped her purple shoes and kicked them off. As she got up to pour herself another brandy the telephone rang. Surely the press hadn't heard of her calamity already? Perhaps it was Martyn ringing to say that the whole thing was an enormous joke. Or perhaps he had called it off. She picked up the receiver and gave a non-committal 'Hello?'.

'Amanda,' gushed a voice, 'I've been ringing you for an hour. Where have you been?'

'Who is that?' Amanda was still suspicious.

'Darling! It's Evadne!' Evadne Rivers was one of her oldest friends but it had been some time since they had worked together. 'How could you fail to recognise the *voix d'or*, darling?' said Evadne reproachfully. 'What are you doing tonight?'

'Nothing,' said Amanda with some venom.

'Perfect. I've just decided to cook.' Evadne was a good cook, Amanda remembered. A better cook than actress. 'It'll just be the three of us,' she cooed. 'Lance is coming over – Lance from the BBC. I thought it was time I jogged his memory.'

Amanda agreed. Anything to get out of the flat. As she put down the phone she was puzzled. Surely Evadne was, how to put it? Away, in care, being looked after? Stupid thought. Obviously she was better. Her poor mind had healed. How nice, Amanda thought. Perhaps she was the first friend to whom Evadne had turned on her return to the world. From being a port in a storm, she quickly converted Evadne into a good cause. She would have to be careful with Lance, who was strategically placed to spread her news through the profession.

As she changed, Amanda speculated on just how Maximilian must be looking. She remembered her first glimpse of him when she – when Ruby – joined the company at Margate all those years ago.

She sat in the stalls watching her new colleagues in *The Sign of the Cross*. Maximilian was playing Marcus Superbus and she caught her breath at the easy elegance with which he moved in the Roman tunic. She knew the play for the romantic tosh it was: but although she had played it in another company she was suddenly excited at the thought of appearing opposite this charismatic figure. She sat forward in her seat at the back of the stalls, her attention to the strengths and weaknesses of the production diverted by her single-minded concentration on the handsome leading man.

The company manager slipped into an empty seat behind her.

'Quite a sight in full flow, old Max, what?' he hissed.

'He's wonderful. I've never seen him in London.'

'Happy on the road is Max. Lewis Waller suggested he join him once, but Max said what would he play? Waller had no answer.'

'When do we do *The Sign* again?'

'Tuesday. If Max takes a fancy to you he'll want a quick run of the wordies. If he doesn't you'll be thrown to the lions. He's an idle devil when he's not interested; but it's my bet you'll be rehearsing on Tuesday if not before.'

'Will you take me round?' Ruby asked.

'I'll take you to the Royal next door. There's bound to be a crowd of MAMS at the stage door.'

'Mams? Mothers?'

The man laughed. 'No, dear. Stupid girls! "Mad about Milmans" they call themselves. Max does pull 'em in.'

'Is Mr Milman married?'

'Is – was – will be? Who knows? He's the noblest Roman on stage and a French farce off it. You'd better go carefully, dear. There certainly was a Mrs Milman but she left the company before I joined. She hasn't shown since. There was trouble with an alderman's daughter in Halifax and we nearly had shotguns in Hull but he always dodges the thunder and gets clear off before the final curtain.'

The company manager took Ruby to the saloon bar of the Royal where he left her with the first actors to arrive. Two young recent Romans clustered companionably around her, swigging their pints as she sipped a lemonade. They fished for information about her background and for signs that she had noticed their performances.

'D'you know what else we're playing, m'dear?' asked the taller, whiskered, young Roman.

'I know those in which I am appearing. *Aurora Floyd, The Unknown, The Corsican Brothers, The Snowball . . .*'

'The lady knows her stuff,' said the shorter, rounder, clean-shaven Roman. 'Who were you with before?'

'A stock company at Northampton,' said Ruby. 'But I had been in pantomime as a very young girl and that more or less got me going.'

'What did you think of our little show?'

'I have never seen the play performed better,' Ruby enthused, though in truth she had not seen much at all, apart from Maximilian Milman.

Before the two young Romans could enquire further, the noblest Roman of them all appeared, attended by the deferential company manager. Maximilian Milman looked even more impressive to Ruby in his street clothes than he had in Marcus Superbus's short skirt. He stood fully six foot three. The eyes were bright and scanned the bar in a moment. She hardly had time to take in the long, brown, curly hair, the open friendly smile, or the strong chin above the green, knotted scarf, before he crossed the room and ushered her into a snug murmuring, 'You must be Miss Bollington. No one else in this hole comes anywhere near Phillpotts's description. Stout for me, Phillpotts – and I'm sure the lady will take a glass of champagne to celebrate our new stage partnership.' As Phillpotts disappeared Max added, 'And our off-stage friendship?'

'Oh, yes, I do hope so,' said Ruby, reckoning that there was little doubt that they would be rehearsing on Tuesday afternoon, if not before. 'I did enjoy your performance,' she offered.

'Old Marcus?' He dismissed it. 'Gives me a chance to flash the hams.'

'I am amazed that I have never seen you before.'

'You live in London, don't you?'

'It's my base.'

'Ah well, y'see, I don't play London. Never have. Got my public up and down the land. "Cock of the North" they call me above the Wash.'

'Never played in London?' She tried not to sound shocked.

'No. A touring life for me. Don't look so sad, little Miss Ruby. I have been up West, you know. The last time I was a call-boy at the Vaudeville. I must have been about fifteen. I soon had enough of that. I got out and worked in a few fit-ups – mostly proved to be dry-ups; but I crammed it in. It broke the ice. I played Utility first, later Walking Gentlemen, quite soon a good Juvenile and then, at Christmas, a Witch in pantomime. And Harlequin. I managed to play most things in the first couple of years, even Pierrot, but never Clown or, I was going to say, Policeman, but, as I've been on for Constable Bullock as well as every other male part in East Lynne except the babe, I've done the lot!'

'My goodness, you have!' Ruby clapped her hands in admiration and took the flute of champagne Phillpotts offered.

'See you at Treasury, old boy,' said Maximilian, waving him away to join the two young Romans. 'Then I joined Dacre Dawson,' he told Ruby. 'Dear old Dacre! Gone now, but he ran a very respectable little Number Two company. At sixty-five he reckoned he was getting just a bit long in the tooth for Romeo so I stepped in.'

'And you've never looked back?'

'Not so much as a peek over my shoulder – unless a pretty little girl was following me.'

He smiled over the disappearing froth of his stout and leant forward across the small marble-topped table. 'You and I are going to have to do quite a lot of rehearsing, my dear.'

Ruby smiled back. 'I love rehearsing.'

As Amanda got out of her cab she saw Lance Baverstock, the BBC drama producer Evadne had mentioned, paying off his driver. They met on the steps of the old Embankment house and mounted the interminable stairs together, resting on every other landing. Lance, tall and dapper in his charcoal suit, gave Amanda a gentle helping hand from two paces behind. As she looked down to smile her thanks she could not help noticing that his toupée had grown again. It had first appeared as a tiny decoration in the centre of his forehead some years ago. Then, as the hair grew scarcer on either side, it had to expand to cover the gaps. By now it resembled a small furry pet. At Brighton, where Lance took his weekend swims, it was worn bravely above the water, confirming Lance's firmly-held belief that no one had noticed. Amanda knew better than to compliment him on his unique growth; besides, she wanted to find out how much he knew about Evadne's condition.

'When did Evadne call you?' she fished.

'About five o'clock.'

'How did you think she sounded?'

'Full of beans.'

They stopped to rest at the penultimate landing. Amanda lowered her voice. 'I thought . . . I thought she was away. She was always highly strung. We go back to touring days. Then I met her on the *Orsova* coming back from Australia. We were both in H B Irving's company for a time. "Flighty" was the word we used for her in those days.'

'Funny,' said Lance. 'I thought she was away too, but then she rather suggested on the telephone that it was time I found her a role. I almost put my foot in it and said, "But I thought you were . . ." I just stopped in time and said "on tour". She was very sharp, said I knew perfectly well she didn't tour nowadays, so I said I'd see what was coming up in Saturday Night Theatre.'

Rested, they set out for Evadne's eyrie on the top floor. She opened the door with a flourish and 'Darlings' flew freely. It was some time since either guest had visited the flat which overlooked the Thames. They took their sherry glasses to the big bay window and made trite comments on the fascination of an endlessly changing river. Presently Evadne flew through to her kitchen and trilled an invitation to demolish her soufflé.

When Evadne produced the next course, 'Something clever with veal and mushrooms', they marvelled at her ingenuity in the face of tiresome rationing. Evadne simpered and confessed that one of the King's Road butchers had always been a fan. Then Lance directed the conversation to dangerous territory.

'I'm working with Maude at the moment,' he said.

Amanda tensed. 'How nice,' she offered. 'What's the play?'

'*Candida*. I was hoping to get Martyn too. He wanted to do it desperately, but unfortunately he was engaged on something big . . .'

Amanda jumped in with apparent interest. 'Who did you cast instead?'

'Godfrey . . .'

'Oh, he'll be so good. Did you see him at the Haymarket in *The Heiress*? I thought he was better than Ralph. How lovely!'

Before Amanda could develop her enthusiasm for Sir Godfrey Tearle, Evadne had divined the possibility of more work for herself.

'How exciting for Martyn!' she cooed. 'Something big. Do you know what it is, Amanda? Of course you must.'

'Martyn never tells me anything,' Amanda stonewalled. 'I shall be the very last person to know,' she said untruthfully.

'Maude thinks it might be a musical,' said Lance. 'Martyn's been spending an enormous amount of time in the music room and Freda August – you know, the woman who helps him with all his musical manuscripts – has been round to St Leonard's Terrace several times.'

'A musical!' said Evadne. 'Do put in a word for me. I had wonderful notices for *Riverside Nights* at Hammersmith. If it's a game old girl he's after, tell him I'm the one. Wouldn't it be lovely if we were both in it, Amanda?'

'It is highly unlikely that I shall be.' Amanda adopted her Mrs Danvers voice. 'Martyn has never put me in one of his plays. I don't see any reason why he should break the habit of a lifetime.'

Evadne followed her delicious veal with a blackberry and apple pudding which – with the wine that had accompanied the meal and the brandy which followed – induced a benign atmosphere in the room.

'It's been a wonderful evening, Evadne . . .' said Lance.

'Wonderful,' Amanda echoed.

'We must see each other more often,' Lance rattled on. 'It's so good to see you looking so well.'

'So good!' Amanda agreed. 'You see . . .'

'You see,' Lance took over, 'well, we, we both thought you were away, in care . . . Not too well.'

'Oh, I was!' Evadne lowered her voice conspiratorially. 'I was in a ghastly place! My dears, I *escaped* this morning!'

Martyn

Back at St Leonard's Terrace the scene was confusion's masterpiece.

'You have been rather sneaky about this, darling,' said Maude. 'Zelda Fane will look like one in the eye for me and you must have known that Amanda wouldn't hug her sides with glee at the prospect of being reunited with your father.'

'Bloody woman,' Martyn said. 'Why can't she see the commercial possibilities? It's a marvellous story! The press will lap it up.'

'How do you know if your father is up to it? You haven't seen him for forty years and he hasn't shown the slightest interest in you.'

'I had him checked out. He's been married three times since Amanda. He's still acting – just. His last engagement was with a bunch of pretentious amateurs outside Sydney. They paid him to play Tiresias: as usual there weren't enough men to go round.'

'Shall we have to find a bed for him here?'

'We might at first. He can have Darcy's old room.'

Darcy had fled the coop for his first studio flat.

'Do you think you can talk Amanda round?'

'I'll have to.'

'Can't you forget the old boy before it gets too complicated?'

'No. I've engaged him. I don't want to finish up with my father suing me for breach of contract. According to my man in Sydney he's pretty hard up. It was a lifeline.'

'You don't remember him at all, do you?'

'I *think* I do. Just. I remember a tall man. A big smile. And a funny smell. It could have been whisky. It was very different from mother's smell.'

'That's not much to be going on when you're casting.' Martyn snorted impatiently but Maude was in full flow now. 'And how are you going to change Amanda's mind?'

'I'll talk to her agent in the morning. The little creep is always sucking up to me. He'll have to do the work. Mother can afford to pass up a West End salary but he needs his ten per cent pretty badly.'

Martyn was being unfair to Billy Little and disingenuous to Maude. Billy had not been an agent for long and Amanda was one of the few established artists on his books. He had inherited her when his previous employer died and he had taken over the list. Neither Maude nor Amanda knew that Martyn had put up the money to enable Billy to embark on a course of self-promotion. But neither Maude nor Amanda knew of Martyn's off-and-on relationship with Billy, when he had played small parts in his company a few years earlier, or how useful he had made himself to Martyn since then.

'At least the children seemed pleased,' Martyn changed the subject successfully.

Maude was always happy to speculate on her brood, which contained no ugly ducklings.

'Darcy should be awfully good as Goring,' she enthused. 'He's so funny in that revue.'

'I hope so. I'm taking your word for it.'

'I do wish you could find time to see it yourself, Martyn. It would mean so much to him. It's on for another fortnight.'

'You're right, I really should.' Martyn saw the wisdom in agreeing with everything. 'I think it's going to be all right for Imo. I bumped into Kenneth Barnes at the Garrick last week and laid on the Royal connection with a trowel. We only have to decide if she goes back there to finish after the run or if he lets her off for good.'

'That leaves only Lysander . . .'

'When is his army medical?'

'Any moment. But he's bound to be all right. His asthma's always been even worse than Darcy's. They couldn't possibly pass him.'

32

'Good! So it only remains for me to reconcile the aged parents. God! What have I taken on?'

Billy Little carried on his agency business from a mews flat off Cadogan Square. He lived next door in a similar but vastly more comfortable and elaborately furnished flat. It was there that he welcomed Martyn at eleven o'clock the next morning.

'Amanda telephoned at the crack,' he said.

'I'm relying on you, Billy. I don't care how you do it, you've got to change her mind.'

'It does sound an attractive idea – Milmans at every turn! No pun intended – but it's not going to be easy. I've never heard her so steamed up. Was the old boy such a bastard?'

'I rather think she thought she could "save" him.'

'Fatal, dear.' Billy slipped off his velvet jacket and helped himself to another chocolate finger with which he stirred his coffee. 'Fatal! There was a period, brief, thank God, when women seemed bent on "saving" me . . .'

'Yes, but from a very different fate. My father's weakness appears to have been wine, women and the gee-gees. I don't think his head was ever turned by little boys – or big ones, come to that. I just hope the charm has survived; he'll need it for Caversham. Do you want to represent him?'

'Certainly not, he doesn't sound like my sort of man at all. Besides that, if he and Amanda are at daggers it's not going to be the easiest tightrope to walk – assuming, that is, that I can persuade her to say yes in the first place.'

They finished their coffee and planned their campaign. Billy had promised to ring Amanda back mid-morning. Martyn briefed him and then sat back, hoping to listen to Billy's performance.

'Oh no, dear,' said Billy firmly. 'I'm not doing this one with an audience. You pop upstairs . . . I've got a big surprise for you,' he giggled. 'Pop upstairs and stretch out in a nice warm bath. I don't want to have to lie to my client and pretend her great hulking son isn't in the room when he is.'

Martyn obeyed his instructions and trudged reluctantly upstairs. Half-way up he considered sneaking back and eaves-dropping, but knew it was beneath his dignity. In Billy's ornate

33

bathroom he filled the bath and amused himself with the comprehensive array of bath salts and finally dozed off.

Downstairs, Billy harnessed his most persuasive telephone manner for his assault on Amanda. He opened by suggesting lunch the next day.

'You see, darling, I want you to consider one thing before we meet. Apart from the fact that it's a good part in the original – I haven't read Martyn's script of course – I gather he's already committed himself to Mr Milman, so the show's going to go on. We have to avoid the appalling publicity if it gets out that you wouldn't do it. I mean, Martyn *is* your son and although he's not a babe in arms, you can see what the press would make of "Actor knight's mother refuses theatrical liaison with son's father".'

'Huh!' Amanda grunted. 'It's not much worse than "Son unites Estranged Parents in Love Drama". I don't even know what sort of old bugger's going to turn up.'

'You might have a pleasant surprise,' Billy said, pushing his luck.

There was a long, unamused silence at the other end of the line.

Eventually, Amanda said simply, 'I'll see you at lunch, Mr Little.'

'Good,' said Billy. 'Caprice. One o'clock. I'll telephone Mario now.'

'I haven't said I'll do it.'

'Of course not, darling. Sleep on it.'

'I doubt if I shall sleep.'

'Beauty sleep,' murmured Billy, cherishing some hope as he put down the phone.

Martyn came out of his beauty sleep in the bath, to find a large, dark young man in overalls standing over him.

'I just delivered some wine to Mr Little, sir. He said to bring you a glass of champagne, personally.'

'How very thoughtful,' said Martyn, taking the glass and recognising the delivery boy as Billy's big surprise.

The man hesitated, but, as he turned to go, Martyn decided to take advantage.

'Just a minute,' he said with a smile, 'would you mind putting your hand in the bath to see if it's the right temperature?'

Half an hour later the delivery man came down to Billy's sitting-room damper, wiser and, as Billy slipped a couple of notes into his hand, richer.

Martyn lunched at Rules with his impresario, Harry Harmon. Rules was where they had met when Martyn pitched his first project to Harry back in the 1930s. Since then, everything had been hatched at Rules and everything had prospered.

Harry Harmon was small and dapper, pink and plump. He liked producing Martyn's plays because Martyn was his only class act. He enjoyed his circuses, his annual ice shows and the very occasional boxing-match which he promoted, but it was Martyn to whom he looked for cachet, for a better class of customer, for a first night foyer with a buzz and proper reviews in the less popular papers. And backing Martyn was not an idle, culture-chasing whim which threw something incomprehensible and pretentious on the stage and emptied the theatre. Martyn had made him money.

'Put me out of my misery, Martyn,' he said. 'All right, I know it's a musical – is it a big musical? Is it a small musical? Is it *Bitter Sweet*? Is it *The Co-optimists*? Is it British? Is it a match for these American shows which are flooding the market?'

Martyn let him burble on, knowing that he was building up suspense for his own pleasure; but sharing some of the excitement of finally exploding his secret. The arrival of the head waiter provided another delay which increased the dramatic build-up. They both settled for the duck *à l'orange*.

'What are you having first?' Harry asked. 'I always have the potted shrimps.'

Daringly, Martyn plumped for an avocado.

'What's an avocado?' asked Harry.

'We had them in Hollywood,' Martyn told him. 'They grew on trees in the garden. They're just catching on here.'

When the curious green object arrived Harry inspected it suspiciously across the table. Martyn offered him a spoonful, placing it beside the pile of thinly sliced brown bread which accompanied the potted shrimps. Harry approached it gingerly, pushing it around his plate with his fork before raising it to his lips. Finally he popped it into his mouth, rolling it around for a moment before swallowing it.

'Taste's like dead man's flesh – not that I've ever had any.'

Martyn smiled. 'It's an acquired taste. In a couple of years you'll be wolfing them down, wait and see.'

Discussion of the great enterprise could no longer be delayed. Martyn revealed the source of his musical, agreed to play Harry the tunes as soon as possible and then explained his plans to cast the family.

Harry was intrigued. 'Brilliant!' he said. 'What state's your father in?'

'All in one piece, apparently.'

'How is Amanda taking it?'

'Billy's taking her to lunch.'

They discussed theatres and Harry agreed to open negotiations for the New Olympic in the Strand which had housed some of Martyn's earlier triumphs. The only problem was the choice of choreographer. Martyn had always worked with the deceased Dominick.

'I'll make a few enquiries,' he said. 'I can't think of anybody immediately. Perhaps there's an American – though it's elegance we need for Wilde, not energy.'

'When does Zelda Fane arrive?' asked Harry, trying to sound casual.

'End of February, I should think,' said Martyn. 'I'll send her my new discs of the songs so that she can learn them before she gets here. Do I detect some small romantic interest, Harry?'

'Well,' Harry puffed, 'I mean, she is a fine figure of a woman.'

'I haven't heard anybody say that in a hundred years,' Martyn laughed. 'Don't get your hopes too high. She's asked for travel for two.'

'Oh.' Harry was crestfallen. 'Has she got a boyfriend?'

'Or a girlfriend,' Martyn said. 'One can never be sure with Zelda.'

36

Max

Max Milman sat at a desk in the reading room of the Sydney public library. It was the first time he had ventured into the building but he had to fill his days until Ingrams, the solicitor, tracked him down again. He had coaxed breathing space out of his sceptical landlady but not enough cash to enjoy himself.

He pulled out the massive *Collected Works of Oscar Wilde* and lugged it across the room. 'Enter Lord Caversham, an old gentleman of seventy,' he read, 'wearing the riband and the star of the Garter. A fine Whig type. Rather like a portrait by Lawrence.' He grunted. I'll have to play it young, he thought. He was three years older than Wilde's character.

He enjoyed his first exchange with Mabel Chiltern, unaware of Martyn's masterplan to cast his entire family, and wondered who would be playing her. Then he arrived at Ruby's entrance. Lady Markby is described as 'a pleasant, kindly, popular woman with grey hair *à la marquise* and good lace'. Pleasant, he thought. She'll have to work at that. He was much more interested in the description of Mrs Cheveley. 'Lips very thin and highly coloured, a line of scarlet on the pallid face. Venetian red hair, aquiline nose, and a long throat. Rouge accentuates the natural paleness of her complexion. Grey-green eyes that move restlessly. She is in heliotrope, with diamonds. She looks rather like an orchid, and makes great demands on one's curiosity.' Max paused to take it in. Clever old bugger, Wilde, he thought, he's got me going. Might be in with a chance there. He read on. 'In all her movements she is extremely graceful. A work of art, on the whole, but showing the influence of too many schools.' He smiled and flicked over half a dozen pages until he came to his next entrance. The only things Max ever read were his own lines and the descriptions of the female characters in order to weigh up his prospects of a fling on tour. He belonged to that school of actors who, when asked if there was a physical romance between Hamlet and Ophelia, invariably answered, 'Always on tour, never in the West End.' He had grown up in a theatre where he was handed cue sheets rather than an entire text. He was relieved to see that his exchange with Lord Goring was only eight speeches long; all he had to do in the rest of the act was stand around and eventually walk Ruby off stage. Well within his range, he decided.

As he counted his lines in Act Two a severe-looking but young and quite attractive librarian hovered behind him. He turned the twenty-eight pages and smiled as he found that he would be able to put his feet up for the entire act while Ruby had quite a lot to learn. He was counting his lines in the third act and had got to forty-nine, including one speech of no less than a hundred and thirty-eight uninterrupted words – better learn 'em on the boat – when the timid librarian approached.

'It is Mr Milman, isn't it?' she whispered.

'At your service, my dear.' Max rose with an elaborately courtly bow, his actor's voice producing a shudder of hushes across the room.

'Hush!' the librarian joined in. 'We mustn't talk in the reading room.'

'Lay on, Mrs Macduff,' said Max gesturing gallantly towards the door with an expansive movement of his right arm.

'I didn't want to interrupt your reading programme, Mr Milman,' said the librarian when they were both safely outside, 'but I'm about to go off for my lunch and I was afraid I might miss you.'

'I'm glad you did, my dear, a little Oscar Wilde goes a long way.'

Max wondered if this was a fan, an autograph hunter or (why not?) a future romance. He followed the trim, suited figure down the stairs and into the hall.

'I would enjoy taking you to lunch, but I seem to have emerged from my lodging without cash – royalty and mummers,' he joked.

'Oh, that's all right,' said the librarian. 'If you can manage on a beer and a sandwich, I'll stand you.'

She led him to a bar nearby and Max's curiosity grew. It must, he told himself, be his body she was after if she was buying him lunch. He watched her neatly negotiate the crowded clientele as she piloted their plates and glasses back to the corner table he had bagged. Max decided that the severe office costume she was wearing admirably set off her pretty round face. Did her highly respectable exterior conceal a passionate interior? He wondered if, having taken the initiative so far, this surprisingly single-minded young woman would continue to lead. He flashed one of his professional smiles at her as she settled.

'Thinking of going on the stage, my dear?' he enquired.

'Oh no, Mr Milman. And by the way my name is Mae. Mae Madely.'

'Cheers, Mae. What can I do for you?' He leaned forward and smiled again.

'I've been thinking of you for a long time. I didn't want to get in touch with you, but when I saw you at the desk I thought, why not?'

'Why not indeed? No old chap like me is going to be offended if a pretty girl takes a shine to him!'

Mae backed away. 'Oh it's not that, Mr Milman. It's not that at all.' She said it with a fierceness that he thought excessive. After all she had picked him out. 'It's just that I thought ... I think ... that you are probably my grandfather.'

Max flinched.

'It was always a bit of a puzzle at home, but when Gran died I was going through her things. I found a box of programmes and cuttings – they were all about you.'

'A lot of young ladies were keeping souvenirs when I first came out.' Max braced himself for shameful revelations. 'What was your dear grandmother's name?'

'Maisie Mary Hannigan.'

This was worse than Max had feared. It sent his mind spinning back to his very first visit to Australia over forty-five years before. Before he'd even met Ruby. The headlines in *Truth*, a Melbourne paper with a theatrical slant, were something he thought he had succeeded in putting from his mind. Australia had been forgiving and forgetful when he returned with Ruby and Martyn after the disgrace.

Little Mae's revelation was a bombshell from the past. 'Mucky Mummer Milman' headlined *Truth*. Neatly underneath was written: 'Belts his wife'. 'Adulterous Actor' was added for good measure. The first paragraph was a sermon – printed under a crude but not unflattering woodcut of his face. 'The morality of stage players is often a byword in the mouths of goodie-goodie folk,' the opening text had read, followed by a lambasting of Max's philandering. It all came back to him.

At the time he was playing in an interminable piece of melodrama called *All is Lost* at His Majesty's, and the notices were good. He owed the job to the leading lady, an established Australian star, Miss Romany French. She had spotted him at the Britannia, Hoxton, on one of her visits to London looking for plays and strong leading men. His marriage to Nona, his first wife, had broken up and he reckoned an engagement on the other side of the world would put him in the best place when the proceedings came to court. He had not expected the Australian press to be so alert but plainly someone in London knew they could make a quid or two by speeding the bad news after him.

They opened in Melbourne on a Sunday and he woke on the Monday morning to find all the papers confirming his success. The praise stayed with him for two weeks before the bombshell exploded. *Truth*'s man in London had done his job thoroughly. 'Max is of the class of man who has backed out of his sworn obligation to protect, cherish and love his one-time sweetheart, Edie Nona Poke.' He revealed that Nona had a stage name and so did Max. Fred Milman did not sound nearly as classy as Maximilian so Max had changed it. Somehow the paper made it into an act of deception. Had he not deceived his wife and abandoned his only child? 'Well, all the world knows now, Fred,' *Truth* had thundered, 'and perhaps you thought in far distant Australia you might wait until the clouds rolled by. Whoever would have thought that what took place before Mr Justice Grant in the London Divorce Court on Monday, 5th February, would be public property in Melbourne on 24 March?'

Max certainly had not; but *Truth* had still not finished with him. First it confirmed that: 'The facts above related were told to Mr Justice Grant by Maximilian Milman's wife, who sued on grounds of cruelty and, what is more *damning to Milman's character* as a man, the Judge granted a decree nisi, with costs, and custody of the child of the marriage.' There was a sting in the tail before *Truth* gave its final body blow. 'Nona now resides with her parents in Plymouth, but her husband is on the stage of His Majesty's. How is the women's idol fallen!'

Max recalled the irony of *Truth*'s next barb. 'No doubt after this friendly little "puff ad" his presence in His Majesty's company will bring an added zest to the performance of *All is Lost*.' He remembered that in its theatrical gossip column the paper announced that 'Tommie Kingston has been fixed to play Romeo to Miss Romany French's Juliet'. Max had been expecting the role of Romeo.

Max's other transgression – his run-in with Mae Madeley's grandmother, Maisie Mary, was listed as an adjunct to the main broadside. Maisie Mary's mother, Nancy Lola Hannigan, the licensee of Melbourne's Civil Service Club Hotel, had sued him for repeatedly failing to pay for his drinks and dodging the rent for his lodgings. 'In June last year she told the District Court of Max Milman's capers. She sued the mean mummer, the lead of the Romany French Company, for £1.10s.6d and obtained a verdict for the amount with 5s. costs.' Finally Max was dismissed as an 'impertinent theatrical bounder'.

He looked across at little Mae and tried to see Maisie Mary's features in her prim face. It was not easy. This was not surprising – the memory of Maisie Mary had all but faded until he had been reminded of it a moment ago. He had last seen her at a tearful lunch in Weiser's Restaurant in Little Collins Street in Melbourne. The day had stayed in his mind because it was one of the few on which he had eaten two lunches.

Maisie Mary was pretty, Max was young and dashing, and afternoons on a bend in the Yarra River – almost an island, concealed under a tangle of blackberries and huge river gums – had produced moments of passion and a legacy of complications. Maisie Mary's urgent summons, left at the stage door of 'The

Maj', pleading for a meeting during her early lunch hour, had put him on his guard. Her tears, shed quietly in the corner of the restaurant, shielded by her hand from the throng of lunching ladies, confirmed his worst fears. She picked at her vegetable fritter while he attacked his crumbed Adelaide whiting. Max's only comfort was the previous experience he had had of this sort of situation. He talked to her gently and reassuringly. Did she want to have the baby? Would she welcome his hand? Would her mother consent after all the bad blood between them – she knew he was free to marry – she must have read it in *Truth*. Would she prefer him to help arrange . . .? He let the question hang in the air. They decided to put the question of marriage to Mrs Hannigan on Sunday and she dried her tears and hurried back to work. For Max it meant a quick dart down Collins Street and along Exhibition Street so that he avoided the Civil Service Club Hotel and a last lap through Bourne Street to the Grand Hotel where Miss Romany French was staying.

He entered from the door in Lang Lane.

Miss Romany French was sitting stiffly at a corner table in the oak-panelled room, looking as severe as the starched napkins. Max panted himself into the chair which she indicated imperiously. She eyed him through the tall cruet with the inevitable bottle of Holbrook's Worcestershire sauce and the spindly nickel trumpet which harboured a handful of dusty orange and yellow Iceland poppies perched dispiritingly at the top of their hairy stems.

Max was immediately aware that charm was not going to work. Miss French was a determined vision in mauve and heliotrope, her forehead hidden by a half-veil. There was little of the brave, frail heroine of *All is Lost*, or her forthcoming Juliet.

'You're late,' she opened.

'I'm sorry,' Max apologised, 'I'm sorry.'

'I've ordered for you. The crumbed Adelaide whiting and a T-bone steak. You'll need some food inside you when you hear what I've got to say.'

Miss Romany French toyed with her soup spoon.

'I run a respectable company,' she said. 'I am battling to improve the public perception of the arts in this country. When

42

I engaged you I did not intend to import to my homeland a drunken derelict who would overnight become a byword for debauchery the length of Little Collins Street and drag me and my company's name across the public prints and into the more sordid law courts.'

Max did not know what to say. He concentrated on his whiting, hoping he need never taste it again, let alone twice in the same lunch period. Miss Romany French sipped her last spoonful of consommé and waved it away. 'Bring him a beer,' she told the waiter.

'But you've been satisfied with my work on stage?' Max asked, unwisely.

'You are a competent actor,' she said, 'but, even if they aren't two-a-penny, actors can be hired. What *is* above the price of rubies is my reputation.'

'Everybody knows you are above suspicion,' Max tried lamely. 'Melbourne's answer to Caesar's wife . . .'

Miss Romany French did not smile.

'Surely a chap sowing his harmless wild oats doesn't reflect badly on an artiste of your stature.'

Max'd always thought there was more than a little of Queen Victoria about his employer and leading lady – besides her tendency to stoutness.

The T-bone steak, the beer and Miss Romany French's fish arrived together.

'You may have read that Tommie Kingston is to be my Romeo.'

Max nodded.

'An excellent actor – and a minister's son,' she added.

If a little young to play opposite a forty-year-old Juliet, thought Max.

'I had intended to give you Mercutio. Have you played it before?'

'Many times,' said Max, adding hopefully, 'and I've played Romeo. Perhaps we could alternate?'

'I am giving you nothing, Mr Milman. Nothing but the sack. I am firing you after tonight's performance. Young Tommie has learnt your role in *All is Lost*. He is a quick study and with the beard he will be very convincing. I am going to give you your return ticket, even though I don't have to, in view of your behaviour. There is a train out of Melbourne in the early hours which will take you to Perth. You will join the boat at Fremantle. Australia will be well rid of you, Mr Milman. We are a proud young country and we do not need the dregs of the British stage to bolster our artistic endeavours. I hope you are enjoying your steak.'

Suddenly Max felt easier. He was getting the sack but he was being sent back home straight away – before his appointment with Maisie Mary's mother. He tried to look disappointed, wondered whether aggrieved or even annoyed would yield better results, and finally settled for enjoying his especially succulent T-bone steak – he knew he would be unlikely to meet its equal in England.

Relieved that she had not faced an explosion or a demand for substantial compensation, Miss Romany French tucked into her sole with vigour. After all, they both had performances ahead of them.

Darcy

Maude finally persuaded Martyn to see his son's revue. It was the last night at the Little Boltons Theatre and the atmosphere was already charged before the cast realised that the great man was in the house. Not by coincidence Louis Armbruster was also in attendance. He had taken to dropping in and standing at the back during Act Two before whisking Darcy off to Hollywood Road. However, for the last night, Darcy had got him a seat next to his mother and father and Louis was committed to both acts.

Darcy had not warned his parents of the presence of his new friend. He knew that they were taking him out to dinner after the show and reckoned that he could manoeuvre Louis into the party. Louis, more calculating, monitored the arrivals in the foyer, watching with amusement as the seedy front of house manager put out the red carpet for the Milmans, soliciting their interval drinks order, introducing them to the revue's young director and finally piloting them to their third row seats on the aisle.

Slipping politely past them to his own place next to Maude, Louis thought he caught a flicker of encouraging interest from Sir Martyn. He had never discussed the father's sexuality with the son but as an avid spreader and collector of gossip it had not taken long after his arrival in England for him to inform himself of Martyn's versatile tastes.

He watched his lover's parents out of the corner of his eye as the revue progressed, joining in with Maude's enthusiastic applause whenever one of Darcy's numbers ended. Martyn, he saw, was studying the action through clearer eyes, laughing and applauding little but making a keener, more professional appraisal.

At the interval the front of house manager came to collect the Milmans.

'Isn't Darcy good?' he enthused.

'Yes,' Martyn agreed, 'a little rough around the edges but his timing is terrific.'

The manager ushered them towards his small office which had been hastily tidied.

'Who did the choreography?' Martyn enquired. 'I'm looking for someone to stage the numbers for my new musical.'

'I don't think you'd want Jean,' the house manager said. 'She's terribly slow, poor dear – they did an awful lot for themselves. Jean comes from the ballet and she's quite clever with the footsies, but the wordies confuse her.'

The crowded little dressing-room was communal. After the show Louis hovered at the door watching Darcy greet his parents and then lead them around the dressing-tables to present each overawed member of the cast. He was impressed by the way Martyn managed to find something complimentary to say to each performer without committing himself to endorsing the actor's personal certainty of stardom, the show's obvious potential for a West End transfer or the possibility of there being a perfect part going in his forthcoming musical.

Finally the little semi-royal caravan arrived back at Darcy's changing space near the door where Louis had draped himself.

'Ah,' said Darcy to Martyn and Maude, 'this is an American friend of mine, Louis Armbruster – Louis, my parents.'

'You seemed to be enjoying it, Mr Armbruster,' offered Maude, proud of her son's success. 'You got more of the jokes than I did,' she added, 'and I've seen it before.'

Louis was not about to admit that he had seen some of it several times. 'I'm getting acclimatised rapidly. It's been a crash course.'

'Are you working here?' asked Martyn.

'Yes, I'm a choreographer. I'm working on *Pennsylvania!*, the big show at the Scala.'

'Oh, we saw that! It was wonderful!' said Maude.

'Come and have a drink while Darcy changes,' said Martyn.

'I'd love to.'

A couple of minutes' cross-examination elicited that, although Louis had only recreated the dances for *Pennsylvania!* from Don Ericson's original Broadway staging, he was not without experience as a dance director.

'Won't you join us for dinner?' asked Maude.

'What a good idea,' Martyn echoed, as Darcy joined them. 'Your friend's dining with us, Darcy.' He turned to Louis. 'We can all pile into one taxi. We're going to the Tyburn. It's a little theatre club near Marble Arch. Quite new. They've got a tiny restaurant which is rather fun. The waiters dress like sailors but the food is definitely officers' mess.'

Louis did not let on that he already knew the Tyburn or indeed that he had started an affair with one of the waiters, which had ended only when he met Darcy. He wondered how discreet Bobby would be and half-hoped that it might be his night off.

When the Milman party was settled in an alcove he saw that it was not. At least Bobby was not waiting at their table – until he registered the party and, after a quick word with a colleague, changed stations.

Tight-trousered waiters were a new phenomenon and he made the most of his undulating progress as he advanced on the table.

'Good evening, Sir Martyn, Lady Milman,' he said. 'Such a long time since we've seen you here, Mr Armbruster.' His glance swivelled to take in Darcy. 'Something tells me you've been unfaithful to us.'

'You know what a hit the show is, Bobby. It's been the Savoy and the Mirabelle every night – but it's good to be slumming again.'

'Oh, Mr Armbruster,' said Maude, 'I do hope you'll enjoy it here. We could . . .'

'Don't worry, Maude, Mr Armbruster was only joking with the waiter, weren't you, Louis?'

'Of course. The Tyburn was a home from home for me when we were rehearsing. It was how I got to know the who's who of the British theatre.'

'Does everyone come here? We've only just heard of it.'

'No, Lady Milman,' Bobby reverted to semi-proper behaviour, 'but the dishes are all named after favourite or notorious stars.

47

You can start with Scampi Cedric Hardwicke – much more interesting than the real thing – pass on respectably to Pork Chop Patricia Kirkwood and finish off with a bang with Banana Brenda Dean Paul.'

While the others laughed Maude chose to be soulful. 'Poor Brenda. What a wasted life!'

Bobby was not easily diverted. 'How are you enjoying Hollywood Road, Louis?' he asked, advertising their earlier intimacy. 'Got it finally sorted out?'

'Settling in nicely,' said Louis, wishing Bobby would go away.

Martyn intervened. 'I think we might order, waiter,' he said, making it clear to Bobby that he was there to do a job, not to make trouble. 'Which page of *Spotlight* do you recommend?'

'The Avocado Aubrey Smith goes down a treat,' said Bobby. 'God knows who Aubrey Smith was!'

'Careful,' said Martyn, 'I played with him in Hollywood.'

'Clever old you,' giggled Bobby, pushing his luck and receiving one of Martyn's most severe stares. 'And to follow?' he recovered.

'Mixed Grill Godfrey Tearle, I think. It sounds a nourishing, hearty platter.'

'Dear Godfrey,' murmured Maude. 'He was such a good Morell.'

The party ordered and settled down to discuss Darcy's performance, the revue in general, and Martyn's new project in particular.

'When are you going to play us the score, Dad? You usually let us hear bits much earlier than this.'

'I've been more secretive this time,' Martyn admitted. 'It's some time since I tried a whole score. Times have changed,' he smiled at Louis, 'we've been invaded by Americans. I had to be sure I could keep up. I hope I have.'

'I'd love to hear the score, Sir Martyn.'

'I'd value your opinion.'

'Do you play yourself, Sir Martyn?'

'Only a little – but I've made a demonstration recording with Freda.'

'Freda?'

'Freda August – she's my musical secretary. She's a wonderful character. She sees me through from start to finish; transposes,

48

provides four copies, liaises with the orchestrators and she's price-less when we get to the auditions. No nonsense with Freda. If some ghastly girl has far too shrill a soprano, Freda sidles across and whispers, "She's been at the birdseed, dear." She knows everybody in the musical theatre. "Nice little arteeste," she hissed to me when we were auditioning dancers for *Fanfare*. "Nice little arteeste, but she's a bit too grand to do onsomble!" '

Freda August stories kept the family in a rich vein of remi-niscence through the meal and Louis was able to interpolate the occasional Ethel Merman anecdote, having been a chorus dancer with her on Broadway. On one first night, standing beside her in the wings, he had ventured to ask if she was nervous. She looked at him incredulously, said, 'Why should I be nervous? I know my lines' and strode on stage to massive applause. The Milmans were impressed.

The atmosphere of relaxed, jovial intimacy, heads bent together in casual communion, was having a bad effect on Bobby who, when not ferrying plates and refilling glasses, stood, hands on hips, by the kitchen hatch helping himself to generous gulps of House Red.

'I'm very keen to hear what you think of the music, Louis. Do you think you could find some time tomorrow afternoon?' As Sunday was a sacred family day in the Milman household Darcy and Maude registered the invitation as an important step.

'Certainly,' said Louis, sensing that he was doing well. 'What time?'

'Come and have lunch – Grace can surely manage to squeeze one extra slice out of the roast, can't she, Maude?'

'Of course, dear. Can we listen to the music too?'

'I think I'd like to try it out on Mr Armbruster first – perhaps we can have an encore for the family in the evening – if he approves.'

'God, what a responsibility,' Louis laughed.

'I might want to make some changes after you've heard it.'

'You know what Merman said to Irving Berlin when he wanted to make a late change in one of her songs?' The Milmans leant forward to appreciate a Broadway gem. 'She said, "Irving, call

49

me Miss Frigidaire, the show is frozen!" ' As they laughed an unsteady Bobby slammed down the coffee.

'Into her Broadway gossip, is she?' he enquired of the table. 'She tells Merman stories in her sleep. I should know, I've been there and had to listen.'

'Shut up, Bobby,' Louis muttered.

But Bobby was on a roll. 'They think they're special when they come over here, these American hoofers,' he sniffed. 'Let me tell you, back in the US there are more boy dancers than there are people!'

This proved to be Bobby's parting shot, digested in speechless embarrassment by the table. Before anyone could break the silence, a disturbance in the open kitchen distracted them. The chef-owner of the Tyburn had observed Bobby's behaviour in a state of rising shock. Bobby was in no mood for a lecture and, downing another glass, picked up an iced chocolate sponge and hurled it at close range into his boss's face.

Catching Sir Martyn's eye the man surveyed the shocked restaurant – 'Chocolate Gateau', he said, 'is off.'

Back in Hollywood Road, to which they had separately made their ways, Louis and Darcy conducted a lengthy post-coital post-mortem.

'Does your father know about us? Does he know about you?' Louis asked, after they had resolved the inevitable row over the Bobby incident and made up with the predictably passionate fuck which such jealous anger so often inspires.

'We've never discussed it. I haven't got to the age when I *have* to be married.'

'Do you know about him?'

'What d'you mean?' Darcy blushed.

'You must have heard gossip.'

'Of course we know. We simply don't talk about it. Mother doesn't mention it so why should we?'

'It all sounds very British – make no waves.'

'There was one squall. Years ago. It was Christmas and we were in Edinburgh with Mother. She was giving her Mrs Darling in *Peter Pan* and Dad brought Imo up on the overnight sleeper.

She had a nightmare and ran into his compartment where he was entertaining the steward in a particularly athletic display. Imo thought he was being attacked and went into shock. They stopped her just before she pulled the communication cord, which would have meant far more than the five pounds for improper use. Lysander and I sort of pieced it together from scraps of unconvincing explanation Mum and Dad offered and bits that Imo let slip. It gave me a permanent ambition to travel on the London to Edinburgh night sleeper, but I haven't had the chance yet.'

'You never know. If your pre-London tour takes in Edinburgh you might get lucky.'

'Oh no,' smiled Darcy sleepily, 'I shall be sharing a compartment with you.'

Martyn

At noon the next day Darcy left Hollywood Road and got to St Leonard's Terrace a carefully agreed thirty minutes before Louis. On arrival he hurried to the kitchen to gossip with Grace and Tony.

Maude greeted the choreographer and enjoyed his exclamation of delight at her impressive hall. Impulsively she offered to show him the rest of the house which she had arranged with a careful balance between family warmth and the grandeur which she felt Martyn's leading position in the theatre demanded. She had been determined not to let Rachel Redgrave, Meriel Richardson or even Vivien Olivier find fault. The dark-green, large-leaf pattern of the William Morris wallpaper had not yet become a fifties cliché, and it was new to Louis. He touched his toupée nervously as he spotted an imperfection when he passed the tall, gilt Chippendale looking-glass. Maude led him first into the dining-room which gave off the hall, laid for lunch. The claret, just decanted by Martyn, glinted with a ruby sparkle in the chilly winter sun. Two large portraits of his host and hostess by Ruskin Spear faced him as he entered. He considered them, his back to the window. Maude in cornflower-blue smiled down serenely. Martyn, who had chosen to be captured in his Hamlet costume, in spite of Agate's dismissive notice, was in sombre contrast. Louis realised how handsome he had been. 'Still is,' he thought. On an opposite wall hung smaller pictures of the three children, painted five or six years earlier when they were entering their teens. Louis inspected the faces of Lysander and Imogen.

'He's certainly caught Darcy,' he said.

'Isn't it good?' Maude agreed. 'And Darcy did fidget so.'

Louis turned and saw his own face again in another large glass, behind him the green of the playing-fields outside. He checked his hair piece again and smiled. Now it was perfectly in place. He followed Maude out to the back of the house where she indicated the terrace and its stacked white metal furniture, and then steps leading down to the large garden sulking in drab winter clothing.

'I do hope you're here in the summer, Mr Armbruster. The children live in the garden and it's so good for parties.'

'I hope so too, Lady Milman.'

'You must call me Maude. Everybody does.'

They climbed the wide stairs together, Louis stroking his hand along the smooth mahogany of the bannisters and pausing as Maude explained the provenance of the pictures on the walls. As the staircase wound upwards he could see posters of the Milmans' stage and movie triumphs. Maude ushered him into the oak-panelled, L-shaped drawing-room. Martyn was hovering at a drinks table poised with a cocktail shaker.

'I'll bet you haven't been able to find a decent Martini in this country, Louis?' he said heartily.

Louis wondered if Martyn's booming *bonhomie* concealed a nervousness about the new show. He had not found a decent Martini; but as Martinis were not his drink he had not missed them. However, he thought it politic not to disappoint his host and possible employer and accepted the cocktail happily.

The door of Martyn's music room upstairs was firmly shut as soon as luncheon was over. As they settled in two large armchairs Martyn started to give Louis a resumé of Wilde's plot.

'It's strong stuff,' he explained. 'There's a perfect junior minister – the ideal husband – that's me, and his wife – that's Maude. Then an adventuress turns up, Mrs Cheveley – that'll be Zelda Fane . . .'

'Zelda?' said Louis, raising an eyebrow, 'I toured with her once. National tour of *Anything Goes*.'

'And . . .?'

'She was certainly a draw. As much for the gossip as her performance.'

'Gossip?'

'It was Zelda's return to the stage. She'd been on Broadway before *Society Scandals* of course, she understudied Ruby Keeler in *Show Girl* and Ziegfeld gave her a bit in that last disastrous *Follies* in 1931.' Louis laughed. 'She loved to tell the story. Old Flo hired Reri, the dusky south Pacific beauty from Flaherty's documentary film about Tahiti, *Tabu*. The moment Ziegfeld saw her he wired some guy in Papeete, "SEND ME TABU GIRL WITH BIG TITS." "WHICH ONE?" came the reply. "THE STAR YOU FOOL" Ziegfeld cabled back. When she got to New York she couldn't sing or dance so she had to be shipped home; but not before she'd scandalised the city. She used to lean out of the apartment window and yell down to passers-by "Fifty cents to come up to my room". That was about all the English she knew. Joseph Urban had designed a great island set and Ziegfeld wasn't going to waste it so Zelda browned up, put an hibiscus behind her ear and sang "Dusky Dancing" in pigeon-English.'

'Was it a hit?' asked Martyn, doubtfully.

'God, no! Ziegfeld was *passé* by then. It was the next season when Zelda was spotted by Hollywood, in *Ballyhoo of 1932*. Luckily the show only ran ninety-odd performances and she was on the Super Chief in a flash. She was kind of the Queen Bee of the *Anything Goes* tour. All the gypsy dancers used to gather round her in her dressing-room, in the hotel, on the bus. God, she used to let them use her bathroom! And Zelda loved to reminisce. Boy, did she love to reminisce! She was a great fairies' friend.'

'A what?'

'You know, a queens' moll. We were in Des Moines one night when she opened up about your romance with her just before the war.'

'It hardly amounted to a romance,' Martyn said primly, 'but we did become friends.'

'Just good friends?'

'What was her performance like?' Martyn enquired hastily. He did not want to be drawn into the details of his time in Hollywood.

'Zelda always delivers,' the choreographer confirmed. 'She was no spring chicken but they surely knew who she was in the mid west. There were a lot of movie broads then taking their names and in some cases their talents out to the big arenas and the tents. That's where the standing ovations started. The audiences were her contemporaries. They were so moved to find she was still alive and could stand that they got up and stood for her themselves.'

'She can't be much more than forty – if that,' said Martyn defensively.

'And she still looks great. Anyway, audiences got so used to standing in the sticks that when they came to Broadway to see a show they thought they had to do it there.'

'What a horrible habit.'

'It doesn't seem horrible if it's you they're standing for, Sir Martyn.'

'Thank God it hasn't caught on here. We'd better get back to the plot. Sadly, Sir Robert – that's me – long ago sold a secret to a foreign power. Mrs Cheveley knows all about it. She tries to blackmail me into promoting a very dubious commercial scheme she's involved in. She threatens to expose me publicly if I don't pilot the scheme through the House of Commons. There's some very smart dialogue. "Scandals used to lend charm," she taunts me, "or at least interest, to a man – now they crush him. And yours is a very nasty scandal." '

' "Scandal" sounds like a song,' said Louis.

'It is,' said Martyn proudly. 'Very quick of you. I think we're going to enjoy working together.'

'Are we going to work together?' Louis asked directly.

'I've made up my mind. I made a few phone calls, too. Now it depends on what you think of the score.'

'Darcy says you're casting your whole family – is that wise?'

Martyn was surprised by his American directness, but relished it at the same time. He had assessed Louis as an ambitious professional and he knew he needed an injection of professionalism if he was going to succeed in the new climate of musical theatre.

'As it happens, they're all impeccably cast,' he said. 'Lady Chiltern is really a dull part but that's Maude's speciality and she has a pretty soprano. Darcy's playing Lord Goring, the playboy man-about-town who outwits Mrs Cheveley in the last act – and you know he can handle that sort of thing. What did you think of Imogen?'

'She was charming over lunch and very pretty, but in the States we don't audition over lunch.'

'She sings like a dream, she'll look lovely – the only thing is that as Mabel Chiltern, my niece and ward, she has to marry Darcy in the end.'

'So you'll have to put the brake on the passion in the duets?'

'They're playful rather than passionate. I don't think it'll be a problem. Lysander's a risk, he's practically tone deaf, but the French attaché is a tiny role and he's a good comedian.'

'What about your mother and father – how do they fit in?'

'With extreme difficulty! Oh, it's not the parts. Amanda is a natural for Lady Markby, a sharp old trout, and Lord Caversham is a peach of a part. All the best lines and not many of them . . .'

'But you haven't seen your father since you were two . . .'

'Darcy *has* been filling you in,' said Martyn. 'Nor has Mother. He needs the money and apparently can't wait to get out of Australia. She doesn't need the money and can't bear the thought of appearing with him.'

'Happy Families!'

'However, I've worked on her and I think she's going to come round. I'm not looking forward to rehearsing their duet . . .'

'I suppose I shall be handed that . . .'

'What a good idea!' Martyn laughed. 'I can see you're going to be very useful!'

'I aim to please, even if I have to punish,' said Louis. 'Discipline is a choreographer's first commandment. That leaves the chorus and small parts for us to audition.'

'We'll audition the chorus. For the small parts I'm more or less tied to what we call my Pensioners. I think an audition might come as an unpleasant shock to them.'

'And I shall also come as an unpleasant shock. Why don't we get it over with at the audition? I want to see them move and hear them sing.'

There was an ominous note in Armbruster's voice which startled Martyn. However, he was aware that he was investing in the professionalism of a new era and was surprised to find that he was already feeling a certain dependence on his new protégé.

'That leaves Zelda . . .' said Louis.

'Ah yes, Zelda . . .' Martyn mused.

Martyn stepped off the Super Chief at Pasadena early one morning in the autumn of 1938, having awoken in time to flush his face in water, put on a clean shirt and select his best Savile Row suit in case he should be met by any sort of official welcoming party.

As the bright Californian sun dazzled him he became aware of a bustle of activity, a dozen or more photographers and a short, stocky, dark man, immaculately dressed in a camel-hair coat and off-white fedora, smelling strongly of expensive perfume. He was pumping his hand vigorously but not looking him in the eye. 'Welcome, Martyn, welcome,' he was saying, exerting some pressure on Martyn's elbow with his left hand, until the visitor realised that he was being manoeuvred to smile directly at the battery of cameramen. Between routine displays of white teeth he took another look at the enthusiastic greeter and realised that he was Gottfried Saxon, the producer/director whose contract had brought him to California.

Martyn mumbled a few platitudes about how happy and excited he was to be in California, how it had been a long-held ambition and how he was a devotee of Gottfried Saxon's work. To star in Mr Saxon's production of *Middlemarch* was, he emphasised, a peak in his career. 'A career,' Saxon interpolated, 'of the utmost distinction.' Their pictures taken, none of the photographers showed much interest in these homilies and as they melted away Martyn was escorted by his producer to the largest car he had ever seen and driven to Bel Air.

Martyn threw himself into preparations for his first Hollywood movie, fittings, readings, and script conferences which Saxon encouraged him to attend, making him an unofficial consultant on idiomatic nineteenth-century English. On regular visits to Saxon's home he was introduced to Saxon's movies in the plush screening-room and to Saxon's galaxy of star acquaintances.

Gottfried Saxon had bought his seven-acre estate for a trifling twelve thousand dollars soon after his arrival in Los Angeles in the first years of the decade. In the following years it had been his hobby to develop it to cushion and facilitate his sybaritic tastes. Situated by a winding hillside road, it had been fenced with a twenty-foot brick wall which concealed the crazy-paving steps, the terraces studded with oleanders and camellias, the classical statues imported after his sorties to Greece and Italy and the spectacular swimming-pool from prying eyes.

Picturesque guest-houses were dotted around the grounds and allotted or occasionally rented to favoured friends and hangers-on; but the central mansion looking down over the estate and across to the Hollywood hills was the particular pride of its owner. Saxon's Picassos and Lautrecs, Bracques and Renoirs, and his Matisse, hung alongside a motley collection of awards and other showbusiness memorabilia – a sketch of Modjeska, a poster of Irving's last tour of America, a signed close-up of Sarah Bernhardt's eyes and an autographed letter from Junius Brutus Booth.

Saxon was guided by a couple of friends who found that, thanks to their high-pitched voices, the advent of sound had ended their careers as film stars. However, their erstwhile popularity and innate flair admirably equipped them for new careers as decorators. With them he remodelled the old house, already an echo of a handsome Italian villa, with shining parquetry, walls covered in subtle suede, sky-blue ceilings, ornate fireplaces of copper and pewter, deep coral sofas and armchairs ideally placed to give a commanding view of the manicured lawns through the enormous floor-to-ceiling bay windows.

To Martyn's impressionable English eye Gottfried Saxon's estate was all he had hoped to find in a Hollywood director's domain. At the frequent evening screenings he realised what a formidable body of work Saxon's was. Although the director's range was wide, his speciality was the European classics. Dickens and Thackeray had been raided profitably and staged lavishly alongside Hugo and de Maupassant.

One evening Saxon and his decorator friends settled down to screen *Bel Ami* for Martyn. The atmosphere was benign. The decorators twittered over the soundtrack, at camera angles, costume triumphs and old friends as they appeared. Martyn was admiring the ambitious, beautifully orchestrated ball scene when he became aware that the camera was lingering on a character, a darkly handsome young man whose function in the plot he was unable to identify.

'What role is he playing?' he asked as the camera sought the boy out for the third or fourth time.

The decorators giggled and looked at Saxon whose tubby figure shook with laughter. 'That is Braden Jefferson, Martyn. He is playing the role of a friend who needed a job,' he said.

'He's incredibly good-looking,' Martyn observed, 'but there doesn't seem to be any good reason to feature him *quite* so prominently.'

Saxon smiled again. 'Oh yes,' he teased, 'there was a *very* good reason! Would you like to meet him?'

Martyn knew what he was being offered. He had been expecting some sort of suggestion since his arrival. Far from home, enjoying the louche atmosphere of California, he admitted to himself that he had been looking forward to it.

'Why not?' he said, and saw Saxon nod to one of the decorators who padded obediently out of the room.

When Martyn retired to his guest cottage he was surprised to find the lights were lit and, as he opened the door, a fire blazing in the hearth. Naked on the hearthrug lay the young man from the movie.

'Hi, I'm Brad.'

'Do you think there's a part in *Middlemarch* for me, Marty?' Brad asked hopefully the next morning.

'I'll have to read the book again,' said Martyn cautiously. He could not see Brad's heavy southern accent fitting snugly into an English industrial town in the 1830s; but on the other hand he was reluctant to deny himself more of the delights which the previous night's initiation promised. 'It's a big canvas.'

'Have you read that whole book?' Brad was open-eyed.

'Several times. It's my favourite novel. I keep coming back to it.'

'Yeh, I do that with my favourite strips.'

'Has Gottfried offered you a role?'

'The old faggot said you were the best person to advise me.' Gottfried was making it clear that the gift of a role was in Martyn's hands. 'I'd like some lines this time, Marty. The close-ups were okay in the French movie but I'd really like to progress to dialogue. I think I'm ready for it.'

Martyn considered it tactically safer to stem Brad's flow of dialogue with some more live action and Brad, who reckoned he had made his point, joined in enthusiastically. But at the next intermission he returned to the business at hand.

'What's the name of the guy you're playing, Marty?'

'Tertius Lydgate,' said Martyn.

'Tertius? What kind of a name is that?'

'It's taken from the Latin for "third child". It wasn't an uncommon name in Victorian times. He's a young doctor. He turns up in the town of Middlemarch on a market day in 1829 bursting with idealism, and can't stop thinking of the improvements he's going to make, the good he will achieve, the hospital he's going to smarten up.'

'Doesn't he have a buddy?' asked Brad, hopefully.

'Not really. He gets involved with a vain, pretty, spoilt girl called Rosamond and makes a foolish marriage and then everything starts to go wrong.'

'Sounds as though he needs a buddy!'

Martyn broached the subject to Gottfried at lunch in the studio commissary.

'Trust Brad,' said the director, laughing. 'Lydgate's buddy! I don't think Miss Eliot would have approved. We'll find him something.'

'He was hoping he might have some dialogue this time. He said he thinks he's ready for it.'

'I bet he did. We'll make him the coachman who drives you in to town. Then he can say "whoa!" or "gee-up".'

'D'you think he'll be happy with that?'

'He'll be happy, Martyn, and if he's not, he isn't the only butt in Hollywood that'll be happy to accommodate you. Don't cramp your style too soon. We've got a long schedule and I don't like my stars getting bored.'

In the event, Braden accepted the role of coachman with good grace and turned up at Martyn's caravan to show off his costume.

Saxon had cast Zelda Fane as the pretty, shallow and frivolous Rosamond Viney. Zelda was moving into her heyday after a succession of frothy song and dance spectaculars that had made her the nation's sweetheart but not given her much acting clout.

Martyn considered their vastly different backgrounds and wondered what their working partnership would be like. Saxon introduced them at one of his grand dinners. This was the public Saxon, snobbish, lavish and on his best behaviour. He directed the meal like a major movie. The planning stage involved secretary, housekeeper and cook. A day was allotted to devising the menu. The florist was advised of the colour of the linen as soon as Gottfried had padded into his vast closet to select it, along with the appropriate dinner service, the crystal and the silverware. The florist's van was often driven up the hill to his estate five times, with five different specimen arrangements before he was satisfied. Nothing was left to chance or to anyone else's taste.

Ostensibly it was a feast to celebrate one of Somerset Maugham's visits to Los Angeles and scattered around the enormous drawing-room were Theodore Dreiser and Aldous Huxley along with Ina Claire, Dorothy Gish and Fanny Brice – a regular guest at the house when Saxon felt that the mood might become unbearably solemn. As he entered the room Martyn was immediately impressed by the company he found himself keeping. Gottfried chaperoned him proudly around the group, diligently explaining to his other guests what a valuable contribution Martyn was making to the script and sketching in his English successes for those he felt might not be aware of them. Martyn's whispered suggestion as they passed from one group to another, that this was a rather different guest list from the one last assembled in the room, was greeted with a frosty stare which melted only with the next introduction.

'Zelda, my dear, I know you've been dying to meet your filmic fate – and here he is, Martyn Milman, Zelda Fane.'

Martyn took in Zelda's petite figure, her delicate features and her huge, violet eyes. He knew them from the screen but he saw that she had turned herself out carefully for this demanding audience.

'I did enjoy you in *Society Scandals*,' he said, as Saxon oiled on his way, 'Gottfried screened it for me last week.'

'It was crap,' Zelda said. 'Let's keep it up front, Marty. There's so much bullshit around this town and a lot of it ends up in this house.'

Martyn laughed. 'I think we're going to get on well,' he said, 'but we'll have to shovel our share.'

'Did you know we were having an affair?' enquired Zelda, with a conspiratorial smile.

Martyn answered in the same vein. 'No, when did it start?'

'Tonight. You'll read about it in the columns tomorrow.'

'Do we consummate it now – before dinner, or are we allowed to build up to it gradually?'

'The studio ain't interested in that. Anyway you've got a wife and I've got a girlfriend. A romance makes sense. It'll get people more curious about you and less curious about me.'

'Perhaps I should warn Maude.'

'Who's Maude?'

'The aforementioned wife. She's in London with my children. They're too young to travel.'

'My!' Zelda raised an eyebrow, 'all alone in li'l ol' LA. I hope Gottfried's looking after your youthful enthusiasms.'

Confronted by her extraordinary frankness Martyn was not sure how much to confide. He got as far as, 'He's a wonderful host,' when the wonderful host led the company in to dinner.

It was to be Saxon's last big soirée before shooting began in earnest. At the dinner table he flanked himself with Ina Claire and Dorothy Gish. Maugham had Ina Claire on one side and Zelda on the other. Martyn was on her right. He could hear his director loudly describing the opening sequences of the movie to Somerset Maugham. 'I open with sheep grazing,' he was saying, 'that's pastoral, innocent, beautiful. Then I pan left to the roadside where a coach is approaching – someone is coming, we don't know who, but the feeling is urgent, dramatic and we know we're in olden times.'

'The m . . m . . m . . moment they see your name on the credits they kn . . n . . now they're in olden times,' Maugham interjected.

'Now, you know that's not fair, Willie. I must screen my chain-gang movie for you some time – though it wasn't one of my major successes. Anyway, as the coach rolls on I pan again to reveal a replica of Stephenson's Rocket steaming past the sheep in the opposite direction – I hold it as it disappears down the railroad. So I have established period and progress in one simple set-up.'

Maugham turned to Zelda. 'What are you playing, Miss Fane? Dorothea Brooke?'

'Stop kidding, Mr Maugham, my public would never accept me as a pious beauty with wrists like the Virgin Mary's. I'm no bluestocking who's going to get hitched to a dried-up old pedant like Edward Casaubon. Can you see me signing my money away so that it ends up in his will where I can't get at it? I've settled for Rosamond and Martyn here. I shall enjoy leading him a dance – and this way I get to wear those gorgeous clothes. Dorothea looks like a nun and acts like an idiot.'

'M . . m . . my, M . . M . . Miss Fane, you don't think m . . m . . much of our greatest lady novelist, do you?'

'She's got class, Mr Maugham, I'll give her that; and at least Dorothea gets to have a fling with Ladislaw after the old bore's dead. Keate Watershed's playing him. He's the latest dreamboat.'

Maugham showed more interest. 'Is he here?'

'No, he doesn't do the social round. He'll be out drinking with the boys.'

'And how are you and M . . M . . Mr M . . M . . Milman getting along?'

'Famously,' Martyn intervened. 'So well that I've just been told we're having an affair.'

'Does M . . M . . Maude know?'

'Not yet.'

'You'd better warn her. You and M . . M . . Miss Fane m . . m . . make a handsome couple. I suppose you didn't see his Hamlet,' he turned to Zelda, 'I thought it was very fine.'

'Agate didn't agree with you,' said Martyn, bitterly. 'He wrote, "Mr Milman speaks his words as though Hamlet were complaining of the management of his service flat... Mr Milman does not speak poetry badly. He does not speak it at all."' Zelda laughed.

'Actors,' said Maugham, 'can always recite their bad notices. You know what Sir Henry Wotton used to say, "Critics are like brushers of noblemen's clothes." You're a nobleman.'

'Well, isn't that the nicest thing?' said Zelda. 'Look at Martyn, Mr Maugham. You've made him blush!'

Martyn duly saw Zelda home and was faithfully photographed escorting her into her apartment house and leaving a few minutes later; but the next morning they opened the trade papers over their separate breakfasts and read that they were indeed 'an item'. Martyn spent the rest of the morning trying to get through to Maude. When he finally did she was putting the boys to bed.

Over the crackling transcontinental, transatlantic line she could only hear parts of Martyn's explanation. 'You're having what, darling?... Oh, you're *not* having it... Well, what is it you're not having?... Be quiet, Darcy, I'm talking to Daddy... This line is terrible, Martyn. Can you hear me?... Oh, that's good... Now you're *having* something... Is it good or bad?... Oh, an affair! Martyn, how could you? And why are you telling me about it?... I don't care what the studio wants! Our marriage is none of their business... I think you'd better come home. No, Darcy, Daddy isn't coming home, not yet...'

Mercifully the line cleared for a moment and Martyn was able to give a brief run-down on his fictional romance with Zelda, explain that it was a routine part of Hollywood studio politics and pass on Willie Maugham's love to Maude, who felt flattered and did not need to be told that it was one of Martyn's inventions.

Long after the call, long after she had got the boys to sleep, as she prepared to sleep herself, Maude wondered if she should telephone Martyn's mother. Amanda took the news in her stride.

'It's Babylon out there, dear, if one believes all one reads in the papers; but if Martyn says he's being a good boy and it's all a publicity stunt I should be inclined to think he's telling the truth. Of course, she *is* very pretty, this Miss Fane, isn't she? Archie took me to see her in *Society Scandals*. Now if *he* was the one on the loose in Hollywood I think there'd be much more cause for alarm!'

Maude smiled. There was little chance of Archie Durrant, Amanda's famously dull and upright second husband, straying. He had come to Amanda's rescue when she abandoned Max in Australia, all those years ago. He was a comfortable clubman knight in neatly polished, light-weight armour who had, for nearly forty years, provided her with the ease and security which had been anathema to Max. Archie worshipped Amanda and she accepted his homage happily.

And so Maude went to bed with an easy mind, and continued to sleep and wake unworried through most of the months of Martyn's absence. The occasional squib in the magazines brought some of her friends rushing around to offer condolence and advice and stir the pot – in that selfless way which is the speciality of really good friends at the first whiff of scandal. Maude was more concerned with her brood and brushed their sympathy politely aside.

In Hollywood the filming of *Middlemarch* ground on its stately way. Martyn's working relationship with Zelda was smooth and he even struck up an unlikely friendship with Keate Watershed, the young cowboy star, who cautiously welcomed his help as he wrestled with an English accent.

They were an odd pair. Keate had graduated from cowboy to stuntman to playing youngsters in Westerns. Straying into *Middlemarch*, he was in awe of Martyn's European composure but yet protective of his place in Hollywood Babylon.

'How are you making out with the chief faggot?' Keate enquired over a beer.

'Mr Saxon has been kindness itself. He's a wonderful host and I've met some fascinating writers . . .'

'All right, buddy, you're old enough to look after yourself.'

On the set, Saxon's behaviour was impeccable. His conservative camera angles and detailed concern for the actor's problems –

born out of his apprenticeship in the theatre – inspired confidence. Vincent Price as Casaubon, Lilian Gish as Dorothea, Nigel Bruce as Mr Brooke, C Aubrey Smith as old Peter Featherstone and even the moody Charles Laughton, providing a cameo as the drunken Raffles, responded to his precise instructions and his meticulous line readings.

'I guess it's why he's called a woman's direction,' Keate offered, 'he's kinda soft and caring behind the camera. In Westerns, the most you get told is the set-up. Are you a white hat or a black hat? Saxon actually let me in on the script. It's more than a mood he gives you. I'd have been all at sea with this Ladislaw character if he hadn't gone over every line of dialogue and every emphasis. When he asked me across to his place at first I thought it was just a come-on – you know – I'd heard all the stories. All the guys on the last movie cracked don't-bend-over jokes when they heard I got the job; but he was so simple and vivid about the scenes and he seemed to know so much about the characters that I found I was grabbed by his thinking. I couldn't get out of his concept. I couldn't be free, be myself; and I reckoned I had to go along with that. I'm about as different from young Ladislaw as you could get. He's not exactly a Republican, hard-drinking cowboy, is he?'

Martyn laughed. 'I was a little surprised when I heard you'd been cast, but I think it's worked out wonderfully.'

Keate took even Martyn's farewell present in his stride.

In a West Hollywood book store Martyn had come across an early Victorian pamphlet, dating back to the 1830s, in which an older actor offered sententious advice to his aspiring young colleague. He presented it to Keate, expensively wrapped, on the last day of shooting. The idea of an end of picture present was new to the young Western star and he tore open the packing with childlike excitement. When he saw what was inside he burst into laughter and hugged him happily. 'Bastard!' he said. 'Bastard! You wait till you make your first Western – you know what I'm gonna send you?'

'What?' asked Martyn, controlling himself as he found that he was enjoying the embrace.

'Liniment, you bastard! A truck-load of liniment for your sore ass!'

And he bounced off to display his prize to his friends on the crew.

'It's a wrap,' Saxon said as Zelda and Martyn completed their last recriminatory encounter. He walked with them to their dressing-rooms and kissed Zelda affectionately before she closed the door. Then he turned conspiratorially to Martyn. 'Come over to the house Saturday night,' he said. 'Don't bring Brad.'

'One of your literary evenings?' Martyn asked.

'Not exactly, I'm planning something a little more enterprising. Seafood,' he said enigmatically. 'Come casual.'

For Gottfried the end of shooting meant a profound feeling of relief and a positive need to relax. His habitual lifestyle had been rejected in favour of monk-like discipline over the past twelve weeks. Now he looked forward to a weekend in louche contrast.

When Martyn arrived at the mansion promptly at eight he found Saxon's inner circle of cronies assembled around the bar.

'How far did you get with Keate, Martyn?' was the first question after he had accepted a very large Martini.

'We got on extremely well,' Martyn told them. 'But not in the way you mean.'

'We heard about your end of picture present,' someone giggled. 'What did you give Zelda?'

'Something very English,' Martyn replied. 'A Crown Derby teapot. I think she was pleased. She gave me a big kiss.'

'Did Keate?'

Martyn was saved from having to reply as round, pink and smelling expensive, Saxon entered the room and immediately became the centre of attention.

'Time to eat, you guys,' he said briskly, 'before we take Martyn on the town. Come through. It's only meatloaf but,' he added melodramatically, 'it's *my* meatloaf.'

'I thought you said something about seafood,' said Martyn, surprised when everyone started to laugh. 'What have I said?'

'Meatloaf first, Martyn, seafood after.' Saxon was smiling along with the others. 'We're going down to Long Beach. The Fleet's in and it's our duty to entertain the boys.'

Martyn pondered his predicament as he toyed with his meat-loaf. The high-pitched conversation played on around him. He wondered what this further plunge into Saxon's world was doing to him. He had long been aware of a confusion in his attitude to men and women, though at the time of his courtship of Maude and the early days of their marriage he had assumed that he had resolved the problem. His affair with Brad had settled into a pleasant routine. They liked each other's company. They made love with ease and enjoyment. Martyn had done a little to help Brad's career and Brad's reaction had been simple and under-standing. He knew that Martyn would be leaving when he had finished dubbing his dialogue. He was probably already casting about for an equally congenial alternative. Martyn had begun to wonder what his fate would be when he returned to England. He convinced himself that Brad and all he represented were neatly compartmentalised in his American period. It was something he could put behind him when he was reunited with Maude and the children. He felt like a serving soldier exploiting a foreign posting without the feeling of responsibility he might have had at home. He was puzzled by Saxon's new initiative, alarmed as well as intrigued by the prospect of an adventure. Brad had come into his life gift-wrapped. He was disconcerted to find that his attitude to the present, more chancy proposition was a guilty excitement.

After dinner the posse of men piled into two of Saxon's large cars and set off for Long Beach. Martyn sat in the back with two of Saxon's cronies who giggled with pleasure as their limousine approached the chosen bar. It was around eleven. The room was crowded but the group pushed through to the back of the dark, low saloon. As he shouldered his way with the others, Martyn sized up the clientele. Plainly Saxon's party was slumming.

He negotiated a couple of beer-bellies. Two girls laughed in amazement as he excused himself politely for forcing his way through in the wake of the others. Dotted in clumps around the room he could pick out a scattering of young sailors highlighted by their white uniforms. The noise level from the juke-box made conversation irrelevant. A beer landed in Martyn's hand as he caught up with Saxon's group.

Six pairs of eyes searched the dim interior for signs of interest from the sailors. The pair nearest, fully occupied with two girls, seemed unaware of the new arrivals. Martyn saw Saxon nod to the barman whose eyes in turn flicked a message across the room to another white-clad figure. Soon enough three sailors had materialised. Their empty glasses were rapidly refilled on Saxon's orders, and the group bawled joshing remarks at one another. As the sailors sank their beers and accepted refills they were joined by the two who had previously been concentrating on the girls. Martyn watched fascinated as Saxon and his friends fell into easy shouted conversation with the men. Harmless subjects – ship, tour of duty, length of shore leave – disposed of, they drifted towards girls, frustration at sea and boredom on land, cash. Eventually Saxon decided that the encounter promised well and gathered up his group.

'Christ!' he said. 'It's hot in here. Fancy a breath of air, you guys?'

Welcoming the developing action they pushed their way back out through the long bar. Martyn sensed a different atmosphere. Their entrance had excited little attention or comment. Now their exit, accompanied by the five sailors, produced raised eyebrows, a parting of the crowds and the odd whistle as they passed conspicuously through. Skirting the two beer-guts he had nego- tiated on the way in, Martyn tripped and nearly fell, fairly sure that one had stuck out a foot as he passed. There was a titter from the nearby drinkers and another mocking whistle from the far side of the bar. One of the sailors who was following steadied him and Martyn emerged from the bar virtually on his arm. As the cleaner night air of El Portos Beach hit him, Martyn realised that the beers in the bar together with the Martinis and the wine he had drunk at Saxon's were having a big effect. He found himself leaning against the sailor for support only to discover that the man was in similar need of support from him. Locked together in what was becoming an increasingly affectionate embrace they stumbled after Saxon who led the group along the beach towards a clump of dusty palms standing back from the Ocean. Each of Saxon's cronies had paired off with another man. Reaching the rough turf under the trees Saxon lowered himself cautiously to the ground and watched the others struggle to join him.

'All alone, Gottfried?' slurred Martyn.

'Don't worry about me, Martyn. The night is yet young. I'm just examining the merchandise.'

Saxon had established his seniority during a covert negotiation with the sailors in the bar. Now he settled back to assess their potential. He intended to pick up the tab and claim the most promising material for himself.

As they grew more engrossed in exploring one another in what light the stars afforded, Saxon suddenly was aware of an alternative illumination, an altogether rosier glow, in the dry brush behind him. He heard a sinister cackle. Focusing sharply, he saw flames racing through the tinder. He staggered to his feet to alert the others. As he rose he could pick out the silhouettes of a handful of men behind the fire. At first he thought they might be fighting it. Then he realised that they were fanning it, driving the flames towards the beach and the fringes of the sand where his little group were corralled.

'Quit it, you guys,' he yelled.

As the flames burnt nearer he could see the undignified spectacle of men struggling to their feet, trying to pull up their trousers, catching one leg and missing the other and falling to the sand again.

'What the fuck's happening?' yelled one of the sailors.

'Get out of the scrub,' Saxon commanded, 'make for the sand and the sea.'

From the other side of the flames they heard a yell and a cry of 'Burn the faggots'. The shapes of their tormentors showed clearer through the flames. Martyn thought he could pick out the two beer-guts from the bar leading the advance.

Saxon gathered his group to make their escape along the narrow strip of beach, but more tormentors materialised from the shadows, blocking their way. From over the flames came a hail of rotten fruit. As the objects hit their target, catcalls rang out from the attackers.

Martyn, bemused by the suddenness of the assault, stood rooted in the sand as Saxon's party was surrounded. The crowd's attitude became more menacing. The five sailors made a break. Saxon, seeing his assailants part to let them through, tried to follow. Immediately his path was blocked.

'Where d'ya think you're going, fatso?' shouted one of the beer-bellies, who appeared to be the leader, poking a finger into his plump stomach. Saxon stuttered to a halt. For a moment the mob seemed unsure of what to do next. The two groups stood in uneasy silence eyeing each other. Behind them the flames in the thin scrub began to die down. A police siren sounded and, before the mob could disperse, a patrol car, flanked by two motorcycle outriders and followed closely by a large wagon, bounced along the beach. Two cops leapt from the car and ran towards the circle, picked out in the lights of the motorcycles. Most of the attackers slid off into the surrounding shadows and away over the flame-scarred scrub but the beer-bellied ring-leaders and Saxon's party lost the chance to escape.

'What's going on here?' the leading cop shouted. 'What's with this fire?'

'They started it,' said Saxon, limply.

'And who are you? What are you doing down here? What's your name?'

'Arthur Smith,' lied Saxon. 'We had a couple of beers in that bar back there and we came out here to cool off.'

'They're faggots,' said the leading beer-gut, 'they were out here friggin' around with sailors.'

The cop turned on him. 'Did you start that fire?' he snapped.

'We don't like faggots down here. It ain't safe.'

'I didn't ask you that. Did you start the fire?'

'No.'

'I'm taking you in.'

'What about them?'

'I'm taking them in too.'

Saxon gave a little whimper of alarm. 'You can't do that . . .'

'Can't I?' said the cop. 'Get in that wagon – the lot of you.' Prodded and pushed by the cops the oddly assorted group climbed into the back.

Martyn's nightmare continued at the precinct. Following Saxon's example he and the others gave false names and Saxon managed to telephone his lawyer. The bedraggled Hollywood party shared their cell uneasily with their two beer-bellied attackers and it was morning before they were released, bleary, rumpled and unshaven, into the sun. After frenzied night-long haggling between studio chiefs and the police commissioner any charges against Saxon and Martyn were dropped. Saxon's acolytes took the rap.

'They gave false names, they lied,' the commissioner protested.

'What do you expect them to do?' countered the studio head.

'But that guy Saxon is famous . . . I could have made an example of him.'

'Okay he's famous – so he comes more expensive . . .'

The offer of a bribe having been tacitly accepted the policeman moved to increase it.

'And the Limey actor – he's famous, too, isn't he?'

'He is in England. And he will be here. We have to keep this under wraps.'

'But he's a faggot, for Chrissake!'

'Okay, so he's a faggot. But he's *my* faggot.'

A chastened Martyn hastened to leave Los Angeles as soon as possible. Saxon, still shaken by the incident, hurried his dubbing schedule to get him out before the rumours could damage him. Saxon did not turn up at Pasadena station to see Martyn off on the Super Chief; but Brad discreetly did and so, to Martyn's surprise, did Keate.

'Had a little bother, I hear . . .' he said.

'How did you know?'

'I was up at Saxon's for dinner last night – so was Leonard, one of those decorators who took the rap. The one whose picture was in the paper.'

'I thought you kept clear of Saxon's evenings?'

'Naw, now I'm half-way to legit I get to go to the respectable nights. Tallulah was there. She was really funny – but she wouldn't stop talking about this critic, some reviewer guy who called her a circus acrobat. Finally Leonard got pissed off. "For

Chrissakes Tallu," he screeched. "Forget that shit. It's not as bad as being called a cock-sucker on the front page of the *LA Times*!" It was real funny. She thought about it for a minute, then she said, "Oh, I'd much rather be called a cock-sucker than an acrobat." '

Martyn managed a wry smile.

Keate continued to reassure him. 'It always gets around. Don't worry about it. They'll forget it tomorrow.'

'You think so?'

'I know so – but they may never cast you in that cowboy movie now.'

'I shan't need the liniment,' Martyn said wanly. 'So long.'

They hugged. As Martyn stood waving, the Super Chief started to move and Keate turned to Brad.

'Like a lift, kid?'

As Martyn's last demonstration disc ground to a halt there was a moment's silence in the room in the house in St Leonard's Terrace. Martyn, who was standing at the window, looked down across the cricket fields to the Royal Hospital. He could not bear to turn round for his new protégé's verdict. Suddenly Louis burst into an enthusiastic round of applause.

He saw Martyn relax a little, crossed the room and placed his hands firmly on his shoulders.

'My, you're tense,' he said. 'And you're only playing to a Broadway gypsy.'

'You are the first person to hear it – apart from Freda.'

'Sit down. Let me loosen you up a little.' He manoeuvred Martyn to an easy chair and massaged his shoulders firmly and expertly.

'That's good,' Martyn breathed. 'That's very good.'

'Another gypsy skill,' said Louis. 'We can't have the star tense. Now you've got to play it to the family.'

'That's nothing compared to playing it to you. Did you really like it?'

Louis's thumbs delved deep into Martyn's blades. 'We'd better understand each other, Sir Martyn . . .'

'Martyn, please.'

'Okay, Martyn. We shan't have time for any bullshit or any

73

drawing-room manners or British reserve if we're going to kick this show into shape. I don't say I like something if I don't. I have ideas, of course. There are some things I think need tightening. It's wordy. We need to find room for the show to breathe. I think I can see a place for a ballet to give the poor bastards' ears a rest and the plot is sound. The old queen knew how to tell a story and he knew how to make a joke – and so do you. What's more you can make jokes in a song. The funny numbers are very funny – though whether they'll sound as funny with some half-assed singer as they do when you do them on the disc remains to be seen. I'll reserve judgement on the romantic numbers until I've heard them again this evening. I think the big ballad's fine but it's odd what a room does to a song. Play it to one set of people with smiling faces and tapping feet and it sounds terrific. Play it the next day to a crowd of doubting Thomases and you can wonder why you wrote the damn thing.'

'I'll call up Harry Harmon, my tame producer,' said Martyn. 'It's time he heard it and it's time he met you. He's practically family.'

Picking up the internal phone he spoke to Grace down in the kitchen. 'How many can you cope with for supper, Grace?'

There was a pause. 'Any amount if you're happy with cold cuts, Sir Martyn.'

'Fine.'

'And I could do some soup. It's bitter out . . .'

'Splendid, Grace. I'm going down to Lady Milman now. I'll tell her I've spoken to you.'

'Yes, Sir Martyn.'

At nine thirty the music room was full. The family was out in force, bolstered by the supper and some of Martyn's better bottles from the cellar. Only Amanda was missing. Martyn did not want to rush her. Harry Harmon had scurried up from his weekend home in Angmering, and paced nervously. Tony and Grace insinuated themselves into the room on the pretext that 'people might be in need of a refill, you never know'. Hanna, who had delivered some needlework to Maude, begged to be allowed to hear the score.

'I haven't been so excited since Brecht and Weill played me *Happy End*,' she repeated to anyone who would listen, 'even if there isn't anything in it for me,' she added wistfully nearly as often.

'You will all have read the play by now,' Martyn said, 'even you, Darcy. I assume you've caught up?'

'Oh, yes, Dad,' said Darcy. 'Juicy part!'

'I hope you've read it all, not just your lines.'

'Of course, Dad.'

'Good. It doesn't look as if that Christie play at the Ambassadors which opened in November will run. If it doesn't, you'll have young Dickie Attenborough to contend with.'

'Darling,' said Maude indulgently, 'don't threaten the poor boy. He really has read it. He was telling me the plot only last night.'

'Just as well,' Martyn turned a stern gaze on Darcy, 'I doubt if your grandfather will have done more than glance at his "sheets"; but still, here we go.'

Martyn was standing by the cumbersome gramophone placed beside the grand piano. On top of the piano he had arranged the pile of discs which he and Freda had been recording over the last months. Louis sat at the piano-stool, installed as a co-director of the material.

'I've tried to make this a piece for the 1950s,' Martyn said with a nervousness which surprised even himself, 'not just shake out the 1890s mothballs. It's about class. It's about money. It's about greed. It's about ambition. It's also about loyalty and love inside a marriage trying to survive money and greed and ambition. That's where I find the musical passion that seems to elude Wilde. That's what I hope will make a musical which sings and has a life of its own – not just a pretty adaptation with a few songs thrown in.'

'We open,' no one was more surprised than Martyn when Louis joined in, 'in Rotten Row, in the servants' quarters, upstairs, downstairs, in my lady's chamber. It's a kaleidoscope of London society in the 1890s. Play the opening number, Martyn . . .'
Obediently Martyn flipped the first disc into action. Freda's piano accompaniment tinkled away. Nervously he turned up the volume

before his own voice rang out into the room. 'It's a chorus number,' he said apologetically.

'Hush,' commanded Louis.

> Society! Society!
> Society is hardly what it was before;
> And this deterioration is because
> Of Suffragettes and Socialists
> And Militant Salvationists –
> All of which our Nation lists
> A bore.

Martyn managed in his opening number to weave a comprehensive pattern of late-Victorian society, rhyming in Mrs Bloomer and Blondin, Rosebery and Campbell-Bannerman, Swinburne and G F Watts, Irving and Ellen Terry, General Booth and Sir Garnet Wolesley. He had raided Wilde's other plays for good lines. 'I'm not political, I insist/ I am a Liberal Unionist' . . . 'Oh that, of course, is fine with us/ We even let them dine with us/ Or come in after dinner.'

Martyn relaxed and became more expansive as he felt the family warming to the piece. A couple of the songs he performed himself from the piano. Lysander's patter number as the Vicomte de Nanjac who loves everything English, especially the colloquial phrases which he always gets wrong – 'It captivates me utterly/ the way that up you butter me' – was a hit, above all with Lysander who reckoned even he could sing it. The duet for Lord Caversham and Lady Markby, a song Martyn had added for his parents to cover a scene change, was another, more sentimental, success. Harry Harmon actually got out his red spotted handkerchief as Martyn intoned. 'The Art of Living/ is easily learned/ The Art of Living/ is not lightly spurned/ The days go by/ swift as a sigh/ But we don't have to try/ To be wiser/ And that is why/ the older you are/ The better you are/ as adviser.' There followed a catalogue of appalling advice handed out gratuitously and disastrously by various old fools down through history.

'Well,' said Maude, as the loyal applause died down, 'if Amanda still has doubts, that'll get her!'

Martyn smiled and placed the next disc on the gramophone.

'This is yours, my dear,' he said as the title song rang out. 'My Ideal Husband/ my perfect spouse/ The man whom I respect/ as Master of my house . . .'

Maude insisted on checking the range and making sure that she could reach the higher notes. Martyn patiently thumped them out for her and only when she was happy did the performance continue. Mrs Cheveley's ingenious, vamping arias were loudly clapped. No one had any doubts that Martyn's final ensemble, 'Luncheon is on the Table', which cleverly tied up the end of the plot after the villainess's melodramatic schemings had been defeated, would send the public home happy.

'You've done it again, Martyn!' Harry Harmon rejoiced as Tony and Grace materialised with celebratory champagne. 'I did have one worry, when you were playing the piano the music sounded a bit loud. I didn't get all the words.'

'Harry,' Martyn explained with elaborate patience, 'you were sitting on top of it. Those songs are very lightly scored.'

'I used to be a violinist,' said Harry, not convinced, 'I know about music.' He turned to Louis Armbruster. 'So, young man, you're joining Martyn's team, I hear.'

'I hope so, Mr Harmon, I'm really looking forward to it.'

'We'd better make a deal. Who's handling your business over here?'

'Sir Martyn is going to introduce me to Billy Little. I guess you'd better talk to him.'

They toasted the enterprise. Glasses clinked around the room. Maude dropped a proud kiss on Martyn's forehead.

Max

Vic Ingrams had caught up with Max – much to the old boy's relief. It was the day of his visit to the library. Everything seemed to be happening at once. He had fobbed off Mae Madely with a well-practised lie.

'What a charming story, my dear,' he said when he collected himself in the crowded pub. 'Fancy your grandmother keeping those old programmes of mine. She must indeed have been a devoted fan. Surprising as it may seem, I had them in those days.'

'Did Gran never try to contact you when you came back the second time? You went home to England when you finished with Romany French's Company, didn't you?'

'Yes. You have been doing your homework, young lady. I sailed from Perth – on the *Orantes*. Lovely ship!'

'Did she sack you?'

'What put that idea into your young head?'

'There were lots of cuttings and programmes in Gran's box – I know you used to go to our Civil Service Club Hotel because Great Grandma, Nancy Lola, got a judgement against you – one pound, ten shillings and six pence – with five shillings costs.'

'And you think your late grandmother would have gone with a man who had trashed her family in that way?'

'It's not unheard of.' Mae was implacable and looked it. 'And you'd had all that trouble with your first wife at home. I assume it was your first wife,' she added.

'Oh, yes,' Max insisted. He decided he had better try a bit of acting. As he had finished his beer, he played the oldest card, frailty.

'Is there, perhaps, a glass of water?' he whispered.

Mae ran for it.

'Thank you, my dear. It is so sad to encounter a recrimination echoing down some fifty years,' he managed. 'There were lovely young girls in Melbourne. There were happy nights at the Civil Service Club Hotel; but I am prepared to swear that, that . . .' he acted old age with considerable conviction, 'I am prepared to swear that I am not your grandfather. Who was the official husband of Miss Hannigan?'

'Gran never married.' She stood and picked up her little purse, dismissing Max's elaborately feeble attempt to rise.

He summoned as much of the old Milman charm as he could muster and looked at her. 'We shall probably never meet again, my girl,' he said. 'I am bound for the Old Country. My son has engaged me for a role in his coronation musical.'

'You never know, Mr Milman. I might be off there myself in the summer. I've got a cousin who lives in Earl's Court.' And with a faint hint of a threat she turned, throwing over her shoulder, 'It could be a family reunion.' She left the pub.

When Max got back to his lodgings he found Ingrams sitting in the sun on the doorstep.

'Mrs Tussoch wouldn't let me in,' he explained. 'A hard woman.'

'And you are here to take me away from her?' replied Max, still shaky from Mae's inquisition.

'I've got the ticket. I've got the back rent. I've got a few expenses and I've got a copy of the play for you – the original,' said Ingrams.

'Bugger the play. I read that at the library. Let's see the expenses.'

'I have very strict instructions, Mr Milman. I am to deliver you to the *Orcades* in two days' time. She is a fine new ship and very fast. On her first voyage to Melbourne she reduced the pre-war time by ten days to twenty-eight. She could make four complete round voyages a year.'

'So you've settled with the Tussoch woman?'

'I have.'

'Until when?'

'Thursday.'

'Couldn't you get me into a hotel till then? This place is the pits. I need to clean up. Buy some clothes.'

'All right, Mr Milman. We have a little leeway. But I have to keep an eye on you. Sir Martyn is very worried lest you do another disappearing act.'

'I didn't bloody disappear. You did. Why didn't you leave me your card?'

'I did, Mr Milman. Mrs Tussoch has told me about your bad luck.'

'I'll bet the old cow didn't call it that.'

'No, Mr Milman. Perhaps we should move you to the Onslow for tonight.'

'A bit snooty.'

'It's convenient for the shops. We shan't have time to have things tailored for you.'

'As long as you get me out of this hole I'm your man,' said Max. The prospect of room service was already tickling his palate.

Room service at the Onslow lived up to his expectations. That night he ate and drank happily in his room. He slept like a log and awoke to stare at the bright sun glancing off furniture finished with a hideous walnut veneer and chairs covered in vivid chintz. Happily untroubled by a hangover for once, he turned luxuriously and stretched out an arm towards the telephone to order breakfast. Over a plate of bacon and eggs he pondered his good fortune. Cocooned like this for the first time in years he felt entirely relaxed about the journey home. This was the life for an old actor. No more hand to mouth existence.

As he shaved he considered the irony of his encounter with Mae Madely. Fifty years ago he had abandoned her grandmother, boarding the boat for England. Now he was quitting the girl who he was fairly sure was his granddaughter, in the same way. He tried to remember what Maisie Mary had looked like and failed. He looked at himself in the mirror hoping to recall what he had looked like at the time, and failed again. He had lived with the ever-changing portrait for so long. His mind ranged to Ruby and he was surprised to find that here his memory played him no tricks. The image which persisted was her face at the moment when he first met her in Margate in 1911.

Max and Amanda

Rehearsals in the Margate Company had been a delight and, as the tour progressed around the south coast, Ruby and Maximilian's affair flourished. It was consummated in Eastbourne. Only really big touring stars stayed in hotels – the rest took rooms in theatrical lodgings. Although Max was more familiar with the northern circuit and had his favourite landladies there, he was expert at judging the prospects of the digs in the seaside towns they visited. Ruby, hopelessly in love by now, meekly accepted his offer to sort out their accommodation. They presented themselves at the front door of Seaview, which had, of course, no such prospect, early on a Sunday evening.

They were greeted by a plump landlady who looked them up and down and said briskly, 'Fifteen shillings a week for husband and wife, but a pound for the usual theatrical arrangement.' She darted a glance at Ruby's unringed hand. 'You look like the usual,' she said, showing them up to a small sitting-room which adjoined a bedroom featuring a large double bed. Ruby wondered if she should demur. However, seeing that both Max and the landlady appeared to consider it the most natural thing in the world, she kept silent. 'My cooking's plain,' said the woman, 'but I doubt you'll say no to chops and steaks. The bathroom's down the hall. In my house it's only used for bathing so you needn't think you'll find coal in it.'

Ruby looked round at the oilcloth floor, the palm leaf fans, saddle-bag chairs and the clusters of photographs of actors, mostly on the Halls, inscribed 'to dear Ma'. She flicked idly through the visitors' book – marvelling at the number who had commented 'A Home from Home' or 'Have been most comfortable, and hope to return'.

Noticing her preoccupation, Max said, 'Looks perfect, Ma.'

'Never had no complaints,' said the landlady.

'D'you know what old Charlie Brookfield wrote in a book once, Ruby?' Max smiled at the memory. 'Quoth the Raven.'

'What did he mean?' asked Ma, perplexed.

'It's a quotation from Edgar Allen Poe,' Ruby laughed. 'Quoth the raven, "Nevermore!"'

The landlady looked unenlightened.

'It meant he wasn't coming back,' Max explained.

'Very rude,' said Ma. 'I shouldn't think he'd be welcome either. Are you playing Venus then, dear?'

'Venus?'

'Aren't you doing *The Merchant of Venus*?'

'No, no,' said Ruby patiently as Max stifled his laughter. 'Not Venus, Venice, it's a town in Italy, you know. It's a play by Shakespeare.'

'Not Venus! Oh, that is a pity; we 'ad a Venus 'ere a couple of weeks ago. She sat all night in a cockleshell. It looked lovely.' She peered at the clock on the chimney-piece. 'I'll bring up your supper in an hour,' she said from the doorway. 'You'll be wanting to unpack.'

She closed the door and Max and Ruby collapsed into each other's arms.

'She's a card,' said Max. 'They usually are. There was a woman in Huddersfield once who was very strict. I visited a couple of girls in her digs with old Holman Horlock and we stayed on a bit. Didn't leave until nigh on two. In the morning she was like a dragon. Said to the girls, "I'll have you to understand, young ladies, that my house is not a Bovril!"'

They laughed again. Then Max led Ruby by the hand into the bedroom. All her doubts and hesitations and prepared excuses and her refuge in modesty vanished in face of Max's singleness of purpose. It was plain that no doubt had even entered his mind and against such certainty she had no defence – even if she had ached to invent one. Which she had not.

By the time they closed in Plymouth, Ruby considered that they were engaged. They returned to London; but suddenly Max was summoned north. Ruby saw him sadly off on the train to Maccles-field. The emergency engagement provided him with six months' work replacing a friend whose illness had threatened the tour. There was no vacancy for Ruby. The roles were all in Max's repertoire and he accepted the offer with alacrity.

Ruby left the station wondering how she would fill her hours alone after the blissful weeks they had spent together. She decided that a matinée might cheer her up and set off for the West End. In Charing Cross Road the front of house display for a comedy playing at the Garrick Theatre called *My Friend the Prince* attracted her attention. It was being presented by George Edwardes. It was one of his rare ventures outside musical comedy and burlesque. Although the comedy did not drive thoughts of Max from her mind she was enchanted by it and soon saw herself in the role of the Princess. To her delight, she discovered from a friend that Edwardes was sending out a tour. Promptly the next morning she presented herself at the Gaiety offices in Wellington Street, and demanded to see the manager who was taking the play out. Assuming a self-confidence she hardly felt she assured him that she would be perfect in the part. Unknowingly she had timed her gesture perfectly. They were about to go into rehearsal and her role was uncast. She was given permission to rehearse it on approval. Eventually she would have to play it before the 'Guv'nor', George Edwardes himself. Only then would she know if he thought she was up to scratch.

In the benevolent atmosphere of Edwardes's empire, she was given every chance. The stage director at the Garrick rehearsed her himself and, when the ordeal was over, told her in tones so reverent that he might have been conferring a peerage on her: 'The Guv'nor is very pleased with you, dear.' There was more splendid news. She could hardly wait to write to Max to tell him of her good fortune. When she was asked to state the salary she expected she was told that she would be paid two pounds a week more than she had asked: 'The part is worth it.'

With both young lovers on tour their passion was restricted to letters. Ruby was an infinitely more conscientious correspondent than Max. They had hoped that they might at least catch a glimpse of one another at Crewe – the great Sunday rendezvous for actors whose companies were crossing the country in special trains.

Suddenly the correspondence developed new urgency. It began with a letter from Max which hinted that he had met an old flame in Glasgow. Reading between the lines Ruby, at the other end of the world in Birmingham, sensed unfinished business. The princess sat in her dressing-room silently sobbing as her dresser entered. 'What's up, miss?' she asked.

'Nothing. Nothing.'

'Men!' sniffed the dresser.

'How did you know?'

'What else has a touring lady to cry over?'

'I don't know,' sobbed Ruby.

'It could be an aged parent passed away,' the old girl offered, taking off her crêpe bonnet and smoothing down her red blouse and black skirt, 'but it don't look like it.'

'No.'

''Ave you got it for definite, miss?'

'No, Mrs Meddings.'

'Then my advice is to get after him. When you've got it for definite there's not a lot you can do. When Meddings went off I kicked up no end of fuss. I went round to the house where he'd set up with his fancy woman. Rang the bell I did. She comes to the door 'erself, opens it 'erself, bold as brass. "Is Mrs Meddings at 'ome?" I says. "I'm Mrs Meddings," she says going all shades. "If you're Mrs Meddings," I said, very quiet, "oo the 'ell am I?" Of course, it didn't settle nothing. I'd left it too late. 'E's still with 'er an' I'm still on me own, but the point of my story, miss, is don't let it drag on. As soon as you 'as doubts get after the bastard an' bring 'im to heel. That was my mistake, miss. When I felt somethin' rumbling I let it run on. Nip it in the bud!'

Two days later Ruby was confirmed in her suspicion that she was pregnant. The revelation gave her new strength. The tour of *My Friend the Prince* would be over in two weeks. The company were to play Liverpool and Blackpool and then she would be free. She calculated that Max would still be in Scotland and was determined to join him. She debated whether to surprise him or let him know that she was coming. She had not written to warn him of her pregnancy. Sitting on her bed in her lodgings she weighed the various courses open to her. Why was she choosing to spend her life with this wayward actor? Because she loved him of course, she told herself, as she brushed her long unbraided hair. Because he was her first lover – a wonderful lover. Surely she was the one person in the world who could 'save' him. Men loved him and women adored him but she would save him. He would turn his back on the nights of carousing and disturbing the peace. The dear boy! She would make a home for him and the child. Perhaps it was time for him to conquer the London stage. With her new-found contacts she would help him. Surely he must be growing tired of bucketing around the country in second-rate plays. She must set his sights higher. As she finished combing her hair she reflected more desperately that she must marry him. She would get no sympathy from her own family if she brought home a child without a father. Nor would she be able to make ends meet in London if Max declined to settle.

As Ruby looked at Max's face smiling at her from the silver-framed photograph on her dressing-table she felt her determination strengthen. This was a prize not to be thrown away. She allowed herself to drift into sleep sure that in the morning she would do the right thing.

'My darling,' she wrote the next day. 'I have wonderful news. News so precious that I cannot put it on paper. I must tell you with my own lips. After two weeks I shall be free of this tour. You, I know, dearest, will be in Dundee. I shall fly north to you by the very first train on the Sunday morning. Will you meet me?'

The correspondence gathered speed with an exchange of wires. Max cabled within minutes of receiving Ruby's letter. 'My dearest, dare I guess at the happiness you promise? Do I dare? All my love Max.'

'Darling, you may dare,' Ruby replied, her heart lighter than it had been for days.

It was now Max who wrote with urgency. 'Marry me, darling Ruby. I have arranged everything. We can marry by licence here in Scotland at the Registrar's office. All we need is two witnesses to vouch that we have lived in Scotland for twenty-one days. I have two chums in the company who are willing to vouch for you. It will be as legal and binding in any part of the world. It is as good as twenty-one days' notice and the banns and the church and the clergyman and all that rigmarole. I shall not be with this company when the future happy event occurs so the fewer people who know the exact date of our wedding the better. Wire me yes or no as soon as you open this and in two weeks you will be Mrs Milman. Now I must on stage to act the noblest Roman once again. Goodbye, my dear little Ruby wife, Your Max.'

And so at 10.30 a.m. on a cold Monday morning in Dundee Ruby did indeed become Mrs Milman. As Max continued his tour she was installed in lodgings in Balham where Martyn's arrival was joyously received. Max even secured a London engagement – not West End, but at the indomitable Sara Lane's Britannia, Hoxton.

The Noble Vagabond was the sort of piece in which he could believe implicitly and to which he brought all his charm and vigour – a preposterous tale of a penniless but aristocratic wastrel in Carolean times who after much swordplay and adventure on behalf of the damsel whom he loves, sacrifices himself on the gallows to save her lover whom he closely resembles. It was a plot stolen shamelessly from *A Tale of Two Cities*. The author had simply changed century and costumes and crammed in various familiar incidents from his shaky knowledge of the history of the period. Max played two parts, distinguishing between them with flamboyant costume changes and sharply contrasting characterisations. He performed a variety of athletic feats, jumping from oak trees, swinging from castle walls and diving into a moat – a hundred gallons of water in a massive tank, proclaimed the posters.

His leading lady was an up and coming star, Fanny Forsyth, and Ruby had moments of alarm when he arrived home from rehearsals full of enthusiasm for her emerging performance. She need not have worried. In the first flush of fatherhood Max's libido ran for a time on one cylinder and young Miss Forsyth was a professional virgin who loved to flirt with her leading man but had no intention of capitulating. She was indeed mildly irritated that Max, whose reputation had preceded him, made no overtures. She had looked forward to leading him on and then rebuffing him. The play was an enormous hit in Hoxton and a tour was announced. Miss Forsyth took herself off to the Lyceum to join the Melville brothers in a revival of their melodrama *The Girl Who Took the Wrong Turning*. 'My mother says it's time I took a title role up West,' she explained to Max, 'and I always do what mother says.'

'So I've noticed, my dear,' said Max. 'I wish you a long and happy engagement.'

'You just love touring, don't you?'

'It's in the blood. Had a grandfather. One of the pomping folk. Never knew him but mother told some tales. Played in fit-ups and hay-barns. Slept under hedgerows.'

'I am looking forward to the West End,' said Miss Forsyth, emphasising the words. 'I'm told it's a different class of audience. More alert. I suppose you'll be asking if your little wife can tour with you – she would surely be up to one of the smaller roles.'

'Actually,' said Max, not bothering to rise to the bait, 'they've already asked her to take your role, Lady Belvidera.'

'Oh, I am glad for you – and for her. But is it wise? Belvidera has quite a range. An actress's reputation can be damaged by being forced forward too soon.'

'Ruby will bring it off,' Max predicted. And so she did. In truth the role did not have the range with which Fanny Forsyth had invested it. Some smiles, some tears and a good deal of simpering were all that was required and in those arts Ruby Bollington was easily a match for Fanny Forsyth.

Martyn was despatched to Somerset to be looked after by Ruby's mother and sisters, coddled in comfort on their High-bridge smallholding and taken regularly down the road to Burnham-on-Sea where he was pushed along the front or played with on the thin strip of sand.

Ruby always looked back on the tour of *The Noble Vagabond* as one of the happiest periods of her life. Max was being a good boy. He put behind him the late-night carousing, the midnight japes, the noisy returns to his digs, which had been a feature of his bachelor life. No longer would he sway down alleys dragging his cane noisily against corrugated iron sheets to rouse the neighbourhood. Rather, after acknowledging the fans at the stage door, he would sink one Guinness and as soon as Ruby had finished her lemonade, or occasionally a glass of port, 'for the voice', accompany her back to the lodgings where a succession of Mas complimented her on the change she had wrought. 'He's a different man, Mrs Milman. Just as nice, he is; but so much more manageable. You've done wonders.'

Ruby basked in the reflected glory which playing opposite Max brought her and truly believed that her plan to save him had succeeded. However, the tour was drawing to a close with every prospect of a second to follow it, albeit in smaller theatres and for less money, when Max suddenly announced that he was off to Australia again.

The offer had arrived out of the blue. The money was good. Donaldson's, the management, were reliable. The old unpleasantness was forgotten. Max had read in the *Era* that his old employer and enemy, Miss Romany French, was dead. He had such pleasant memories of so many Australian girls that no specific recollection of his run-in with the Melbourne Hannigan family had stayed with him.

'That's where the money is!' he repeated to the weeping Ruby. 'It's the coming place. You'll see when I send for you, my darling.'

'But how soon, Max?'

'That I can't tell you, Ruby girl. Ralph Donaldson's already engaged a leading lady or I'd have put your case. It's the greatest stroke of luck that he needed me. He'd all but made a deal with Cosmo Stanford but Stanford backed out at the last minute. Now Donaldson's congratulating himself on his good fortune. Apparently I'm a deal more suited to the range of parts than Cosmo. He's got no legs, y'see,' he added, patting his own affectionately.

It was a tearful parting at Tilbury. Tearful for Ruby, at any rate. Although Max was tender and concerned for her his heart was already at sea, looking forward to the voyage. There would be the leisurely journey. He remembered how he had enjoyed it nearly ten years before. The changing scenery, the varied climate, the intricate pattern of shipboard romances. He saw no reason why this trip should be any less pleasant. He would laze on the promenade deck scanning his lines, occasionally looking up to assess his chances with this returning officer's wife or that planter's daughter. He wrinkled his nose, sniffing the salt sea-air and the promise of adventure. Then he remembered Ruby and hugged her affectionately again.

'Write to me, Max,' she said, clinging to him.

'Every day, my darling girl. But they only despatch the letters when we arrive in port. You'll get one from Plymouth. Then it's going to be silence until we pull into Gib.'

Max's mind was already at the end of the voyage. He was seeing reception committees, and parties, and being fêted and meeting new colleagues and a new generation of fans. He was already downing Sydney oysters and drinking Sydney beer at the Australia Hotel. With a quick leap of his imagination he was reading his undoubtedly splendid notices in the *Bulletin*. The hoots of the ship's siren, the first one long, the second two much shorter, banished Ruby from the newly-built *Orama*. From the quayside she stood and waved long after Max had faded from her view and had in fact descended to the first-class lounge and ordered his first drink. She stood there until the two black funnels vanished in the Thames fog, drew her cloak more tightly around her shoulders, and turned to catch her train.

Max

Social Sydney took Max immediately to its heart. The Donaldsons' connections were impeccable and he found his treatment different from that which had greeted him when he was on trial with Miss Romany French.

Ralph Donaldson was the only one of his family to take an interest in the theatre. His brothers and sisters, all owing their comfortable lifestyle to sheep farms in the Hunter Valley, were obsessed by the Turf. They might play a little golf at the Royal Sydney, the smart course on the sand flats which lay between Rose Bay and Bondi; but their passion was for horses. They bred them, rode them, backed them and played polo on them. Between the various members of the family they could claim six winners of the Melbourne Cup and had high hopes for their chances at the Easter races in Sydney.

Max arrived, like the sharp, bright weather which traditionally heralds Australia's autumn, in time for that Easter meeting. The damp summer heat which had characterised Christmas was banished as Sydney society flung itself into a frenzy of dancing and shopping. Men visited their tailors and shirtmakers; women their milliners. Children were fetched from school, graziers and horse-breeders gathered, marriages were celebrated and it was all recorded in the *Town and Country Journal*.

Ralph Donaldson's passion for the theatre was tolerated with amusement by the rest of the family, who enjoyed dressing-up for his first nights and meeting some of the exotic acting creatures he imported from England. This year his calculations had gone slightly awry. Before he set out for the Old Country he had prepared his siblings to welcome one Cosmo Stanford who, he assured them, would be a uniquely dashing attraction. Cosmo's photographs had been handed round to flutter young breasts in the Hunter Valley. On Stanford's defection, Ralph had rushed to book Max only the day before the boat sailed. However, he got back to Sydney in good time to revise and remount a campaign on behalf of his new star. Although he had seen Max play on only the one occasion – when *The Noble Vagabond* was ending its tour – Max had not undersold himself.

Ralph drove out to the homesteads with which his family had pimpled the Hunter Valley – giant piles thrown up by Horbury Hunt surrounded by vast, elegant stables and backed by immense shearing sheds. Here, behind red-brick walls framed with iron and lattice he handed Max's likeness round to the excited girls, who peered at the pictures in the large gloomy rooms. Light filtered faintly through ambitious art nouveau windows decorated with sparkling, wayward flowers. The photographs were passed from eager hand to eager hand, held up to the light, returned, passed on, and clucked and cooed over. Dorothy, the youngest Donaldson girl, surreptitiously slid one into her sleeve. She could hardly wait to excuse herself, hurry along the vast hall past the sturdy screens and large urns which bordered its echoing walls. She sped up the impressive staircase flanked by its cedar columns, past trellised balconies and proudly displayed photographs of famous horses and prize rams. She sought the sanctuary of her bedroom. Here, she could pore over Max's image and imagine that she was in love.

All the Donaldson girls were impressed with what they saw. They talked to their neighbours. They wrote to their more distant friends. Some were treated to a precious photograph. The rumour spread with gratifying speed and by the time Max came down the gangplank of the *Orama*, an Antipodean branch of the MAMs was firmly established. A press conference at the Australia Hotel over and his luggage stowed away upstairs, Max was delivered up to the close-quarters admiration of the Donaldson girls.

Stowey, Ralph Donaldson's smart, city mansion at the back of King's Cross, looked out over Rushcutter's Bay. Max was impressed. He had seen nothing like the inside of Stowey on his first visit to Australia. In the hall he admired Mrs Ralph Donaldson's buhl table, on which copies of the *Tatler* and the *Sketch* were casually strewn. Through a door on the left he could glimpse her small 'French' sitting-room and register the tapestry and the gilt 'drawn together' by a large portrait of Mrs Ralph herself. It was by Agnes Goodsir, the Australian artist who had graduated from the Bendigo School of Mines and chose to live and paint in Paris. She returned every so often to gather the rich pickings available when she painted women such as Mrs Ralph.

His hostess and the twittering girls led Max through double-doors into the long drawing-room. Its walls displayed Hilda Rix Nicholas's paintings of the Donaldsons' good grazing country in the Hunter. Fallen on m' feet here, thought Max as he followed his new fans through the french windows at the end of the salon on to a wide veranda. He could see the harbour ahead, admiring it through trunks of palms and an imposing bunya bunya tree.

'You must be hungry, Mr Milman,' said Mrs Ralph, 'talking to those tiresome newspaper people. And I find my appetite deserts me entirely at sea. Do come through.'

One end of the veranda was screened with lattice and behind it Max saw the dark, cool dining-room, its approach protected with fly wire. Again he was impressed, by the burnished Georgian family silver which dominated the large dining table, and by the Donaldsons' best china, white with a broad blue band around the rim and a big gold D in the centre of each plate. Not least he registered the flurry of activity as the Donaldsons' butler moved firmly between the dining-room and kitchen ensuring that the cook and two parlour-maids kept supplies flowing smoothly to the table.

In spite of all this new-found luxury Max was most aware of Dorothy Donaldson's two wide eyes fixed on him from the far end of the table. Nice little prospect there, he thought. Hold hard tho', Max, old boy, he reminded himself, not on your own door-step.

'When is Ralph going to start you working, Mr Milman?' Mrs Ralph enquired.

'Soon, I hope, ma'am,' Max replied. 'I've got myself pretty well up on my words on the boat over – at least on the Roman piece – but I'm starting from scratch with this new bush drama.'

'We've got to give you time to find your land-legs,' said Ralph, 'and not much work gets done during Race week so you might as well enjoy yourself for now.'

'I hear this McMahon's a tough taskmaster,' said Max.

'We're lucky to have him,' Ralph replied. 'He's a bit of a highbrow but he knows his stuff. The deal is that if he fits up these two melodramas for me I give him a financial hand with his experimental work – he's keen on Shaw and Barrie and Ibsen, that sort of thing. I shall lose any cash I put in there, but I get a first-class stage director for your two plays.'

'Have you played *Ben Hur* before, Mr Milman?' Dorothy plucked up courage to ask the question.

'No, Miss Donaldson, but I have given my Marcus Superbus the length and breadth of Britain. *Sign of the Cross*, y'know. Rattling good piece. Very much the same thing, I dare say.'

'Did you ever act with Irving?'

'Goodness that was a long time ago,' Max hedged, not wanting to admit that he had not. 'Let's see, when was the Guv'nor called to that great green-room in the sky? Seven years back wasn't it? Seems like yesterday. What a man! He was an inspiration to everyone in the profession.' He changed the subject. 'Which of your cities are we to visit, Mr Donaldson? I have played here in Sydney, many years ago, and in Melbourne, but never farther west.'

'You'll be seeing the lot this time, Max. Sydney, Melbourne, Adelaide; then we'll trek over to Perth and, I should reckon, Kalgoorlie too. It's a heavy repertory to travel, but if I'm doing something I like to do it properly.'

'What parts did you play with Irving?' Dorothy persisted.

'I was very young then, Miss Donaldson, very young. The parts would have been very small. Practically walk-ons. I'm not sure I can remember. I tell you what I do recall, those moments when the Guv'nor used to arrive for rehearsal,' Max was improvising, 'he had his own door, y'know, at the back of the Lyceum. He'd sweep in. We'd all be laughing and chatting and suddenly he'd be among us doffing his hat and slipping off his great cloak. "Good mornin', Ladies and Gentlemen," he'd say, "shall we commence?" And we would.'

Dorothy hung on every word. Max smiled benignly at her and once more attempted to steer the conversation into safer waters.

'Is there anything interesting playing in town just now?' he enquired of the table in general. 'Delicious duck, Mrs Donaldson.'

'Black duck, Mr Milman. We have them sent up from Timberscombe, that's our place in the Hunter,' said Mrs Ralph. 'And pigeons and kangaroo tails. Have you tried kangaroo tails?'

'Can't say I have,' said Max.

'Delicious. You must dine with us when the next batch arrives. It's a real Australian delicacy. But you were asking about entertainments.'

'Yes.'

'The season is just getting under way. Do you think Mr Milman would enjoy Mrs O'Keefe's *tableaux vivants*, Ralph?'

'It would certainly launch him on the social crowd,' said her husband. 'Great character, Nelly O'Keefe. She's American. She came here in 1903 playing Cio Cio San in Belasco's *Madam Butterfly*. Married Bertie O'Keefe, a businessman. Now she runs all the big charity shows. She's tireless. At her annual *tableaux vivants* she recreates the finest visions of the Old Masters. She's been known to ransack the districts of Edgecliff or Vaucluse to find the perfect face to bring a Rubens or a Raphael alive.'

'Would you like to escort me, Mr Milman?' Dorothy asked, surprising the others by her boldness and not entirely pleasing her sister-in-law.

'Delighted, Miss Donaldson,' Max accepted.

Mrs Ralph intervened. 'We shall all be going, Mr Milman. We shall dine here beforehand and then you can go on with our party. Who knows? Perhaps the kangaroo tails will have arrived.'

Deftly she had diluted Dorothy's impulsive gesture and turned an assignation into a family outing. She smiled indulgently on her husband, the girls and their guest.

So Max's first days in Sydney were spent idylically enough. The Donaldsons introduced him to the delights of the Members Bar at the Royal Easter show and included him in their party for the races. He was on his best behaviour, neither drinking too much nor betting too wildly. Dorothy continued to focus her devotion

95

on him but between Mrs Ralph's careful chaperoning and Max's disinclination to get into trouble with his impresario's sister all was well. The outing to Mrs O'Keefe's *tableaux vivants* was considered a great success. Nelly O'Keefe cast herself as Helen Fourment, Rubens's second wife. Her low-cut dress and ample breasts provided a suitably Rubensesque effect for Max to admire. Her head was crowned with a tilted hat, turned up at one side studded with pearls and stuck with feathers.

'Quite a handful there,' Max mused to Ralph Donaldson, 'even if she do lack some of Mrs Rubens's elfin charm.'

Max made himself thoroughly at home at the Australia Hotel rubbing shoulders happily with the graziers. He was exploring Sydney, unaware as he learnt its map that it would be his home, off and on, for the next forty years. From his visits to the Donaldsons he got to know Rushcutter's Bay Park and the boxing stadium. Darling Point, and its hinterland, Woollahra. Point Piper and Bellevue Hill became his stalking grounds. Darlinghurst and the Cross yielded pleasant surprises and very soon, walking home from Stowey, he came upon Woolcott Street and brightened at the sight of the prostitutes waiting hopefully in their doorways. He selected the prettiest and led her to the sea wall in the Park where he quickly forgot any vows he had made to Ruby and considered the price he was paying very reasonable for the pleasure afforded.

Casting

Billy Little finally persuaded Amanda Bollington that she should accept her son's invitation to play opposite her ex-husband.

'When you deal with Harmon, the manager,' she told him firmly, as they sat cosily on a red banquette at the Caprice, 'make sure he knows how reluctant I am to take this role. It will be a very good bargaining point, Mr Little.'

'Do call me Billy.'

'I may do that after I see what sort of deal you make for me. After all this is your first negotiation on my behalf, and I'm not doing it cheap because I'm the author's mother.'

She fluttered a hand with just the right degree of intimacy and not too much enthusiasm at Noel Coward, whom Mario was showing to a table.

'What's Noel doing for the coronation season?' she asked Billy.

'*The Apple Cart*,' he said. 'The Oliviers have got a comedy by Terry Rattigan – topical, it's about a coronation; Wolfit's at the King's, Hammersmith and Redgrave's up at Stratford doing his nut with three heavy Shakespeares, *très gai*! Martyn's been very clever, doing the only new British musical, if you don't count a Hylton thing with Fred Emney and there's half a show at the Players called *The Boyfriend*. I'm told Martyn's advance is building already. We can't afford to miss it.'

'Nonsense. That's negative thinking,' snapped Amanda. '*They* can't afford to miss *me*. I don't want you giving Harmon the idea that I'm lucky to get the part. I can't emphasise that enough. And of course I must be billed above Milman. Martyn and that Fane woman will obviously be on top. I suppose little Maude will come immediately below . . .'

97

'Perhaps I could get you an "and Amanda Bollington" at the bottom?'

'If Maximilian had his way it would be "*but* Amanda Bollington",' Amanda sniffed. 'No, I imagine Martyn'll want to bill us on the same line like Nervo and Knox or some awful old variety act. If he does, make sure I get the left-hand position. He can't really argue about that, it's alphabetical. One other thing, Mr Little, I haven't seen a script yet. You may start negotiations with Harmon but make it perfectly clear that nothing can be concluded until I have read the play. That should give you another advantage.'

'You would have been a wonderful agent yourself . . . if you hadn't been so beautiful,' said Billy, wondering if he had laid it on too heavily.

Amanda took the compliment without a flicker. 'The way some of my representatives have conducted my affairs in the past I have often thought so. I am looking for a marked improvement, Mr Little.'

'I'll drink to that.' Billy raised his glass decorously to hers and they sipped together. Amanda fell on her dover sole with gusto and Billy began to feel that she was thawing.

In the music room at St Leonard's Terrace Martyn and Louis were in the middle of their first argument. Martyn was not used to having his material challenged. The late Dominick had merely given his characters a few simple steps and arranged the groups of actors gracefully on stage for the ensembles. Here was his American successor demanding movement. Worse, he wanted actual dancers. Worse still, he insisted on auditioning the Pensioners to see how well they could move.

'If you want to put all these dances in, quite a lot of the dialogue's going to have to go,' said Martyn testily.

'Not a moment too soon.'

'I thought you liked the book.'

'It's a strong, melodramatic story, Martyn, and there are some good laughs; but these are the fifties. It's got to move. And if your old hands *can't* move they'll have to move *on*. I thought you said you wanted to stand comparisons with the Broadway article. So far this is a costume parade with songs. They are very good songs which is why I want to stage them but for Christ's sake don't cling to your pre-war ideas. Fucking Novello's dead!'

'Poor Ivor!'

The more positive Louis became the more insecurity racked Martyn. Having convinced himself that Louis was essential to the success of his new show, every word of criticism made him feel more inadequate.

'We need to rethink the sets, too.'

Louis sensed he had Martyn on the run.

'I've been up half the night thinking of those designs that old queen of yours brought in. Right now it's built scene, front cloth, built scene, front cloth. It needs to flow. I've got an idea for a number that should do just that.'

'What sort of number?' Martyn asked wanly.

'You know that place where they go to ride. The society crowd . . .'

'Rotten Row?'

'Right. Give me something like "Riding in the Row". I can shift the chorus to it. Release some energy. And we can incorporate that running gag you're so keen on, too.'

'Tommy Trafford?'

'That's the guy – the one who's off stage in Wilde and you want to see proposing to Maude and being rejected every time he appears.'

Martyn was aghast. 'Surely you don't want to lose that!'

'You're not listening, Martyn. I said "incorporate" not "obliterate". Loosen up! Kick ass! We've got to get this show on the road. What was the designer's name? Cedric? You should fire him and talk to his assistant. Now *he* is bright!'

'But Cedric's designed all my musicals.'

'Let him do the clothes then. As long as my dancers can move in them.'

Cedric accepted his demotion with ill grace but declined to flounce out, explaining to anyone who would listen that even if Martyn was not loyal to him, *he* couldn't let Martyn down and he was determined to be at his old friend's side in this moment of crisis.

99

Some of the Pensioners to whom Cedric had moaned talked to each other and agreed that probably Cedric was a bit past it. The smile was wiped off their faces when they were summoned to audition. Suddenly, 'the young American' was transformed into a monster.

'What has got into Martyn? The *idea* of auditioning! What can there be that he doesn't know about us? No less than we know about him, dear.'

When Harry Harmon's office sent out the summonses, some of them refused to believe that they were being subjected to the indignity.

'Surely he can't mean *me*!' they protested to their agents. 'He must mean the supers – Martyn always has a few small parts hanging about to dress the stage.'

'I'm afraid Harmon's office was quite specific,' the agents all replied. 'Miss Oates has been ringing around personally so that there will be no misunderstanding.'

'I'll bet she loved that,' they chorused to their various representatives. 'It's just the sort of mean victory Dymphna Oates has been looking for.'

'She actually had the nerve to tell me that to appear in a Milman show was not a God-given right when I was off during the last weeks of *Wonderful Moonlight*,' moaned one.

'She's power-mad, dear,' said another. 'Has anyone met this American yet?'

'Soon enough when we have to sing for the little blighter.'

'I'm told he's going to make us dance, too.'

'I'm bound to be out. I've got two left feet. Always have had. Martyn knows that perfectly well. It's sheer sadism.'

'Perhaps that's what appeals to Martyn?'

'Ooh! Back in the knife box, Miss Sharp!'

Auditions were held at His Majesty's. Martyn, Harry Harmon and Louis sat in the centre of the stalls, attended by Dymphna Oates who was in her element, armed with sheaves of notes and lists, photographs and resumés of the candidates. Freda August hovered in the row behind them. A piano had been pulled out from the wings and a naked light lit the stage. Martyn, too embarrassed to conduct the ritual himself, left everything to Louis.

'Good morning, Martyn,' each candidate would gush, only to find themselves handed over summarily to the implacable choreographer.

'What have you done?' he asked one veteran.

'You mean since breakfast?' snapped Adela Skelton, whom Martyn wanted for Lady Basildon.

'No, I meant when did you last work?'

'Surely Martyn has told you, we've done so much together.'

'What are you going to sing?'

'You really want me to sing?' Adela was not going to give in without a fight.

Louis turned to Dymphna Oates. 'Didn't you tell her agent?'

'Of course I did. Haven't you brought your music, Adela?'

'Certainly not. Martyn knows my range.'

'Martyn is not staging the musical numbers. I am,' said Louis evenly. 'I don't know your work.'

'That makes you unique, young man,' Adela said unwisely.

Freda August tapped Martyn on the shoulder. 'Shall I pop up and play "Happy Little Home" for her?'

'Good idea, Freda. That was her number in *April in Provence*,' Martyn told Louis.

Freda edged her way along the row and up the temporary steps which gave her access to the stage over the orchestra pit. 'Martyn wants me to play for you, dear,' she said to Adela, who had been scanning the stalls, her hand shading her eyes as she peered into the darkness, trying to work out what was going on down there. 'You remember "Happy Little Home", don't you?'

'Of course I do. Does he really want me to sing it again? He had to listen to it for three hundred and forty performances when I was playing opposite him.'

'It's for Mr Armbruster, dear,' said Freda, making her way across to the piano and displacing the rehearsal pianist who got up and lounged against it, watching with amusement as Adela Skelton reluctantly made her way to stand in the well.

Taking a chiffon handkerchief from her pocket Adela turned and nodded to Freda, who embarked on the introduction.

'Stop,' snapped Louis from the stalls. 'Put that handkerchief away. Just stand and sing.'

Adela swallowed, opened her mouth to protest, shut it again and replaced the handkerchief in her pocket. Freda played the introduction once more – this time a little louder. Adela's usually firm contralto quavered as she launched into the first verse. However, by the time she reached the chorus some of her confidence had returned. 'Ours is a happy little home,' she was trilling, as Louis ran down the aisle clapping his hands and yelling, 'Stop! Stop!'

Adela looked stunned as Freda's accompaniment tailed off.

'All right, Miss . . . Miss . . .'

'Skelton,' said Adela.

'All right, Miss Skelton. The singing's okay. There's a call back for movement at twelve tomorrow. It'll be a group audition. Come at twelve, bring your dance shoes and something you can move in.'

'You want me to dance?'

'I want to see you move.'

'I hope you haven't turned Lady Basildon into a Gaiety Girl,' muttered Adela Skelton as a parting shot and stalked off into the wings feeling slightly better for having had the last word. Unfortunately she walked straight into a cul-de-sac formed by two pieces of scenery so she had to creep back on stage and around the set. She heard Dymphna Oates snigger in the stalls.

Martyn's spirits sank as the day continued. More of his old colleagues were subjected to Armbruster's brusque inquisitions. They reacted with varying degrees of co-operation but no one was allowed to get away without performing. Darcy, Lysander and Imogen were among those paraded for the choreographer's approval. The only exceptions made were Maude and Amanda and, of course, Max, who was still in Australia.

'Do you think Lady Milman could come to the dance call tomorrow, Martyn?' Louis asked. 'It's not to audition; but I'd like to know how she moves so that I get some idea of what I can push her to.'

'I'm sure she won't mind,' said Martyn, 'and it'll be good for the others if they see Maude co-operating. I'm glad you haven't asked Mother to shake a leg. That might be the last straw.'

'I think we've finally got Amanda on board, Martyn,' Harry Harmon interrupted. 'I had a long chat with Billy Little this morning. He's being very tough about the money and very fussy about the billing. Seems to think she's indispensable – which in a way I suppose she is since we're making such a splash of this family thing.'

Just as the little group was preparing to leave the stalls at the end of the afternoon a breathless young man appeared in the wings. Clutching some sheet music he advanced nervously to the front of the stage.

'Excuse me, Sir Martyn . . . Sir Martyn,' he said, 'I'm afraid I don't have an appointment but Lady Milman rang me. She suggested that I should sing for you. I just did Marchbanks with her on the wireless and she said you might need someone for Tommy Trafford. She told me you'd written him in . . .'

'What's your name?'

'Oh, I'm sorry, Sir Martyn, Adrian, sir, Adrian Arbuthnot.'

'What are you going to sing?'

'Lady Milman said he was a sort of silly-ass type so I've brought a Gershwin number. "Stiff Upper Lip". It's frightfully British.'

He handed the music to the pianist, then launched into the song in a confident light baritone. Soon his audience was purring with pleasure. When the song was over they advanced down the aisle in a phalanx to the front of the stage to congratulate him.

'Mr Arbuthnot,' said Louis, 'that is the first professionally presented audition we have heard today. Come back at twelve tomorrow so that I can check out your movement. Do you want to read him, Martyn?'

'Oh no, I don't think so. I'll ask Maude about you tonight, Mr Arbuthnot. That was very pleasant,' he added. 'I'm sure you can handle the dialogue. You're exactly what I'm looking for for Tommy Trafford. Now it's just a question of whether Mr Armbruster here likes what you can do with your feet.'

'Thank you, sir. I'll come at twelve then.'

Adrian Arbuthnot disappeared through the stage door leaving behind him a happy team beaming with the satisfaction that only comes from knowing that they had found at least one actor perfect for his role and, better still, a new actor, a new face.

'I wonder why Lady Milman didn't tell you he was coming?' Louis asked Martyn as they shared a taxi going west.

'It's often better not to crack somebody up before an audition,' Martyn told him. 'There's always the chance my hopes would have been too high and then the disappointment would be greater. And, *now* we have the feeling that we've discovered him for ourselves, haven't we? That makes *us* feel good.'

Martyn had a shrewd idea why Maude had sprung Adrian Arbuthnot on him and an equally shrewd idea of her long-term strategy. It could be very convenient, he thought, if she had a young admirer on tour. The more he worked with Louis – the more he saw of his determined, confident, demanding behaviour – the more he remembered the physical attraction which he had felt on their first meeting. He reckoned that Louis was likely to reciprocate. He put from his mind the speculation that Louis's motives might be more professional than personal. Martyn was used to being admired. Already he was reluctant to cross Louis in their theatrical discussions. He wondered if this was his opportunity to discover whether his instinct was correct. Their taxi was taking them along Piccadilly.

'What did you make of my Pensioners?' he asked.

'We can use some of them. They're going to have to learn some new tricks. And some new disciplines. God knows how you got performances out of them! Did you find today very awkward?'

'A bit. Some of them have worked for me over nearly twenty years. It did leave me a little worn.'

Louis stretched out his right hand and felt the back of Martyn's neck. 'Christ, you're tense again! Do you want to come back to my place for a rub?' He tapped on the glass partition of the cab. 'Hollywood Road,' he said.

Darcy let himself quietly into Louis's flat. He wanted to know how the day had gone and more particularly how his own audition had been received. He was disappointed to find the hall in darkness. He had felt sure Louis would be back by now. Perhaps he had gone on to the Scala to check on *Pennsylvania!* He usually looked in once a week. Darcy thought he would telephone the theatre and check. He opened the sitting-room door and pressed the wall switch, flooding the room with light. In front of the bright gas fire he saw his father, naked on the hearthrug, kneeling at Louis's feet. Louis was also naked. His toupée was hanging on the wing of an armchair.

Several hours and many drinks later Darcy was walking aimlessly through fog-blind Chelsea streets. Gay London surrounded him, scarcely apparent to those who did not inhabit it. Discreet, secret, concentrated in small clubs and particular pubs, it was invisible to the man looking down from the Clapham omnibus even if he could have pierced the shrouding gloom. It was not so invisible to the police who might swoop on a bar which had grown in notoriety as an increasing number of homosexuals found it a congenial rendezvous. On a 'warning' the clientele would all migrate to another pub in some mysterious, mutual, masonic movement. The specialist clubs were more closeted, low key and decorous. A single room, a small bar and an upright piano supplied a background against which a tentative lock of hair could be let down. Proprietorial caution saw to it that 'disreputable incidents' were frowned upon. To a suspicious suggestion from a pair of visiting coppers that the club's membership seemed to be entirely male, it was a foolhardy proprietor who pointed out that you could say the same about the Athenaeum, the Navy – or indeed the police force. Safer to sweeten the officers.

Darcy was aware of the risk of seeking satisfaction in the streets, although it had its dangerous allure. Some months ago, before he met Louis, he had been walking home towards Cheyne Walk when he passed the metal, open-to-the-air lavatory which stood at the end of Lots Road, known as the 'Iron Lung'. As he approached he saw two loiterers. Darcy crossed to the other side of the road. As he did so he was passed by an elderly man, neatly dressed, with grey hair, who walked by the two men who lounged against the embankment wall. He headed for the lavatory. The younger of the two swiftly followed him in. Curious, Darcy stood in the shadows, out of the glare of the street lamps. Very soon he heard a disturbance inside the Iron Lung. The second loiterer ran inside. Darcy, assuming that the two were roughs engaged in robbing the old man, hurried across to protest as they dragged him out. They twisted their victim's arms up behind his back. He writhed and wept. Summoning his courage, Darcy advanced on them and shouted, 'Stop that! I'll call the police.'

'We are the police,' snarled the older man.

'Filthy old pervert!' said the younger, better-looking officer.

The two policemen now had their victim bent over the embankment. He started to scream.

'Go and phone Chelsea police station,' said the older. 'Tell 'em to send the van to the Iron Lung. They'll know what you mean.'

Darcy felt sick. He wanted to refuse; but as he saw the frail old figure struggling more violently he was afraid he would injure himself. He ran to a call box by Battersea Bridge and dialled the number he had been given. The phone was picked up immediately. The duty sergeant took the information in his stride. By the time Darcy had returned to the scene of the attack the police van, which had obviously been standing by, was screaming to a halt. Darcy hovered horrified as the younger, 'prettier' policeman, the bait, and his partner, together with two heavier men from the van, manhandled what was now a bloodied wreck into the vehicle. Doubtless there would be commendations all round in the morning, thought Darcy bitterly. He resolved to give the Iron Lung and its equivalents a wide berth.

However on this traumatic night, unable to stand his own company, he dragged himself to the Queen's Head, the pub where he had first met Louis. He drank steadily until closing time, ignoring the other drinkers as the pub filled up. By the time the kilted pianist got round to playing his selection from *Pennsylvania!* Darcy was too drunk to feel the pain. At closing time he refused to go home alone. His befuddled mind was still debating whose betrayal he resented more bitterly – his father's or his lover's. He decided that he hated them both and was surprised to find himself harbouring thoughts of revenge. As Darcy was a self-centred young man, his first idea was not to damage Martyn and Louis, but to gratify himself. Bastards! he was thinking, I'll show them! However, showing them was the last thing he intended. He made his way down to the King's Road, crossed to Cheltenham Terrace and made for Royal Hospital Road. A plan was forming in his mind as a dense fog swirled and far-away footsteps clattered anonymously.

Darcy had been living on his own for some months since he had moved out from St Leonard's Terrace and rented his studio. There had been odd encounters and one-night stands. There had been the more serious affair with Louis, but, he thought, I still haven't had a guardsman. Everybody I know has. The idea obsessed him. He stood on the corner by the barracks peering into the fog, listening for a solid tread. None approached. He turned and felt his way back up Lower Sloane Street, confident that as the pubs were out he would soon score. For a time he was unsuccessful. He patrolled the length of Sloane Street, turned at Knightsbridge and retraced his steps down the opposite side of the road. A friend had, on such a foggy night, pleasured a guardsman in a sentry-box outside Buckingham Palace, dropping half-crowns into his boots as he did so, reassured that the soldier's colleague in the next box was keeping a look-out. Darcy did not feel quite brave enough for this.

Frustrated, he decided to spread his net wider and struck out from Sloane Square towards Victoria. Here too the streets were barren of promise and he sank on to a dank bench in Grosvenor Gardens and listened for signs of activity. Presently, padding through the fog, came a wizened, adenoidal teenager in stringy cords held together by a black, studded, leather belt. Darcy's spirits sank as the boy asked. 'Got the time, mate?'

'Around midnight,' he replied. The boy stood staring at him. Noticing the belt Darcy bridged the awkward silence by pointing at it. 'What's that for?'

'Yah,' said the teenager slyly.

Darcy reckoned that he could not be more than fifteen.

'Yah,' he repeated. 'That's for the mattakicks. Tickle their bums with it. Makes the buggers go mad. Want a go?'

Darcy declined and walked back through Eaton Square to Sloane Street. The occasional taxi limped by at five miles an hour. He was alone but for occasional night prowlers, illuminated by the diffuse orange glow of the street lamps. They cast nervous glances at him, pretending to peer into shop windows. They looked back over their shoulders as they moved on. For Darcy, they were not right. By now the determination to possess a guardsman was all-consuming. As another figure flitted by, Darcy began to despair and to lose the instinct for the chase in a wave of self-pity. Suddenly, as he rounded Sloane Square for the second time and walked along the side of Peter Jones, he spotted the bulky figure of a man, perhaps six foot five tall, plodding purposefully on the other side of the King's Road. Darcy stopped in his tracks and studied the window display, ostentatiously looking round as his quarry drew near. The message was clearly understood as the man, perhaps a guardsman judging by his physique though he was not in uniform, crossed the road. He took up his position, looking intently at the next window display some twenty feet away. Seeing that the man was studying an elaborate table decoration, an improbable interest, Darcy's heart leapt. Their eyes locked briefly. Darcy registered an open face and questioning eyes. With a slight beckoning inflection of his head he walked slowly round the corner into Cadogan Gardens and waited to see if he was followed. The man approached and came into foggy amber focus under the street lamp.

'Like a cup of coffee?' Darcy mumbled. 'I live near here.'

'Yes,' said the man, adding slowly in a soft Welsh accent, 'They call me Nicky.'

They moved off together.

Welsh Guards, thought Darcy.

'I'm David,' he lied.

They hardly spoke as he led the soldier back to his flat. Suddenly he was possessed by misgivings. The man was so tall he must be a guardsman. On the other hand policemen were invariably tall. What if this policeman was not alone? What if he was a decoy? In the fog they could easily be shadowed by a colleague. He half-reassured himself that he had committed no offence so far. He felt a measure of relief when they reached their destination. Letting his prize into the block as quietly as he could, he made quickly for his own front door. After they had entered, he secured it behind them. He took the soldier's coat, still not sure if he was a soldier, and hung it behind the door and went into the kitchen alcove to boil the kettle.

'Would you rather have a beer?' he called out.

'No, coffee's fine.'

'Black or white?'

'White, please. Two lumps.'

When he returned with the coffee, Nicky was sitting on the bed, staring in front of him. Darcy registered his large feet in black highly polished shoes and once again wondered – guardsman or policeman? His nervous uncertainty returned and when Nicky said 'What do you do, David?' it was a moment before he remembered the false name he had given. He decided to keep up the deception.

'I work in a bank,' he improvised, 'very boring.'

They lapsed into a long silence. Occasionally Nicky would raise his eyes from the mug of coffee he was cradling in both hands and dart a glance across at Darcy. Was it uncertainty? Was he nervous or was he waiting for his partner in crime prevention to burst through the door and catch them *in flagrante*? Darcy found it hard to rid himself of the fear that he was being set up.

'Would you like another cup?'

'No, thanks,' said Nicky, dully. At that moment his eyes lit up as he looked across at the sideboard in a corner of the studio. Darcy watched, puzzled, as he got up eagerly and moved towards it. On top stood a cheap toy which Darcy had bought to amuse his cousin's baby. He was due to visit the family that weekend. It was a fluffy, yellow squeaking duck. Nicky lifted it in fascination and pressed it until it gave a high-pitched quack. Gurgling with pleasure he brought it back to the bed and continued to play with it.

Fuck this for a lark, thought Darcy, whatever else he is, he's not a copper. He crossed to the bed and sat beside Nicky, who looked at him without surprise. Darcy unbuttoned Nicky's flies, then he motioned Nicky to unbutton him. Obediently, after a final quack, the young man set aside the duck and helped Darcy to exorcise his betrayal.

When the ceremony was completed the actor unlocked the

door and reached for his coat to find some cash. He had no idea what a guardsman charged.

'Er – how much?' he asked.

Even if his partner had seemed to enjoy the experience, Darcy knew he hadn't come for free.

'Ten bob, please,' said Nicky.

Darcy handed him a ten-shilling note.

'Thank you,' said the young man and hesitated for a moment.

'Is there something else?' asked Darcy.

'Well . . .' Nicky moved from one foot to another. 'Would you mind if I took the duck?'

Darcy stifled his smile. 'Please,' he said, gesturing towards the toy.

Delighted, Nicky leapt towards it, gave it a triumphant squeeze and then placed it with a care approaching reverence in the large pocket of his overcoat.

'Good night, David,' he said as he let himself out. 'See you.'

As he heard the front door close Darcy let out a yell of laughter, flung himself on to his bed and hugged his sides. What a story! he thought. What a pity I can't tell Louis. Then he reconsidered. Maybe he could.

The next morning Sir Martyn decided not to attend Louis's dance call. If the blood of some of his old friends was to be spilled he would prefer not to be a witness. Nor was he keen to encounter Darcy. As Darcy had slammed out last night, Louis had commanded: 'You're not to follow him. He had to find out sooner or later. Sooner is better.'

Conveniently Billy Little telephoned to confirm that Amanda had agreed to play Lady Markby. Martyn rang her and asked her round to hear her duet, 'The Older You Are'.

After he had played the disc twice, he tinkled the tune at the piano and was pleased when Amanda came across with her script and began to bring the song to life. He joined her on Max's lines.

They had run it through a couple of time, and she smiled. 'You know, Martyn, I'm beginning to believe this might be fun. Do you really think we'll be asked for those encores?'

Martyn, who had already written three, insisted that they would stop the show.

'If only Maximilian can be relied on to behave,' she pouted.

'I'll have to be responsible for that,' said Martyn.

'You don't remember how he went off the rails in Australia.'

'I don't remember Australia at all.'

'Why did I ever go?' Amanda asked the walls of the music room, dramatically. 'What madness it was! I was just getting used to life without Maximilian and I assumed he would be back. I had resigned myself to awaiting his return when I heard that his producer, a man called Donaldson, was in London. He was mounting *Ben Hur* and he was in trouble. Apparently he had engaged an avant-garde Australian stage manager – that's what we called directors in the old days – and they weren't getting on. I was never sure if he was incompetent or if he simply couldn't stand that fustian dialogue. Anyway Mr Donaldson postponed the whole thing with Max on full salary and came to England to persuade Ben Teal, an American who had done the original Drury Lane show at the turn of the century, to take over. I heard he was staying at the Carlton and I made him see me. Such a civilised man. Not at all my idea of an Australian. As luck would have it the girl who was playing Tirzah, Ben Hur's sister, a Miss Fitton, had walked out too and Mr Donaldson said I could have the part. I cabled Maximilian immediately in great excitement. He was so thrilled.'

Max and Ruby

'Christ! The wife's coming out,' Max exploded in the bar of the Australia. 'She's taking over from that pretentious cow, Doris Fitton.' He was drinking with a couple of the actors who were also becalmed until rehearsals could be restarted.

'When does she arrive?' asked one of them.

'She's sailing with Donaldson. Ben Teal's loading a lot of the Drury Lane machinery for the chariot race and bringing it with him. Ruby's hauling along the son and heir.'

'Nice to have the little woman with you, Max.'

Max looked doubtful.

'Still fighting off young Dorothy?' asked the other actor.

Max shrugged. 'We'll be hard at it when Teal arrives. There won't be much time for socialising.'

'Is he a bit of a taskmaster?'

'That's what they said at the Lane,' lied Max, having been touring far away in Scotland at the time.

'You know the feller then?'

'Not exactly know . . . mutual friends . . . that sort of thing.'

'We'd better keep in with you, Max. Drink up. Always good to have friends at court.'

'My shout,' said Max.

Meanwhile Ruby was enjoying the long voyage out. Martyn was as good as gold. She found Ralph Donaldson a congenial travelling companion and she struck up a good relationship with Ben Teal, the irascible American on whom the producer said so much would depend. Donaldson patiently heard her lines, of which there were very few, and Teal, sunning himself on the promenade deck of the *Orsova*, daily explained the complicated mystery of the stage machinery and the tricky genesis of the production. He had originally staged the play for the famous managers Marc Klaw and Abe Erlanger in New York in 1899, and had created a stir with his special effects.

'Lew Wallace, the General, the only begetter,' he said, slurping his mid-morning broth enthusiastically as he lounged beside her, 'wrote his story when he was Governor of New Mexico. Presidin' over fightin' an' feudin' Indians, Mexicans, Yankees an' cow pokes all speakin' different languages and scrappin' for acres. I guess he saw the Holy Land a bit like that – Jews and Arabs, Cypriots, Cretans, Greeks, Egyptians and Romans – all speakin' in different tongues and not communicating. Have I told you this before?' he asked, stopping in full flow.

'I find it fascinating,' said Ruby diplomatically. She was already bored with her character, and was hoping for better things in the new Australian bush drama. She hated the prospect of Tirzah's rags and sores for her appearance as a leper in Act V of the biblical epic.

'I see Judaea as the young America,' Teal enthused, 'keen to throw off the Roman yoke just like the native America banished the cruel British and began to stand for all that is good and free.'

Ruby finished her broth and nibbled her sandwich, occasionally turning to rock Martyn in his cot or shift its position so that the sun would not scorch him. She knew she was in for a long lecture.

'How did you become involved?' she enquired loyally.

'Quite soon, my dear, Klaw and Erlanger came up with a way of keeping Christ in the wings. They knew the General had woven Jesus in and out of his narrative but they also knew the New York audiences would not stand for some nelly, lightfooted actor in a nightshirt comin' on as the Lord. First they hired Bill Young to adapt. Now Bill is a wizard with words . . .'

Having read his play Ruby doubted this.

' . . . and when Bill came up with his solution that's when they needed me.'

'To achieve the effects?'

'The Great Effect! There had to be galley scenes, the Masque of Eros, the Revels of Daphne and of course one helluva race.

But Bill's genius was solving the Christ problem. Couldn't tell a diorama from a treadmill, but he knew how to handle the Son of God. "Ben," he said to me.' Teal paused at the brilliance of the solution. ' "Ben, we'll do it with lights!" '

Ruby managed a gasp of admiration.

'As you know, the good Lord has to cure you and your mother of leprosy in the fifth act.'

Ruby shuddered again at the thought of how she would look.

'You and your mother enter, prompt side. You're in filthy, disgusting rags – haggard, weary, worn,' he paused and lowered his voice to a thrilling bass, 'leprous! Your brother enters OP side, he is searching for you. In the gloom he misses you. You exit, OP. Resting his tired ass on a rock he falls asleep. Scene change! I fly out the drop. We are on the Mount of Olives. Three hundred supers. Every damn one carries an olive branch. Hosanna! They are waiting the passing of the Saviour. My way, they don't even get to see the damned donkey. Just when they expect Jesus on the moke I cram on five limes in a blinding light. I turn 'em on the audience and rake them. I *blind* them. The miracle has happened. You throw off your rags. You rip off your warts and tear off your sores. You are beautiful! Out thunders Edgar Stillman Kelly's great music. Hosanna! In the Highest! That's how we topped the chariot race, Ruby. That's how I did it!'

'Thrilling!' said Ruby, just as Martyn was sick over the pillow in his cot. Gratefully gathering him in her arms, she made her escape.

The reunion was warm. The tugs had nudged the *Orsova* into Melbourne's Princes' Pier. They were due to take the train across the sun-bleached country to Sydney. Donaldson had not stinted. Max and a photographer were waiting. So were the Donaldson clan, in force. Only Dorothy was indisposed and did not make the journey. Ruby was photographed with Max, with Ben Teal, with Max and Ben Teal, with Max and Martyn and, finally, alone. Her wanderings around provincial England had not prepared her for such a reception. Surrounded by strangers she and Max could hardly communicate beyond a public embrace. It was late that night when they arrived in Sydney. Finally she escaped with him to their suite in the Australia Hotel.

'Tired, old girl?' he asked as they settled the baby in his cot.

'I'm too excited to be tired, darling. I expect it will hit me tomorrow.'

'Like the diggings?'

'Very grand! Are you sure we can afford it?'

'They seem to like me out here. Very hospitable people. Then again, a chap has to show the flag, stand his round. Means a lot to the Aussies. Can't take rooms in a back street. That'd be letting the side down.'

Ruby felt a twinge of anxiety. She had never heard Max talk quite so extravagantly before. In England his touring routine of theatre, digs and pubs had been hallowed by habit. It was modest, friendly and familiar. In spite of the odd after-the-show binge, she had always managed to balance the books. Suddenly she realised that she was a long way from home. However, Max took her gently in his arms and in the moments that followed she forgot all her anxieties.

Ben Teal's strength was technical and the actors were left to get on with their parts as best they could. This suited Max who happily devised his own noble postures and thundered out the creaking dialogue with resolute conviction. 'There have been soldiers in my family,' he would intone. 'Fought they not as bravely as the Roman? How oft hast thou told me of their deeds! And how often praised them for their valour and their victories. Mother! Canst thou so misjudge me?'

Most of Ruby's scenes were played down-stage in front of conventional painted scenery but when she was not required on stage, which was often, she sat in the darkness of the stalls and watched Teal putting his spectacular effects together. For the prologue the curtain rose on a gauze drop. Then its dark backing was flown to reveal a desert view with two of the wise men, Balthasar and Melchior, artfully posed on their camels. Real camels. Then Caspar, the third wise man, in Greek garb, arrived on his beast. A star moved across the backdrop, growing in intensity. To swelling music Caspar, Balthasar and Melchior descended from their mounts and prostrated themselves before the star. The backing to the gauze was flown in again and more music, a great deal more music, thundered out and covered the elaborate transformation.

Ruby often found Dorothy Donaldson sitting beside her in the dusty auditorium, a place of chaos with bits of scenery waiting to be transferred to the stage and assembled. Considering herself by now a seasoned campaigner, she was amused by the young girl's admiration for Max.

'Isn't he wonderful, Mrs Milman?' she would say. 'It's so rarely that we get great actors here in Australia.'

Producer's sister, thought Ruby, better be polite.

'I've asked Ralph if I can be your understudy,' Dorothy gushed. 'I'd never thought of being an actress before but now it seems the only thing that makes life worthwhile.'

'It's not all fun and games, you know,' Ruby warned her, 'touring can be rough.'

'Oh, but that's what I'm looking forward to. What a wonderful way to see Australia!'

On the stage, Ben Teal's store of effects was piling up. The episode aboard the Roman galley with Max virtually stripped naked as a galley slave was achieved with traditional scene-building and painting techniques, skilfully carried out in the Sydney workshops under Teal's close supervision. The collision and fight with the pirates was performed with savage intensity and rocking scenery; clever lighting and delicately painted waves enabled Ben Hur and the Roman, Arrius, to give the illusion of a struggle to keep afloat until the rescuing trireme was winched on up-stage-left to effect their rescue from the waves. Ruby observed Dorothy inching closer to the stage the better to observe Max's impressive physique.

Teal's masterpiece was indeed the chariot race. To bring it off he had combined two ancient stage effects. Up-stage three endless belts of backcloth, dioramas, suggested the crowded stadium. In front of them treadmills which could be moved forward or back at the touch of off-stage controls enabled the horses to gallop furiously on the spot. What Teal aimed at was to reproduce

Alexander von Wagner's 1893 picture, *The Chariot Race*. Ralph Donaldson had displayed a large copy in the theatre foyer and had already excited popular interest in Sydney by blazing it across half a page in the *Bulletin*. It illustrated a race in the Roman Circus Maximus, the cheering crowds, the vast space in vivid perspective, crashed chariots littering the track and, in front of them two charioteers – one marginally in the lead – as they drove their violently straining horses into the final laps. Teal had changed von Wagner's layout so that the leading teams raced neck-and-neck. The villain, Messala, harrying his team of two black and two white horses, was clad in scarlet and gold. Max, as Ben Hur, was robed in a white tunic, driving a team of bays.

'Ralph had the bays brought down from Timberscombe,' Dorothy confided to Ruby, 'but we had to scour all the stables in Sydney to track down the black and whites with the right markings. Doesn't Mr Milman look wonderful in white?' she added.

'It's certainly a very effective scene,' said Ruby, increasingly aware of Dorothy's obsessive interest in Max, and equally aware that as she sat there in her leper's rags and carefully applied sores she did not look like very lively competition for the fresh seventeen-year-old who sat beside her.

The background and sides of von Wagner's painting having been broken into the three moving backcloths, Teal spent hours synchronising them to create the illusion of the race course with spectators retreating behind the rapidly advancing chariots. The stage was supported underneath by enormous cross-beams and great uprights so that the eight horses in Ben Hur's and Messala's teams could pound away on their treadmills for dear life. The treadmills themselves, large enough to accommodate both chariots and both teams, were neatly fitted into the floor. Covered with rubber and felt they became part of the track. Such noise as the treadmills made was drowned in the furious gallop of the horses, the whirring of the chariot wheels, and the swelling orchestra. As the great panorama of the crowds in the circus seats moved around the stage and the horses tore along, the illusion had Ruby gasping in the stalls.

Beside her Dorothy clapped her hands in excitement as the horses, rehearsed daily by Teal, set off at a killing pace. As the chariots alternately drew ahead the horses plunged and reared. Powerful electric fans in the wings raised a wind which blew the loose trappings of the horses in the air and flurried the cloaks and tunics of the drivers as they leant out over their chariots. Another mighty blast of air from under the horses' hooves and the chariots' wheels raised what appeared to be clouds of dust, caught up and wheeled away behind the charioteers. The collision in which Ben Hur drives against Messala's wheels and brings about the catastrophe was so realistic that the wheel which was detached was sent spinning across the stage. At that precise moment Teal commanded a black-out and during it, to a triumphant burst of music, a scene drop slipped down between Ben Hur's chariot, which was nearest the footlights, and Messala's wrecked affair. The panorama, upstage of the drop, stopped moving and a crowd of a hundred and fifty supers raced on to the stage in the darkness. Up went the lights revealing Max striking a bravura pose above his panting, foaming steeds, the crowd yelling their hurrahs as he gave his victory salute.

It took Teal two eighteen-hour days of solid rehearsal before the chariot race was brought off to his satisfaction and when he finally pronounced that it could not be done better Max called on the exhausted company to give him three cheers.

'You're a taskmaster, Ben,' he told him, 'but, by God, you know how to make theatre.'

Expansively he invited Teal to dine and, seeing Dorothy and Ralph in the stalls, suggested they should join the party.

Back at the Australia Hotel champagne flowed. Ruby went up to check that Martyn was asleep and, when she returned, was alarmed to find Max expansively ordering more.

'What a night, Ralph!' he was saying. 'Can't wait to get that in front of the public tomorrow. Ben, you're a genius!'

'Glad to have you on board, Max,' said Teal. 'I thought Morgan was good in New York, certainly better than Taber, the guy who played it in London; but I've got to hand it to you for sheer power. Your Australian Messala is all right, Donaldson; but I wish I could have matched Max here and Bill Hart who played him for me with Klaw and Erlanger. Now that would have been a contest!'

'Can I quote you on Max, Ben?' Ralph asked. 'It wouldn't hurt to tell the press you think you've found your best Ben Hur yet.'

'Tell the world,' said Teal.

'More champagne!' called Max, flushed and excited. He patted Ruby's hand. 'Don't worry, girlie,' he reassured her, 'a night like this only comes along once in a lifetime. We're riding high, eat, drink and be merry! Tomorrow we open!'

Ruby, who knew better than to puncture Max's mood, smiled obediently and bided her time.

'Have you said yes to little Dorothy here yet, Ralph?' Max asked. 'Is she touring with us?'

'She certainly seems set on it. I don't see why not. Ruby, you wouldn't mind coaching my sister in your role would you?'

'Don't worry about that,' Max interposed. 'Ruby will have her hands full with the boy. As soon as the show's up and running, I'll be happy to rehearse Dorothy. Most of her scenes are with me, so I know the score.'

Ruby remembered Max's enthusiasm for rehearsing with her in Margate for *The Sign of the Cross* and felt a chill of apprehension.

'That's so generous of you, Mr Milman,' said Dorothy, 'but won't you be busy rehearsing the Bush drama?'

'There's going to be a delay before we go into rehearsal there, Dorothy,' her brother explained. 'I'm so pleased with Mr Teal's work on *Ben Hur* that I've persuaded him to stay on to stage the Ned Kelly play. He needs a lot of re-writes. He's going to use the treadmill again for the chase but he wants to introduce some other big effects. We can't have an anti-climax after this show. There's going to be a pursuit up a mountainside, an escape along a log-bridge crossing a ravine and a perilous dive twenty feet down into a tank of water.'

'It all takes time to plan,' added Teal, 'and I want to emphasise the all-Australian nature of the piece. Forget the camels for this show. We need real sheep, more horses, maybe a kangaroo. I can promise you, by the time I burn down Jones's Hotel in Glenrowan in the last act the audience will have seen enough to wipe *Ben Hur* from their minds. *The Vultures of the Wombat Ranges* is going to be a sensation.'

'Don't you think we should change the title?' asked Max. 'They tell me it was an old pot-boiler in the eighties and it certainly sounds like it.'

'Let's just call it *Ned Kelly*,' said Teal.

Donaldson agreed.

'How wonderful to be a part of something new!' said Dorothy. 'Isn't it exciting, Mr Milman?'

'Certainly is,' said Max. 'This is the life for me.'

Later, in their room, Ruby decided that the moment was still not right to tackle Max about the size of the tab he had picked up. However, the next morning as they pushed Martyn's pram through the Botanic Gardens, she finally found the courage.

'You know, Max,' she ventured, 'we spent both our salaries for the week in the dining-room last night.'

'Worth every penny, girlie. We're on to a great thing here with Donaldson.'

'But Max . . .'

'Don't you worry yourself, girlie. We're on a roll,' and, as so often, Max slipped into Shakespeare in default of an argument, ' "There is a tide in the affairs of men, which taken at the flood, leads on to fortune; omitted, all the voyage of their life is bound in shallows and in miseries." '

'But . . .'

' "On such a full sea are we now afloat, and we must take the current when it serves or lose our ventures." *Julius Caesar*,' Max added superfluously but proudly. 'Old William knew what he was talking about.'

With a sinking feeling Ruby left it. She knew better than to nag Max before such an important first night. She also knew that in his book there was no arguing with Shakespeare.

The opening at His Majesty's Theatre was all Donaldson had hoped for when he floated the idea of his season of spectacular melodrama. Social Sydney turned out in pale-pink taffetas, in grenadine and cashmere, organdie, calamanco and Bengaline poplin. Mr Courtauld's new silk cloth, recently imported from England, covered a multitude of shoulders. Three of the Donaldson girls, swathed in Ottoman plush, striped cerise and sapphire paduasoy and *peau d'ange*, draped themselves around the foyer, assuming the role of unofficial hostesses for the event. Donaldson men puffed on their pipes behind their women, not looking forward to an evening in the theatre but consoling themselves that there were going to be horses on stage towards the end of the bleak prospect. Some they might recognise and hail. Dorothy Donaldson in saffron and cinnamon with *passementerie* flitted from group to group telling everyone how wonderful Max was going to be and hinting that in no time at all she might be privileged to be acting alongside him. Nelly O'Keefe sailed into the stalls draped in rhubarb-coloured *gros de naples* with bobbles. Mr O'Keefe followed deferentially two paces behind her.

'What a night!' she yelled across the aisle to Mrs Ralph. 'I've never known Sydney so excited.'

A second cloud appeared on Ruby's horizon. One morning she awoke to find Martyn fighting for breath in his cot. The colour had left his face which grew greyer as he coughed and coughed, weak and frightened. Asthma was diagnosed by Fairfax, the Donaldsons' family doctor. Ruby knew that there were weak lungs among the Bollingtons. Ironically, she had welcomed the Australian climate as an extra reason for taking Martyn to join Max in Sydney. Now her fight for his survival became an obsession.

Max was wrapped up in the success of *Ben Hur* and preparations for *Ned Kelly*.

'Air's good here, girlie, he's a tough little bugger, he's going to pull through.'

'I can't leave him today, Max. I'll have to miss rehearsal.' Once again, in the Bush drama, Ruby was playing Max's sister. 'Wouldn't you agree, Doctor Fairfax?'

'I think you should be with him, Mrs Milman. The little chap won't really know what's happening to him. He needs you to be here and I would not advise parking him in your dressing-room at the Maj. Theatres are notoriously dusty places.'

'How long will the attack last?' asked Max, as he collected his script.

'Impossible to say. We know what causes the attacks. The

lower airways to the lungs, the bronchi, close and fill with mucus. That cuts off the passage of air in and out of the lungs.'

'Is it very painful for the child?'

'When the attack is severe the patient suffers – and this is a nasty turn.'

'What sets it off – dust?'

'We know very little about what triggers the attacks. Some authorities say it is caused by nerves and the victim can cure it by exerting his will. That obviously doesn't work when the child is as young as yours and doesn't know what's happening to him.'

Ruby took Martyn in her arms and gently rocked and comforted him. Doctor Fairfax puffed smoke from his pipe in the direction of the child and continued to explain; 'Others blame the air: some have always said that Sydney is a bad city for chests but then again, out in the bush or up the Hunter the country doctors will recommend bracing sea air for sufferers.'

Max was at the door. 'I'll have to leave Ruby with you, Doctor. Rehearsal call. Ben Teal will go mad if I'm not there. You see,' he added without a trace of irony, 'it all depends on me.'

'What about you, Mrs Milman, can you be spared?'

Max did not give Ruby time to reply.

'Oh yes, Doc,' he said promptly. 'She's got a very good understudy.'

In the days that followed, Dorothy's passionate desire to appear in the play and Ruby's obvious anxiety over Martyn's health readily convinced Ralph Donaldson to let the distraught mother off her rehearsals and performances.

In their rooms at the Australia Hotel Ruby burnt belladonna leaves in a bowl as the doctor had instructed. The sickly-sweet smoke gave Martyn some relief but left him queasy and exhausted. Called in response to another severe attack, Fairfax pumped adrenalin into the baby's arm. He explained to Ruby that the effect of the drug was to relax the bronchi and restore normal breathing. Recognising the panic in the child's eyes he gave him a little morphine to allay his alarm. One night he poured a sticky white solution of ephedrine sulphate down his throat.

'It's to get the adrenalin to the lungs without breaking down in the stomach,' he said in answer to Ruby's query.

It had little effect and when Martyn was hit once again by a severe bout Doctor Fairfax returned to the hotel with another fat syringe of adrenalin. In her anxiety, Ruby hardly noticed how late Max was getting back from the theatre.

The euphoria of his success in *Ben Hur* gave Max an exhilaration he had never before experienced. He was lionised and sought after and he saw little beyond the pleasure which that induced. On days when Martyn was conspicuously better Ruby would bring him to the theatre and give her performance as Tirzah. The fact that Dorothy cleared her things from the dressing-room on these evenings with some reluctance did not escape her notice. On other nights the understudy was always waiting wide-eyed and adoring, longing for confirmation that she was on. After the show, Dorothy carried Max off to a succession of parties and balls, where she hung on his arm with a proprietary air as Sydney society fawned over its latest attraction.

Ned Kelly was as dramatic a triumph as *Ben Hur*. Max found some comedy in designing and donning the tin-can suits of armour which surprised and delighted the Australian public who had seen him only in unrelieved heroics. Once again it was Teal's stage-craft which amazed the crowds. Just when they thought he was repeating his effects with Sergeant Kennedy's posse of police on horseback thunderously chasing the hero, he trumped them with the cataclysmic firing of Jones's Hotel. To achieve this he modified techniques borrowed from James Pain's staging of *The Last Days of Pompeii* in the open air on Coney Island which he had seen twenty-five years earlier. Gun-shots rang out through the theatre and dark figures staggered down-stage while up at the back the canvas flats representing the hotel were hinged along regular horizontal cuts and then propped up with stage-braces. As the gaudily lit conflagration flicked and flared red and orange behind the façade of the building, stage hands removed the braces and the upper storeys appeared to collapse, revealing twisted skeletal frames seen as the wreckage of the fallen walls.

The triumphant Sydney season was followed by the move to Melbourne. The apprehension that Melbourne might dismiss what Sydney had praised was soon dispelled. Daringly Ralph Donaldson decided to hold back *Ben Hur*. He opened with *Ned*

Kelly, giving Victorians a chance to thrill more speedily to the antics of their local hero. The gamble paid off. Only one note of criticism was sounded. Dorothy, who had hoped to open as Ned's sister, was frustrated by a profound improvement in Martyn's health. Ruby was restored to her role, leaving her understudy free to start speculation in the audience about the authenticity of Kate Kelly's accent, a tentative mixture of would-be-Australian and stage-Irish.

The Milmans' bill at the Australia Hotel had been well beyond their ability to pay, but Ralph Donaldson had given Max a hefty advance on the Melbourne season. Once they were there, Ruby hoped to keep her increasingly ebullient husband on a more modest budget. His continued success and Dorothy's determination to drag him to all her Donaldson cousins made her task impossible. As the tour pressed westwards to Adelaide and then to Perth, the rift between the Milmans grew.

It was in Adelaide that Max suggested that Ruby should give up the role of Kate Kelly to Dorothy and confine herself to Tirzah in *Ben Hur*. He made the excuse that it would free her to be with Martyn on some evenings, and that she couldn't cope with the accent.

'But, Max,' she pointed out, 'if I only play in one piece Ralph Donaldson is bound to cut my salary. Things are tight enough already. We'll be deeper in debt . . .'

'I've had a word with him, girlie. You are not to worry. I made it seem like we were doing him a favour – giving his little sister an opportunity.'

'She's not carrying Martyn on in the abduction scene,' yelled Ruby, 'she can use a bloody doll!' She had not sworn at Max before. In the quiet moment that followed she realised that she had never sworn at all.

At the theatre that night Max saw Dorothy.

'So, princess, did your brother tell you? You've got the part. You're the only Kate Kelly from now on.'

Dorothy pretended to be less than excited. 'It was the obvious decision,' she said, 'after those notices.'

Max ignored the judgement.

'I hear that Gretchen Kerin may not be coming to Perth,' Dorothy added.

'News to me.'

'Ralph told me this morning; I think he may ask me to play Esther in *Ben Hur*.'

'You *are* moving fast, princess.'

'You know I can do it, Max. I have the words off pat already and with you to rehearse me . . .' she looked up at him 'I could be so much more convincing than Gretchen. That scene in act six when Malluch brings on Esther heavily veiled . . .' She draped a large lawn handkerchief over her head. Max slipped into the reunion scene he had now played many times with the statuesque Gretchen Kerin. He felt a tender new charge as he spoke the lines.

'Malluch!' he declaimed. 'But this is not Amrah.'

Dorothy whisked the handkerchief off her hair and smiled winningly.

'Esther!' Max breathed the word in his lowest, most throbbing tones. 'Thou' (long pause) 'here?'

Taking advantage of a very explicit stage direction Dorothy threw herself into his arms.

'Oh Judah!' She caressed his face. 'Oh, how thou hast suffered!'

'It is nothing.'

Max cradled her in his arms. 'But, Judah,' she said, 'what sound of surging is it I hear?' Gretchen Kerin at this moment, would have taken a step back and cupped her ear in an extravagant gesture with her right hand. Dorothy stayed in Max's arms as she looked up at him.

'It is nothing,' he said.

'Dost thou hear it? Then it is no fancy. Judah Ben Hur! Thine eyes are mild.'

'I saw Him – the Nazarene. The new light of the world! Oh, was it but a vision of sleep – false like so many another?'

'Vision it was, but it was not false. Oh, Judah, Heaven hath sent thee this token. Thou shalt see it confirmed.'

At this moment in the play Ben Hur's mother and sister arrive, miraculously cured of their leprosy. Dorothy now thought of another way to end the scene. Pulling Max's head down towards hers and reaching up with her lips she repeated her line.

'It is confirmed,' she said, and drew him into a kiss. 'Oh, Max,' she whispered. 'It's so much better acting your lover than your sister.'

Zelda

The kitchen cabinet convened downstairs at St Leonard's Terrace. Grace fussed over her Aga preparing dinner. Tony helped himself to a beer from the fridge. Together they plied the children with questions. Darcy was absent but Lysander and Imogen were full of Louis's dance class-cum-audition which had taken place that day on the stage of His Majesty's. Hanna, equally keen to hear how things were going, materialised with some sewing for Maude. With her was her son, Kurt, a medical student, who never needed an excuse to be near Imogen.

'You should have seen Adela Skelton's face,' said Lysander. 'He actually shouted at her.'

'Do 'er good,' muttered Grace, 'stuck-up cow. She'd never work if it wasn't for your father.'

'She was wearing *brogues*. Armbruster asked where her dance shoes were.'

'She said she hadn't got any.'

'He blew his top. Yelled at her. Told her he'd asked her personally the day before.'

'It was awful,' said Imogen. 'He told her to take her shoes off. She said "What about my feet?" '

Lysander butted in with an imitation of Louis: 'It's your fuckin' feet I want to see, woman! They have to do the dancing, not your fuckin' shoes. Kick 'em off, lady.'

'She climbed down a bit then. She fished in her bag and pulled out a pair of gym shoes. "I have brought a pair of my cleaner's plimsolls," she said, pulling herself up to her full five foot three.'

Lysander took on Louis's accent again. 'What the fuck are

plimsolls? Oh, sneakers. Why didn't you say? Get the goddam things on!'

'I thought Adela was going to faint. I don't think she'd ever been spoken to like that.'

'Oh yes, she has.' Grace abandoned her Aga for a moment. 'I heard Noel Coward bawl her out once. And he didn't mince his words. First day of rehearsal it was and she wasn't up on her part. He had 'er in tears, the Master did.'

'I hope the Yank was more polite to your mother,' said Tony.

'Good as gold. I didn't know Mummy could move so well. She was quite the star.'

'She always was a lovely dancer,' said Hanna, who had been listening enviously, 'light as a feather bed.'

'Light as a feather, Mama,' Kurt corrected his mother. He looked across at Imogen. 'How did this monster treat you, Imo?'

'All right,' she said. 'He didn't seem too interested.'

'Fool!' snapped her admirer. 'If he gives you any trouble, you let me know.'

'Would you challenge him to a duel for me?' she teased.

'There are easier ways to take care of him,' he said darkly.

'I think Lysander might need your help before me.'

'Was he down on you?' asked Tony.

'He did give me quite a hard time,' Lysander admitted. 'You know, he got us all in a line-up – all the chaps – and made us learn a few steps. Unfortunately he put me next to a fellow called Adrian and I'm afraid he showed me up a bit. He was such a smoothie, so light on his feet, I shouldn't be surprised if he isn't a bit of a gigolo – a cake-eater at the very least.'

'Who is a cake-eater at the very least?' Maude, bathed and changed, had come downstairs to join the group.

'The man I was next to in the line-up, Ma. Adrian something.'

'Adrian Arbuthnot,' said Maude firmly. 'A very nice young boy. He was my Marchbanks on the wireless. Such a promising actor. Your father has cast him as Tommy Trafford. I'm so pleased.'

Tony and Grace exchanged looks.

'Is Darcy eating here tonight?' asked Grace quickly.

'No,' said Maude, 'he told me he was going to the pictures. And Martyn's having a meeting with Louis and that young designer.'

'Chops to spare then,' Grace said.

'Why don't we dine down here? Won't you stay and eat with us?' Maude invited Hanna and Kurt, who needed no second bidding.

As they settled at the long kitchen table, Hanna plucked up the courage to say to Maude: 'This Mrs Cheveley in the play, is she not, not English?'

'She's a sort of international adventuress – that's why it's all right for Zelda Fane to play her.'

'I too am not English, said Hanna. 'Could I not perhaps be understudy?'

When Zelda Fane arrived at Southampton, Martyn and Louis, accompanied by an over-excited Harry Harmon, drove down to meet her. Zelda came off the liner looking radiant and fell into Martyn's arms for the photographers. Then she spotted Louis and embraced him with similar enthusiasm. 'Louis Armbruster, I declare! What are you doing in England?'

'You've just kissed your new choreographer,' Martyn explained. 'How does that suit you?'

'Great!'

Then Zelda spotted Harry Harmon hovering in nervous antici-pation.

'But who's this?' She bore down on him. 'This looks to me like a producer.'

'You got it in one,' said Martyn. 'May I present the prince of producers – Harry Harmon. This is Miss Zelda Fane.'

Zelda extended her hand which Harry kissed reverently.

'A great honour, Miss Fane, you're looking w . . wonderful,' he said nervously. 'I think everything's prepared, as your agent demanded, I mean asked. The flat in Hay Hill is ready, and the car. I'm having the dressing-room redecorated as soon as you've approved the design . . .'

'Mr Harmon, please! You make me sound like a monster. God knows what that man has been shouting for. It's all news to me. I'm just a little old gypsy. Isn't that right, Louis?'

'A gypsy with style, Zelda.'

'Where's your luggage, darling?' asked Martyn.

'On its way. My new secretary is looking after it.' She waved the baggage away airily. 'Why are we talking trunks? Martyn, this score is terrific. I can't wait to rehearse it. And the book, it's so strong. That scene where I try to blackmail you. I'm going to love that. You said you were going to give me a dance number. Is that ready?'

'Louis and I were up all night working on it. I think you'll be pleased.'

Harry still hovered. 'Are you sure I can't help with the luggage, Miss Fane?'

'Call me Zelda. I'm certainly going to call you Harry, unless I'm very cross with you.'

She turned towards a tall, bronzed thirty-ish man, who was supervising a gaggle of porters pushing and piloting an armada of hat boxes, cases and cabin trunks through the crowds.

'You see,' she said, 'I've come prepared for a long run. This is my secretary, Braden Jefferson. He's wonderful. He looks after just about everything, don't you, Braden?'

'I try, Miss Fane, I sure try.'

'This is Mr Armbruster, my choreographer. He's a tough task-master. And this is Mr Harmon, my producer, you must be *very* nice to him.'

'How do you do, sir.'

'And, Braden, I think you know Sir Martyn.'

'Oh yes, I remember Sir Martyn. We were in *Middlemarch* together, weren't we, Sir Martyn?'

Perhaps there was a noticeable emphasis on 'Sir'.

'We certainly were,' said Martyn, recovering swiftly from his surprise. He clasped Brad firmly by the hand and pumped it hard, looking at him for some seconds, assimilating the transformation which had taken place from the eager, ambitious, puppyish farm-boy adrift in Hollywood fifteen years ago, into the smooth, assured, professional 'walker' who now confronted him.

'How's the typing?' he asked.

Brad smiled. 'Oh, I hire somebody to do that.'

Max

As the *Orcades* carried Max across the Indian Ocean towards his reunion with Ruby, he struggled to remember the exact circumstances of their parting. He could recall the row when she heard she was being replaced in *Ned Kelly*. He remembered the train journey across the Nullabor to Perth with Dorothy becoming more and more proprietary. Martyn's asthma had flared up again. By the time they opened at the Maj, Dorothy was queening it over the company and he and Ruby were scarcely speaking.

After six weeks the successful season drew to a close. The plays were to be transferred to the gold-rich mining town of Kalgoorlie. The armed truce between the Hilmans escalated into open war. Max still danced attendance on Dorothy. He excused his conduct on the grounds that it was good publicity for the play for the two leads to be photographed *tête-à-tête* in the King's Street cafés. Abandoned, Ruby found herself barely able to pay the rent for the modest lodgings they were about to vacate. To rent them had been an attempt to counter Max's extravagance but, since he was rarely with her and Martyn, she could not control his casual spending.

When Ralph Donaldson arrived at the theatre in Hay Street to supervise the transfer, Ruby asked to see him. She had decided to leave the tour and return to England. Martyn was racked again with asthma. She was divided in her impulses – whether to cosset her son or to make him tough it out. In spite of the heat she layered him in singlets and on advice but against her instincts placed him on a hard hair mattress while he tried to sleep. The child alternately clung to her and pushed her away. Asthma became a weapon, used, at his age, unconsciously.

When she presented her case to Ralph Donaldson she found him sympathetic.

'You really feel the boy's life is threatened?' he said.

'I can't bear to watch him, Mr Donaldson.'

He skirted round Max's predicament, not mentioning the affair with his sister, though Ruby knew he must be aware of it.

'Of course so much depends on Max's contribution. I shall not be able to release him until the end of the engagement.'

'I'm sure Maximilian would never want to let you down,' Ruby assured him.

During the rattling train journey across the desert, Dorothy and Ralph shared a compartment with Max and Ruby. Martyn, exhausted by restless days and nights and lulled by the movement, slept with his head in his mother's lap. The train gathered speed through the shady trees north of the Swan River out into the red, sun-baked soil. They watched in silence as the line crossed and re-crossed dirt tracks and stretched past spindly trees decked out in the tints of autumn. Ruby marvelled at the rich, red foliage until Ralph pointed out that the colour was due entirely to a drenching of red dust thrown up from the primitive roads. Fifty yards away nature reverted to monochrome.

They had been promised an endlessly changing kaleidoscope of shape and colour. In the event the desert stretched out interminably, deadly dull. Occasionally the train clattered by blink-and-miss-'em places, handfuls of houses made of weatherboard with corrugated aluminium roofs, badly painted and down at heel. Haphazard figures by the track straightened their backs to wave a lethargic acknowledgement.

'It's so dry here the frogs never learn to swim,' said Max to no one in particular. 'Where the hell are you taking us, Ralph?'

'Kalgoorlie's a different story, Max, you wait,' Ralph said encouragingly. 'Twenty thousand people, other settlements all around, wide main street, a score of hotels and half a dozen banks. The lode has run out next door in Coolgardie, but the heat, the miners' payrolls and their thirsts keep three breweries going. Seven newspapers to get your face in! Twenty years ago it was nothing. The big gold strikes had been in New South Wales and Victoria forty years before. It wasn't until '93 that Paddy Hannan struck it rich here. There wasn't any water so they built a pipe-line three hundred miles from a reservoir near Perth.'

'The beer sounds more my tipple,' said Max, mopping his brow.

'The Palace is the new hotel, fabulous they tell me.'

'We have rooms at the Exchange,' said Ruby. 'In Perth they said it was very comfortable.'

Max, who had weighed up the advantages of having his wife in one hotel and his mistress in another, had not, for once, demanded to stay in the grandest accommodation.

'Such a pity you have to leave us so soon, Ruby,' said Dorothy sweetly. 'A girl I met in Adelaide said Kalgoorlie was the best fun of her last tour.'

'The miners gamble on the earth's riches every day,' said Ralph, 'and they carry on with "two-up" every night.'

'Two-up?' queried Max.

'It's a uniquely Australian game,' said Ralph, 'you can lose a lot of money at it.'

'Don't worry, Ruby,' Dorothy leaned forward and patted her hand, 'I'll keep him on the straight and narrow once you've gone.'

A week later Ruby stood on the station platform at Kalgoorlie, Martyn cradled in her arms, her luggage at her feet, her husband nowhere to be seen. She recalled his last words: 'Sorry old girl, got to put the new Tirzah through her paces. Can't let the company down. Ralph trusts me. Give my love to the Old Country.' Then he kissed an uncomprehending Martyn and headed for the Cremorne Theatre.

Ruby boarded the train. She resigned herself to three hundred lonely miles of searing heat, dazzling light, the scorching hostility of the sun, the endless desert and the unwholesome company. She was grateful that Martyn slept again. Eventually the sun fell below the horizon but its flames still played games on the heavens, leaving behind gold as the only colour in the world. The moon was there, now swollen, bright yellow and close enough she thought, in her drowsy, drained, defeated state, to touch.

133

If Dorothy had thought that Ruby's departure would leave her in sole possession of Max, she was to be disappointed. In his nocturnal ramblings on Roe Street in Perth, he had gathered from nods and winks that there were pleasures to be discovered in Kalgoorlie. Hay Street was to be his new stamping ground. With Ruby's departure he determined to explore it. Dorothy's clinging attention had lost its charm now that it was not an alternative. Worse, she had run out of socially useful relations in the gold-mining town. Some of the miners had begun to import their wives and families, but they did not constitute a society which Dorothy had recognised and manipulated in Sydney, Melbourne, Adelaide and Perth.

Prostitution was not illegal in Western Australia. Brothel-keeping was, but it was habitually winked at. The increasing domesticity of the town required that the girls be confined to a segregated vice area. The houses of Hay Street were home to most of them.

'It's fairyland, boy,' said Max to Ray Comstock, one of the younger cast members, sinking a beer after an exhilarating performance of *Ned Kelly* in which the effects had thrilled the miners' families and he had been cheered to the echo. 'It's a honeypot!'

Dorothy put her head round his dressing-room door. 'Will you dine with me at the Palace, darling?'

Pulling on one leg of his trousers Max slumped back in his chair, took another swig of beer and played exhaustion. 'Not tonight, princess, not tonight. Slight headache, princess. Early night at the Exchange, methinks.'

Dorothy opened her mouth, closed it again, swallowed, turned on her heel and, while not quite slamming the door, closed it noisily.

Max heard her heels clatter away down the corridor and winked at Ray. 'Now, young shaver,' he said. 'Who's to explore Ma Bray's establishment?'

'Word in your ear, Max,' said Ray, who was playing a younger Kelly and had a few lines in *Ben Hur*. 'I've looked it over already. Lot of battered boilers.'

Max looked disappointed.

'Cheer up, old son, the bloody street's full of houses, an' I'll tell you what, mate, Marie de Bray's daughter, Fifi, runs a much better show down the road. Better beer, bigger beds and girls from all over. Mostly Australian, a few British, a couple of French and Japanese, and one great Eyetalian. Fifi – don't you love the name! – quarrelled with her mother months back and one of Hannan's side-kicks, a regular of hers, took a shine to her and set her up.'

'What are we waiting for, Ray? Just let me get me other leg in me trousers.' He paused wickedly. 'Hardly worth it though, when you think how quickly they're coming off again – still, we don't want to frighten the horses in Maritana Street, do we?'

Jauntily the two actors set off in the direction of the brothel. Comstock, the younger, tapped on the door of the modest two-storey house and gave a thumbs up to Max as a small panel slid back and a girl's voice said, 'Oh, it's you, Ray. Come on in.'

They were ushered into a very ordinary room which its tenant had attempted to transform into a parody of a bordello with heavy red curtains, shaded lamps, full-length gilt-framed mirrors and a scatter of low sofas. On these, a number of bored-looking girls in corsets and wraps sprawled listlessly. As Max entered they brightened and one, cupping a hand to her lips yelled, 'Fifi! Company!'

A click of heels on stairs and a rustle of silk preceded Miss de Bray's entrance through a bead curtain. She took one look at Max, screamed with delight and yelled, 'Girls! Girls! We've landed the Big One!'

Other women materialised from upstairs and from cubicles in the back of the house.

'It's a slack night, tonight, Mr Milman, may I call you Max? But that's all the better for you, isn't it? More choice! Have a drink?' Fifi de Bray said it all in one excited breath. 'Champagne, whisky, beer?'

'I'll have a beer,' said Max.

'I do love to entertain actors – my mother is going to be so jealous – poor old bag . . .'

She handed Max a beer which a plump Japanese girl in a dragon-embroidered kimono had brought from the kitchen.

'*I* run the only place with any class in Kalgoorlie, really in the whole of West Australia.'

She clapped her hands and the girls eased themselves from their sofas and showed themselves off in a little circle around Max and his fellow actor.

'I've been to the Cremorne to see you three times already, Max,' gushed Fifi. 'And I don't know which part I enjoyed you in most.'

'You must come again, my dear, as my guest, of course,' said Max grandly. 'Just mention my name.'

'Isn't that nice? And for tonight, let me tell you, it's on the house – and that goes for Ray, too, because if he hadn't brought you here you might have finished up with Ma and her lot, and I wouldn't wish that on anybody.'

Max and Ray smiled at each other.

'I think we're in for a long run, lady, so what could be nicer?'

Max exercised his free option on the madame, who was by no means the least attractive of the girls being paraded for him. He reckoned that there would be time to sample the rest on later visits. Ray took full advantage of Fifi de Bray's generosity and herded two of the girls, the plump little Japanese and a tall, bony Frenchwoman, up the stairs with him. 'Variety – the spice of life,' he observed to Max on his way up.

Closeted in Fifi's red-draped bedroom Max took his time. Like most working girls Fifi was not averse to telling her life story and, once launched, was unstoppable.

'I keep a clean house,' she told him proudly, as she loosened his tie. 'That's one thing I did learn from Ma. Regular inspections, cleanliness, all that, *and* I watch my girls. Especially the English. Right careless cows they can be, walking water closets for Germans, Chinamen or anyone else who likes to get into them.'

'You don't sound very French for a Fifi.'

'Born in Western Australia,' she said. 'Mother came down from New Caledonia with her bludger. He was on the run for doin' in a vigneron up there. When he heard I was on the way he went on the run from Ma. Never heard nor seen him since, she hasn't. Good riddance. She was working Fremantle in them days. Mainly sailors. That was before the Rush. Got a good reputation for cleanliness. She hit a sailor over the head with a bottle and when it came to court she said she'd refused to do it with him 'cause he was drunk and diseased. Good as advertising her high standards that was. When Pa Hannan found the lode she legged it out here with me sharpish. I was christened Swan back in Fremantle after that bloody river. Swan de Bray! I ask you? Stupid name. When she put me to work she changed it to Fifi smartish.'

'Why did you fall out?'

'Obvious. I was doing all the work. Bringing in all the custom and she wouldn't split it. Stupid cow! She's pushing fifty now and she's still jealous. Mean to her girls, too. Mine can make upwards of five pounds a week. That's six days a week and they get one week off in four. When they was in service, them that was, it was workin' all hours God sends for one or two quid, do your own housework and cooking and lucky if you get a week off a year. No wonder I attract the best. You need class in this business like everything else.'

Beneath the mirrored ceiling, Max sealed her reminiscences with his lips. Then turning over on his back he admired his performance in the long bout of violent exercise.

Eventually they drifted into sleep until Max was awakened by a violent shaking. Opening his eyes he made out Ray Comstock in his long johns, clutching his trousers. He was enveloped in a thick fog.

'Get up, Max! Fire! Fifi! *Get up*!' he shouted. 'The bloody brothel's on fire!'

'Christ!' yelled Fifi, leaping from her bed. 'That'll be bleedin' Ma and her bloody bludger. The bastards! Follow me!' On the landing they found Ray's two prostitutes wrapping sheets around themselves and snivelling, scared out of their wits. There was no escape down the stairs. The flames below licked the bannisters and leapt higher.

'This way! To the front, follow me!' Fifi screamed. She led the way up a half-stairway and through a door to a small veranda, bounded by wooden slats. 'We gotta jump for it, girls,' she shouted. One storey below, a bleary crowd of half-dressed, half-awake spectators had assembled. Max looked down the street, alerted by a harsh, clanging bell. The Kalgoorlie Fire Brigade – horsedrawn of course – was thundering to their aid.

'They got here quick,' muttered Max.

'Tip-off, I shouldn't wonder,' said Fifi, tight-lipped. 'Jump, girl!'

The Japanese girl was straddling the wicker balcony and preparing to jump when it collapsed and she fell into the arms of a miner. Whipping her blanket off her, he called three others to take the corners and hold them as the rest of the women jumped in turn. Comstock and Max, disdaining assistance, leapt the twelve-foot drop and landed on their feet to a scattered round of amused applause. As Madame Fifi checked all her girls and pronounced them safe, Max was confronted by two young men. One carried a camera, the other a notepad.

'Paying a social call, were we, Mr Milman?' said the one with the pad. His companion stood back to snap Max in his semi-nudity.

Water played on the building while Fifi tearfully comforted her sobbing brood. Some had rushed out of the front of the house when the fire started at the back, too scared to warn the couples – and the trio – upstairs. A policeman who arrived to take statements, was deeply unimpressed. Then, from a house a few doors up Hay Street, emerged a woman smothered in shawls and a buttoned-up dressing-gown. She crowned the severe effect with a conservative night-cap, beneath which curl-papers peeped. She sauntered down the street arms akimbo and unconcerned, followed by a tall, saturnine man.

'Ees the fire under control, officer?' she asked the police sergeant. 'Not likely to spread to my property, I hope.'

'Not unless the wind changes, Mrs de Bray,' said the sergeant. 'Should be doused in no time.'

Fifi de Bray flew at her mother, hands and fists whirling. 'Cow! Bitch! Fire-raiser!' she screamed as the tall, swarthy man interposed himself between the two women and let her beat out her fury on his chest.

'You'll need a bed tonight, Fifi,' he sneered. 'You'd better be nice to your Ma.'

'I'll sleep at the Palace,' she flashed back. 'I don't talk to arsonites.'

'Eef they will 'ave you,' said her mother. 'And don't forget zee laws of slander, Mademoiselle de Bray.'

Tossing her head, turning her back on her mother and drawing a blanket around her with as much dignity as she could muster, Fifi strode off barefoot down the road, followed by her pathetic crocodile of girls similarly shoeless and identically robed.

'War of the Brothel Madams' trumpeted the front page of the *Kalgoorlie Gazette* the next morning. 'Noblest Actor Caught with Pants Down!' The 'eye-witness account' was spread over five columns punctuated by cross-headings with which the sub-editors had obviously enjoyed themselves. 'Ben Hur with Her!'; 'Ned in Bed!'; and 'Impromptu Balcony Scene for Limey Romeo'. Parallels were drawn with the conflagration scene in *Ned Kelly* and the contrast was pointed out between the immoral actor and the relentlessly honourable Judah Ben Hur. More pictures were promised and delivered on page three.

Max, who had, as Ray Comstock put it, 'tied one on', when they got back to the Exchange, was unaware of the paper until noon when the door of his bedroom burst open and Dorothy, a small ball of fury, erupted through it and flung a pile of *Gazettes* into his sleeping face. His head splitting, he burrowed his way through them to be confronted by her spitting lips.

'Had a headache, did you?' she shouted.

'I have now,' said Max, peering at one of the front pages and wincing at what he saw.

'I know you like to save your cuttings,' said Dorothy. 'These should keep you going for a bit.' She moved towards the door.

'I'm sorry, princess . . .'

'Sorry won't help you now,' she shrieked. 'And that's not the only news. I'm pregnant.' She slammed the door behind her and left Max in a mess of rumpled sheets beneath a mountain of tattered newsprint.

Amanda

Now that she had accepted her role in *In Society!* Amanda decided that it was time for a *rapprochement* with her grandchildren. She marvelled at how little she knew them – not even well enough to have chosen a favourite. Archie had never been keen to have them run riot over his quiet routine. Still, it was better to have them for her than against her on the tour. She decided to treat them to lunch at the Ivy.

'That was always Ivor's table,' she explained, gesturing airily to the far end of the room opposite the door. Just inside the entrance she pointed to two tables which had been the battle positions taken up by Lilian Braithwaite and Marie Tempest two decades earlier. 'Lilian had such a tongue,' she told her eager audience. 'Dear Ivor once gave her and Fay Compton diamond brooches. I forget why – anyway, as Fay and Ivor walked past one day she stopped them in their tracks. "Fay, dear," she cooed, "what a lovely brooch Ivor has given you! Can you *see* mine?" '

The children laughed and turned to their menus.

'Now,' said Amanda, 'what are we going to call each other?'

'How do you mean, Grandma?' asked Lysander.

'I'm not having three fellow actors calling me Grandma all through rehearsals and for the whole length of the run. One would be bad enough but with the three of you doing it I should feel three-hundred-and-five by the end of the first week.'

'We could call you Miss Bollington,' Darcy suggested.

'Such a mouthful. I think it had better be Amanda.'

'But the other youngsters will be calling you Miss Bollington.'

'Quite right too. They're not related. Anyway, if my experience of current theatrical discipline is anything to go by, they'll be calling me Mandy by the time we get to Bristol.'

'Are you looking forward to it, Amanda?' asked Imogen, pleased with her effort at familiarity.

'In a perverse sort of way I think I am. I shall enjoy watching you all at close quarters and of course I've never actually acted with your father and mother.'

'You've left one of the family out,' risked Lysander.

'Maximilian.' Amanda grasped the nettle by its name. 'I'm not going to pretend that it will be easy. We did not part in a friendly fashion. Your grandfather had enormous charm and he was a rather good actor – of the "dashing" school – but he was not made for marriage.'

'Wasn't that thought rather scandalous in those days?'

'No, Darcy. We were much more sophisticated than you young people seem to think. Sex didn't start with the war and the GIs, you know.'

The three young people began to enjoy their grandmother's company. She was changing before their eyes from forbidding matriarch into sympathetic senior actress.

'Do you like your roles?' she enquired.

'Oh yes,' they chorused.

'Your part is charming, Imogen.'

'I know. I'm looking forward to it.'

'Oh, look,' Amanda interrupted her, 'there's your father. Who is he with? Is that this mysterious American I'm hearing so much about?'

The two men were crossing the other side of the restaurant, Martyn pumping hands as he passed the tables and introducing Louis to the lunchers.

'That is Louis Armbruster,' said Darcy, tight-lipped. He had managed to avoid his father since the débâcle in Hollywood Road and he had seen Louis only at the dance call when they pointedly ignored each other.

'Adela Skelton rang me in tears,' said Amanda with relish. 'Floods! Everyone seems to be in thrall to American musicals, these days. All that energy and high spirits. He'd better not expect me to be energetic and high-spirited.'

'I'm hoping to make a quick trip to the States,' Darcy told her. The idea of putting some space between himself, Louis and his father before rehearsals started had occurred to him at that moment.

'What a good idea! Can you afford it?'

'I think Mother might stump up. I've never been to New York and it would help to see some American musicals on their own ground. I've got a couple of RADA friends I could stay with.'

'You can rely on me for a small sub,' said Amanda.

Before Darcy could thank her, she had caught Martyn's eye across the crowded restaurant. She waved gaily and beckoned him over. When they had kissed he surveyed his children. 'Plotting with Granny behind the director's back?' he joked.

'I keep hearing about your monstrous choreographer,' said Amanda. 'The children tell me that's him over there.' She looked round and raised an eyebrow. 'That one, slouching on the banquette. Do introduce us.'

Martyn crooked a finger to Louis who made his way to the table. 'This, Mother,' he said, 'is Louis Armbruster.'

As Louis stretched out his hand she took it and held it firmly.

'I hear you are an absolute tyrant, Mr Armbruster,' she said levelly. 'I must warn you it's no good expecting me to high kick, and I wonder if my poor old ex-husband can still cross the stage.'

'Thank you for warning me, Miss Bollington,' said Louis. 'I thought I might stage your number with you both sitting down.'

'How sensible,' said Amanda.

'The servants can do the movement behind you,' he added, 'bringing you drinks and fanning you and . . . and . . . things.' He tailed off, catching Amanda's basilisk eye.

'I think we can lose the servants, don't you, Martyn?' Amanda said, ignoring Louis and turning to her son. 'So distracting. We don't want Mr Armbruster to ruin your little jokes, do we, darling?'

'I think servants are out, Louis,' said Darcy, delighted to witness his defeat.

Ruby stood at the rail of the *Orsova*, staring at the low unremarkable buildings which fringed the port of Fremantle. The dockside harboured only a scattering of well-wishers. There was none of the excitement she had experienced when the ship left Portsmouth on the voyage out. Here and there a handful of Western Australians gathered to wave their farewells to sons or lovers off on their great adventure. For a moment Ruby cherished a dream that Max would come loping along the quay.

Before the ship's siren hooted its final warning a tall, good-looking man did turn the corner, but he was in no hurry. He slouched against a wall and lit a cigarette. At the two, shorter bursts of the siren he tipped back his wide-brimmed bush hat and drew deeply on his cigarette. The black hull pulled steadily out into the Indian Ocean, its white superstructure sparkled in the sun and from yellow ochre funnels the smoke spiralled straight up in the heavy, windless air. The blue cross on a white field of the flag of the Orient Line hung limply. Ruby watched the shore until the man who was not Max flicked the stub of his cigarette to the ground, pressed on it with his heel, turned the corner of the building and disappeared. She took Martyn down to their quarters.

'Did Daddy miss the boat?'

'No darling, Daddy has to stay in Australia and make some money.'

Ruby sat beside Martyn on the bottom bunk of their tiny cabin. The smell of the engine room seeped up through the hatches as she contemplated her lonely journey. The last weeks with Max had brought matters to a head. Her contract with the Donaldsons was running out. If she stayed for a second spell they would be under no obligation to fund her passage home. She despaired of saving enough to pay for it herself. It had been as much as she could do to settle Max's debts. Agreeing to sail steerage made up the difference.

On board, Martyn's asthma lifted. They made forays to the long trestle tables plainly laid in the second class dining-saloon. On the third day they braved the promenade deck, moving cautiously along the lines of chairs, dodging the shuffleboard matches and the mattresses moved on deck by passengers in search of relief from the stifling heat.

It was here that at last Ruby saw a friendly face. Beef tea and biscuits were served at eleven to the first-class passengers. Hearing a burst of laughter from along the deck, she saw a group of men and women sprawled in basket chairs. They seemed to be more animated than anyone she had met on board. Suddenly she recognised an old friend.

'Evadne!' she cried, surprised at her own display of excitement after two days closeted with Martyn.

'Ruby!' came the welcoming response.

They flew into one another's arms and Evadne Rivers, having established that mother and son were travelling alone, introduced them to the rest of the party. Their leader, a dashing, fiftyish figure, moustachioed and, in spite of the Indian Ocean heat, draped in a long grey travelling cloak with a shawl, raised his broad-brimmed, black velvet hat with elaborate courtesy.

'Aubrey Desborough,' he intoned, 'and this is my little company – the *Improper Peter* company – returning from an antipodean tour with our tails somewhere between our legs.'

'Did you not enjoy playing in Australia?' Ruby asked cautiously.

'We enjoyed playing. The audience in Perth did not appear to relish our performance. It is perhaps a trifle sophisticated for their tastes. We had been engaged to open at the new theatre, His Majesty's, A fine, fine theatre. Handsomely decorated. The dressing-rooms commodious, the acoustics splendid; but somehow the entertainment failed to take the local fancy.'

'What a shame!' Ruby sympathised. 'Do you think it was above their heads?'

'No question,' insisted Mr Desborough. 'I argued that surely the intellectual level in the East, in Sydney and Melbourne, must be superior; but I met with a blank refusal to book us any further. We have had to cut our losses and skedaddle for home. When I get back I shall consult Counsel and see if the law can be invoked – a matter of compensation, you understand.'

'We had a good season there,' said Ruby, adding quickly, 'but of course we were playing a pot-boiling melodrama.'

'Ah,' sighed Mr Desborough.

'Is Max with you?' asked Evadne.

Ruby braced herself. 'No, the dear boy is doing so well there

I couldn't tear him away. But we didn't want little Martyn to grow up in Australia. We have decided upon a separation – temporary of course.'

'Very sensible,' said Mr Desborough. 'If you are hoping for a future for the boy on stage it would be unwise to expose him to those tainted vocal mannerisms.' He bent down to Martyn. 'Are you going to be an actor, little man?' Martyn hid in his mother's skirts.

'You seem to be taking your disappointment very well,' said Ruby.

'Water under the bridge,' said Mr Desborough. 'We bounce back, do we not, Hermione? We bounce back!'

'We bounce back, Aubrey,' agreed his wife, who had raised her ample frame from the basket chair and was patting her bun into place. 'We have already secured another engagement.'

'Only a one-night stand, my love.'

'Nevertheless it is a beginning. The Captain has graciously asked us if we would entertain the passengers with a gala performance of *Improper Peter* after we leave Colombo. He will be taking on more people there and we are assured of a full house. We shall be playing in the first-class deck lounge. Of course,' added Mr Desborough, 'should demand exceed the available seating we may give a second performance.'

'Look, Aubrey,' Ruby's friend Evadne chimed in, 'here's the answer to your other problem. If you let Ruby play Kate's role we shan't need to look for an amateur replacement from among the first-class passengers.'

'An inspiration, my dear! That's what I call bouncing back in the most practical possible fashion. Kate Cardew decided to stay on a few months in Perth,' he explained. 'She has family there, a brother or a cousin. Would you agree to play?'

'I would love to,' said Ruby. 'Of course,' she added apologetically, 'I'm only travelling second class.'

'I shall speak to the Captain,' said Aubrey Desborough expansively. 'A very congenial fellow. The ship is not overcrowded. I'm sure something can be arranged. Bouncing back!'

Aubrey Desborough's intercession with the Captain worked. There was indeed a spare bunk in Evadne's cabin and a cot was found for Martyn. Assured of Ruby's professional status, the Captain, who had a weakness for pretty actresses, welcomed her to the first class dining-room as well. The days assumed a pleasant routine. Rehearsals were punctuated by deck quoits, followed by dances or a fancy-dress contest. The ship's five-piece orchestra endlessly played its repertoire of Gilbert and Sullivan and the lighter classics. Ruby's part in *Improper Peter* was quite large but she was a quick study and, although she secretly despised the play, had no sympathy with the role of Gladys Pickering and could readily understand its failure in Australia, she was nevertheless aware of the comfort it was bringing to her journey. Martyn was consigned to the fenced-in pen for children under five from which she retrieved him for lunch and in the evenings. Aubrey Desborough, pleased with her progress, encouraged Ruby to believe that he would be delighted to assist her in the London theatre when they arrived back in England.

In Colombo they spent the day exploring the city. Aubrey Desborough led the way. He had not changed his suffocating clothes but he seemed impervious to heat as he stepped firmly from the gangway to the dock. With Hermione Desborough two paces behind, he strode confidently through the noisy crowd of beggars and salesmen offering silks and cottons, past the stores of ornaments, tortoiseshell and oriental beads. Hermione had her mind on a set of tourmalines she had spotted earlier. She urged her husband on. The rest of the company hovered to watch the fun.

'Love to barter, these beggars,' whispered Aubrey conspiratorially as a dark-eyed Bengali in a turban welcomed them with many smiles and much bowing. The shopkeeper produced a stock of small chamois leather sacks and dazzled the actors as he poured out his hoard of zircons, amethysts, aquamarines, star sapphires and rubies. The more Desborough asked to see the tourmalines – 'My lady wife has set her heart on them' – the more the Bengali confused his customers with opals, agates, cat's eyes and cultured pearls as big as garden peas. Finally he produced the gems that Hermione coveted. He listened with practised patience as she explained that she was going to have them set into a bangle. When Aubrey had beaten him down to the satisfaction of both parties and the admiration of the others, Hermione decided that Aubrey owed himself a small present. Finally they settled on eight zircons which it took them another age to match.

'Ideal,' Aubrey explained, 'to be cunningly fashioned into four studs and a pair of links for evening dress. Nothing flashy, mind you. Discreet and distinctive.'

Evadne felt obliged to dip into her purse and purchase an opal pin, explaining to the storekeeper that it was her birthstone. Gerald, the juvenile, wondered if he should do the gallant thing and buy a jewel for Ruby: but he was fortunately relieved of the responsibility when the smiling Bengali, delighted by his total haul of twenty-two pounds, seventeen and six, threw in a garnet crucifix which he hung round Ruby's neck. Thoroughly pleased with their worldly-wise shopping skills the actors went up to the Galle Face Hotel where they attacked a lunch which Aubrey decreed must be the local curry.

'Can't beat Singhalese curry,' he pontificated. 'Best in the world. Take my word for it.'

Ruby was allowed to make an exception for Martyn. As she ordered his simple omelette she caught the eye of an amused older man at the next table. Embarrassed at being spotted staring, he bent over his chop and attacked it fiercely. Ruby thought no more about him until that evening when they had all returned to the ship. This time she enjoyed the departure much more. Surrounded by her new friends and with the prospect of work when they got back to England, she smiled as she watched the farewells – more vociferous than they had been in Perth. She pointed out the lights of Colombo reflected in the harbour water to Martyn, and as whistles blew and bugles brayed she held his hand while the harbour sounds faded in the freshening breeze. Ruby found the dining-room an altogether livelier place than it had been on the voyage from Fremantle. A governor's lady, pale and reserved, joined the Captain's table. Military men, their wives, and in some cases their twittering daughters, filled other seats, the husbands bolt upright in spotless drill, the wives fading with unbecoming blotches, the daughters shy, and with one exception ungainly. A frail old woman occupied three places, flanked as she was by two Chinese amahs. At a nearby table a noisy

American was telling jokes. He produced a gale of laughter from his companions, more newcomers, agents for Standard Oil. Turning away from the laughter and towards the table on her other side, Ruby was surprised to meet the gaze of the man who had caught her eye on shore. This time he did not look down but smiled and then resumed eating with no sign of embarrassment. Ruby smiled back at him and then to herself.

Rehearsals were resumed. Evadne divided her time between a persistent Purser and one of the Standard Oil men, increasing the ardour of both. Deck quoits ceased to be a casual game and escalated into a tournament. A fancy-dress dance produced some weird improvisations and the little orchestra sawed away at more selections from Gilbert and Sullivan, *Merrie England* and *Les Cloches de Corneville*. It was during *Les Cloches* that the man from the Galle Face Hotel introduced himself to Ruby.

Evadne had left her for an assignation with Standard Oil, instructing Ruby not to tell the Purser her whereabouts. As Ruby lay back in her steamer chair on the promenade deck, looking up at the stars and wondering if she could identify the Southern Cross, the man settled into a neighbouring seat. As the orchestra ground to a conclusion he looked across at her. 'D'ye know, that's my favourite show?' he said, almost to himself.

Forgetting the Southern Cross Ruby turned slowly to look at him. '*Les Cloches de Corneville*?' she asked.

'Clever of you to recognise it,' he said. 'I should have thought you were all for this modern stuff.'

Ruby laughed. 'I'm an actress,' she confessed. 'It often turns up in the entracte.'

'An actress,' he repeated. 'Well, I certainly should have guessed that from your colleagues. He has a fine theatrical manner, your leader.'

'Dear Mr Desborough,' said Ruby. 'We are a very happy little company. Of course, you are not in the profession?'

'Alas, no, young lady – but I should have introduced myself – Archie Durrant.'

'Ruby Bollington,' she returned as she leant forward.

She saw a small, neat man, fortyish, with a trim moustache

and a precise manner, clearly determined to press home the introduction which he had just offered.

'I'm in tea,' he said. 'I *was* in tea. It's been jolly good to me,
tea – I've been out here some twenty years.'

'Are you going home for a holiday?'

'No, no, Mrs Bollington. It's a new adventure for me. No more
Ceylon. I'm going to be something in the City!'

'Something grand? It sounds grand.'

'Not at first. I shall find my way gradually, but it is time to
come home. And you? You and your little boy? Are you taking
him back to his papa?'

'No,' said Ruby, evasively. 'His father is still playing in Aus-
tralia but we both felt that Martyn should have his childhood in
England. Australia is very exciting but the life of a touring player
is hard on a very young child. We were there a year and saw
Sydney and Melbourne, Adelaide and Perth, but we decided in
Perth that I should bring him home.'

For the next couple of days Ruby was busy with rehearsals for
Improper Peter and Archie Durrant continued to take his mid-
morning consommé and sandwich alone. However, he was not
without stratagems and familiarised himself with the children's
crêche, establishing a smiling relationship with Martyn. Older
children played hide-and-seek, racing noisily to and fro along the
decks. Martyn, he observed, seemed to be an altogether quieter
boy, apparently engaged in some private game, perhaps of theat-
ricals, with his teddy bear, when he was not scrawling his crayons
across a pad. Artistic, thought Durrant, takes after his mother, I
suppose. He gave it further consideration. Father too, though.
Actor chappie. I dare say I'll hear more of *him* if I give her time.

The performance of *Improper Peter* was due to take place the
evening before the *Orsova* arrived in Bombay, but that morning
the frail old lady with the two Chinese amahs died peacefully as
she sat in her steamer chair. Her eyes were closed against the
burning sun, and the amahs were unaware of her passing until
one of the stewards, brisk in his white coat, swooped down
to deliver her snack. Her stillness alarmed him and his alarm
communicated itself to the Chinese who first fussed and then

wailed when they realised what had happened. As a mark of respect the performance was postponed. In the late afternoon the frail old lady was laid to rest. The *Orsova* reduced speed and very slowly came to a halt. A posse of missionaries who had joined the ship at Colombo sang a brief unaccompanied requiem and the Captain read the short service. 'We therefore commit her body to the deep, to be turned into corruption, looking for the resurrection of the body (when the sea shall give up her dead) . . .' Here one of the amahs, reminded again of her grief, and perhaps of her uncertain future, fumbled to find the corner of her robe and dab her eyes. ' . . . and the life of the world to come, through our Lord Jesus Christ.'

Ruby, who had spoken to the old lady once or twice, flicked a tear from her eye and, turning, found Archie beside her.

'There's nothing more impressive,' he whispered, 'than a burial at sea.'

Together they watched as the shroud disappeared into the Indian Ocean.

'Who at his coming,' the Captain concluded, 'shall change our vile body, that it may be like his glorious body, according to the mighty working, whereby he is able to subdue all things to himself.'

And, with that, six shrieking planters' children raced round the corner of the deck and through the respectful little throng, which sadly broke up as the impromptu mourners moved away and quickly forgot a woman they had never known.

Deprived of their performance that evening, the Desborough company felt a sense of anti-climax. They derived some consolation from various passengers who expressed disappointment at the delay and especially from one who was disembarking at Bombay and said he was desolated that now he would never see them perform.

'Let me buy you a drink,' said Aubrey, 'small consolation, I know, but the least a chap can do.' To his annoyance the man, one of the Standard Oil contingent, cheered up, accepted and forgot his disappointment with the first sip.

By now the temperature had risen to prodigious heights, the

atmosphere below was stifling, and after Ruby had settled Martyn down and pecked at her meal she found herself again observing the stars on the promenade deck. Archie materialised at her side.

'Are you very disappointed?' he asked.

'Oh, no,' Ruby replied. 'It's only a postponement. We are to give the play on the second night out from Bombay. Not the first because the new passengers need a night to settle in.'

'Oh, that is good news.'

'Besides,' Ruby added confidentially, 'between you and me,' she giggled, creating an intimacy which had not existed between them before, 'if you promise not to tell Mr Desborough I told you, it's not a very good play.'

'I say,' spluttered Archie, 'that's frank of you. But I'm sure I shall enjoy *your* performance.'

'You can be absolutely truthful with me,' said Ruby, 'as long as you don't tell me what you think in front of the others. When they are around, if you cannot find anything nice to say about the play or the acting, you must admire the costumes. If we were in a theatre you could praise the scenery, but as we are playing in the first-class deck lounge without any you don't really have that option.'

'What a world of artifice you live in,' Archie said. 'If my tea wasn't up to snuff I don't think I'd go around decrying the blend. I wouldn't be going back to the Old Country in first class if I'd done that for the last twenty years.'

'Oh, actors are very strange creatures,' said Ruby, cheered by Archie's disclosure that his life was settled. In truth, Max's abandonment had confirmed her suspicion that she was not suited to the vagabond life. Oh, yes, she enjoyed acting and she thought she was rather good at it, but she was beginning to see the advantages of a London career – so despised by Max – over the rickety joys of touring.

The departure from Bombay was enlivened by the embarkation of a Maharajah and his substantial retinue, followed by vast silver urns of Ganges water brought along for his ablutions. At the first siren he scattered a handful of jewels into the sea to ensure a safe passage, then went below before he could see a posse of little boys diving off the quayside to retrieve them.

Archie, Ruby and Martyn settled down to observe the now-familiar withdrawal of boat from quay and the widening gap of brown water which followed the third siren warning. Martyn turned to his mother.

'Where do we go next?' he asked.

'Aden, Martyn,' Archie interjected.

'Will Daddy meet us at Aden?'

'No, darling,' Ruby replied calmly, 'Daddy is working hard in Australia.'

'Will we go back to Australia?'

'Not yet, Martyn. Not yet.'

Later that evening Archie and Ruby met for their now-regular late-evening conversation on the promenade deck.

'Little chap seems to be missing his father,' Archie observed.

'I am hoping the memory will fade,' she replied. 'It is unlikely that Maximilian will be following us home. I believe he feels that his future lies in the New World.'

'I say, I am sorry.' Archie assumed what he felt was an appropriately sympathetic countenance. 'Very brave of you to go it alone, very brave.'

'I'm afraid I had little choice. Maximilian is a man of great charm and kindness. Very talented and very handsome. He is a leading player. He is everything that one could wish for in a barnstorming actor but not, I fear, in a faithful husband and a devoted father. We must make a life of our own, Martyn and I. Later, when he is older, he may wish to seek him out: but, for now, that chapter is over.'

Before Archie could decide whether a similar confession on his behalf was appropriate she had risen to say good-night, adding gaily: 'We have a long day tomorrow.'

She corrected herself. '*I* have a long day tomorrow. We have a dress rehearsal in the afternoon and the performance in the evening. I must have my beauty sleep.'

When Archie straightened up from his deep bow she was already descending the solid mahogany staircase.

The performance of *Improper Peter* was not a triumph; nor was it a disaster. The actors had the advantage that the endless round of deck quoits, dances, fancy-dress competitions and the repertoire of the five-piece band were beginning to bore everyone except the passengers who had embarked at Bombay.

Archie sat happily watching Ruby. He even allowed himself a possessive frisson of jealousy when Gerald, the juvenile, embraced her. The Maharajah, who had reserved the front row for his party, clapped and laughed noisily, not always in the right places, and at the curtain call presented the three ladies, Hermione, Evadne and Ruby, each with a jewel. 'Beats a bouquet,' whispered Evadne out of the corner of her mouth.

That night the calm weather broke and the ship was caught in a ferocious storm. The Captain reduced speed but could not lessen the rolling as the vessel pitched and tossed on its way.

Miraculously, Martyn slept. He had been allowed to stay up, sitting solemnly beside Archie. The play was so different from the spectacles in which he had watched her perform with his father that he was rapt. Now, in the cabin, all was confusion. Evadne had left her porthole open and the floor was awash; a vase of tropical flowers acquired in Bombay flew from a shelf to be caught by Ruby just before it could land on Martyn's serene face. The two girls gave up the idea of sleep and sat on the bottom bunk in their lifebelts watching over the cot, convinced that the end was nigh.

First light brought no relief. It did however bring Archie, who made his way past battened hatches and deck doors guarded by patient, tired stewards with orders not to let the hardier foolish passengers go up on deck to photograph the churning sea. He knocked timidly on Ruby's cabin door.

'Who is it?' Evadne called.

'Archie Durrant. Just come to see that you're all right.'

Evadne opened the door, clinging to it for support. 'Just look at Martyn. He slept through it all,' Ruby pointed out proudly. But now Martyn was hungry and excited. Seeing that the girls were in no condition to face breakfast Archie volunteered to escort him.

'My own sea legs are standing me in good stead,' he explained. 'Come on, Martyn – I dare say there won't be much of a rush for tiffin today.'

It was late afternoon before the storm abated. First, those able to take an interest spotted a strip of clear blue sky to starboard and, as the gallant orchestra gamely played on, they watched the strip expand and cheered as the sun finally broke through. It was some time before the ship settled down but the worst was over and the hardier souls, including Ruby, took their places for dinner. The Desboroughs and Gerald, the juvenile, were still suffering and Archie took advantage of the empty spaces to join Ruby and Evadne. They were full of congratulations for his iron constitution and his stewardship of Martyn.

'Wasn't it fun?' said Martyn. 'Will there be another storm tonight, Mummy?'

The two women shuddered. Martyn and Archie laughed in a conspiratorial fashion.

'I think Martyn's going to make a sailor,' said Archie.

'Oh no,' said Martyn, 'I'm going to be an actor, like Daddy.'

At Aden, Archie persuaded Ruby not to disembark. Ruby looked out at the dusty buildings burning in the sun, the sweating port officials and the dirty black coal barges moving like sleepy beetles round the *Orsova* and took his advice.

Port Said was a different matter. Martyn, escorted by the Ruby and Archie, was spellbound by the gully-gully men. Coins vanished before his eyes, chickens appeared and disappeared again, and before they rejoined the ship there was an ice to be eaten outside a café while Archie beat off a seedy but importunate salesman who was flashing a postcard of a venerable oriental nude.

As the *Orsova* slid into the Mediterranean Archie felt ready to unburden himself to Ruby. They were sitting after dinner on the starboard side of the promenade deck. Ruby sipped her coffee as Archie nursed his brandy balloon. The day had passed pleasantly; the air was fresher here. Away in the distance across the placid sea, against a dark sky, they could see Stromboli spurting flame.

'Will you miss Ceylon terribly?' asked Ruby.

'I expect so,' Archie replied. 'I was there for so many years; but I have so much to look forward to at home. I shall probably be too busy to notice.'

'Did you make many friends?'

Archie weighed the apparently simple question and thought of his reply for so long that Ruby wondered what was on his mind.

'It was a very isolated station,' he said at last. 'I had to learn to be self-sufficient, but,' he paused again, 'but I was not quite alone . . .' As his voice trailed away Ruby sensed the reason for his hesitation. 'When I arrived, I was a young man in my twenties. I took over a sizeable plantation and very soon I added to it. I also took over a large staff – indoors and out. They were, I suppose, my new family. Among the indoor staff was a very beautiful young Singhalese girl called Shameen. She was graceful and accomplished and she realised very soon that I was attracted to her. It seemed most natural, indeed inevitable, that we should make love. And so we did.'

Ruby watched him closely. His gaze remained firmly out to sea. 'She is still beautiful and graceful and accomplished,' he said, 'and we have two daughters. I shall never see them again.'

Ruby felt the need to fill another awkward pause. 'Did you not want them to accompany you?' she asked.

'No, my dear, that is not the way of things. That would not have done. They would not have fitted in with my London plans. I have, of course, made ample provision for them. I have arranged an income for Shameen which will ensure that neither she nor the girls will ever want. "East is East and West is West" as the poet said, "Never the twain" and all that. She understands. The girls understand.'

He turned to look at Ruby for the first time since he had begun to unburden himself. 'I hope that you understand.'

'Is it important for me to understand?' Ruby wondered if she had been too direct.

'It is if we are to be friends. And I hope that we shall be friends.'

'I am sure that we shall be. What an odd pair we make! You have left a cosy colonial life for the cut and thrust of the City. I have parted from a dashing husband to try to make a life for myself and my little boy on our own. We are both starting out.'

Ruby was dramatising their predicament rather more theatrically than was her wont but Archie responded to her sentimental summing-up.

'Perhaps we can help each other face the challenge,' he said. 'We must not lose touch when we reach England. Let us say no more now. Ships and the sea can make strange changes in a chap and, I dare say, in a girl too, but I would like to think that we shall not lose touch. My London club is the Travellers. Would you perhaps let me know where you are staying when you have completed your arrangements?'

'Most certainly,' said Ruby. 'I am not sure at the moment. My family live in the country. Bollingtons have been farmers for generations. I am the first to venture on to the wicked stage,' she laughed. 'Of course I do not yet know if I am to be a touring actress again or whether I may be lucky enough to secure London engagements. I am thinking of changing my name. Somehow Ruby does not sound right for the West End.'

'There was Ruby Millar.' Archie offered up one of the few pieces of information to be found in his almost empty stock of theatrical knowledge.

'Ah, but she was very much a part of the lighter stage,' countered Ruby. 'I hope to confine myself to the legitimate theatre. I don't see my future at the Gaiety.'

'All stage-door Johnnies, eh,' laughed Archie. 'I went to Romano's once,' he added, apropos of nothing. 'Didn't see any dukes drinking champagne out of gals' slippers though. Mucky habit. What are you thinking of calling yourself?'

'I haven't quite decided but I must make up my mind before we get home. If I am to make a clean start I must not confuse the profession by returning as Ruby and then becoming someone different later. Mr Desborough has promised to give me some introductions to West End managers, and if I do not win a role in London immediately there is a possibility that I might tour with his company until one comes along. He is very optimistic. He calls it "bouncing back".'

Through the gunmetal seas of the Bay of Biscay, splashed with spray and shivering with cold, Ruby tasted the sound of Spanish names on her lips.

'What do you think of Carmen?' she asked Evadne.

'Lovely tunes.'

'No, not the opera, silly, as a name?'

'Who for?'

'Me, of course.'

'Carmen Bollington? Doesn't sound right. And let's face it, dear, you're more an English rose than a Spanish firecracker. I should forget Carmen.'

'I suppose you're right. But I'm definitely getting rid of Ruby,' she shouted, as the wind gathered force.

By evening the storm had died down, and most of their conversation centred on the ship's concert which was to be held the next evening, officially in aid of the Seamen's Fund, but mainly an excuse for the passengers and the Purser to show off. The *Improper Peter* company was excused duty because of its previous triumph. As her affectionate Purser put it to Evadne: 'You would only show up the amateurs, which wouldn't be fair.'

The Purser compèred the evening, and made a great point of thanking the performers, the audience, and the Captain for gracing the occasion with his presence. Much to the disappointment of a procession of wobbly sopranos who had been counting on another jewellery hand-out, the Maharajah did not appear but remained resolutely in the smoking-room. The men from Standard Oil offered a Barber's Shop Quartet with a repertoire which surprised everyone by being spotlessly clean. The governor's lady caused an unexpected sensation by reciting 'If'. The final item was a selection from *Veronique*.

'Veronique Bollington,' Ruby mused. 'It has quite a ring to it.'

'A lot of letters to go up in lights,' said the practical Evadne and left Ruby to ponder French alternatives.

However, by the time that England was sighted – a blue smudge on the horizon on a cold, clear Channel morning – she was still not satisfied. The proximity of the craggy granite of Land's End, a first sighting of the Lizard, squat among the chopping waves sharpened her search and she remained distracted as Archie pointed out the Cornish landmarks to Martyn. The child jumped up and down in excitement as they passed the slim, white Eddystone Lighthouse and listened spellbound as he was shown Plymouth Hoe and told of the Armada and Drake's game of bowls.

Babbacombe Bay was left behind. The cliffs of Dover were sighted and passed. Packing completed, the little party returned to the deck as they entered the Thames estuary, Kent on one side, Essex on the other. Martyn, who could not remember England, made his first conscious acquaintance with it. Over the flurry of oilers, tankers, tug-boats and cargo ships he stared at the wharfs and factories that lined the river and over to the marshy land still further away. The *Orsova* sailed majestically past the churning paddles of the *Margate Queen* and steamed up to Tilbury. For the last time they heard the siren's triple hoots and watched as the great anchor dropped into the greasy river water.

'Don't forget to write,' Archie reminded Ruby as he handed her into her train.

But Ruby was hardly listening. 'Amanda,' she shouted to him as the train pulled away.

'What?' yelled Archie, stiffly hurrying down the platform, straining to catch what she was telling him.

'Amanda! That's it! Amanda!' she repeated. 'Amanda Bollington.' And Amanda she became.

Max

Martyn went alone to Tilbury to meet his father. Tony drove him down in the Rolls, neither of them knowing quite what to expect – Tony curious, Martyn frankly apprehensive. 'How,' he wondered aloud, 'does one greet a father one has not seen for forty-odd years?'

'With a large scotch, I should think,' suggested Tony, 'from all we've heard about the Aged Parent.'

'Maude wanted to come along, but I thought I had to face it alone. I hope I can recognise him.'

'Recognise an actor?' said Tony, ''course we will.'

'He's unlikely to be "a robustious periwig-pated fellow tearing a passion to tatters", Tony. He'll probably be a frail old gent picking his way through the luggage with a stick.' They were entering the large customs shed. 'He's well over seventy.' Martyn switched from *Hamlet* to *As You Like It*. 'More likely "A lean and slippered pantaloon with spectacles on nose and pouch on side . . ." '

' " . . . and his big manly voice," ' boomed out from the tall, elegant old gentleman just inside the door of the shed, ' "turning again towards childish treble, eh? *Sans* teeth, *sans* eyes, *sans* taste, *sans* everything" – particularly *sans* a drink at this moment.'

Max put his hand on Martyn's shoulder. 'Is the old Tilbury Hotel still going, my boy? I thought I caught a glimpse from the promenade deck.'

Martyn recovered himself. 'Welcome home, father. This is Tony, he'll take care of the bags.'

As Tony busied himself the two men stood their ground, looking each other over.

'Of course, I've seen you in the pictures, my boy, so I had the advantage. Do you have any memory of me? Of Australia?'

'I only remember the heat. And the trams in Melbourne.'

'How's the asthma?'

'I suppose that's *your* last memory of me. Having to nurse me.'

'Didn't do much of that. Left it to poor old Ruby.'

'Amanda, now.'

'Christ, I forgot. That'll take some getting used to. Amanda, yes, that's it? Where did she dig that up?'

'She changed it when we got back from Perth. She wanted to make a new start.'

'Poor old girl. Can't blame her. You know, I didn't behave very well towards your mother, Martyn.'

Martin laughed. 'That's putting it mildly,' he said. 'I've heard the story enough times.'

'So you have no memories of me?'

Max took his hand off Martyn's shoulder and replaced it so that it circled his son's neck in a comradely gesture. 'Thanks for bringing me back. I can't say "home" because it doesn't feel like it. I'll try not to let you down.'

'Mother's the big hurdle.'

'I didn't think she'd be too happy . . .'

'I'm going to bring you together at a press conference. That way you'll both have to be on your best behaviour.'

'Seriously, Martyn, do you think she's up to Lady Markby?'

'Steady on, Father. You can't start finding fault with a co-star when you're hardly off the boat.'

'There's some good laughs for Lady Markby. In the old days Ruby, sorry, Amanda, couldn't get a laugh if she pulled a dingo out of her drawers.'

Martyn tried to look serious without being priggish. 'That was forty years ago, Father . . .'

'As my employer you'd better call me Max.'

'Forty years! She hasn't been out of the West End since then. H B Irving, Shaw, Maugham. She's a good actress.'

'I'll take your word for it,' said Max grudgingly, 'she was a pretty little thing. Tell me, what was her number two like?'

'Archie? Safe, dull, devoted. Something in the City. Good to me. A second father, as they say. They met on the boat coming back from Australia.'

Tony appeared with the bags. 'Is that the lot, sir?'

'Call me Max, old boy. It's a democracy Down Under.' He counted the cases carefully. 'Yes. You got the lot. Your man Ingrams would be proud of me, Martyn. Now let's find the Tilbury, I'm parched. It must be over the yard-arm somewhere in the world.'

They found the hotel precisely as the saloon bar doors were flung open. 'Good omen,' said Max. 'Timing was always my strong point.'

Harry Harmon went to town on his press reception at the New Olympic. In the stalls bar the journalists and photographers were greeted at the noon call by the excited impresario who had laid on champagne, cucumber and smoked salmon sandwiches. After Violet Redding had checked her guest list and reckoned with satisfaction that she had more than a ninety per cent turn-out, she clapped her hands together and said: 'Ladies and gentlemen, if you would care to charge your glasses and take them through to the auditorium we can start . . .'

Reluctantly, they began to move. All except one old buffer with leather patches at his tired elbows, ash cascading down his yellowing shirt-front and a beacon nose deep in a tumbler of whisky which he had somehow conned from the bar. Vi Redding fussed around the rest, reassuring those whose thirst was famous that they would be returning in no time at all for more. The solitary drinker slipped through her net. Settled in the front stalls, they heard Freda August deep in the orchestra pit strike up the jaunty title song from *In Society*! and segue into the big romantic ballad 'My Ideal Husband'.

The *Daily Mail* nudged the *Daily Sketch*. 'A bit brazen of Martyn,' he whispered. 'That's straight out of Ancient and Modern.'

'Probably like the rest of the show,' said the *Sketch*. 'I gather he's resuscitated his dear old Ma.'

Freda thumped the big ballad down on the pit piano.

'It's not Ancient and Modern,' hissed *The Stage*, 'it's an old Welsh hymn.'

'More than you can say for its composer,' the *Sketch* muttered, as the curtain slowly rose revealing a family group – Martyn, Maude, Lysander and Imogen. There was a polite scatter of applause, led by Violet Redding, Harry Harmon and Dymphna Oates in the stalls. Martyn stepped forward to acknowledge it.

'Thank you for finding the time, ladies and gentlemen,' he said. 'Of course, you all know Maude, who is type-cast as Gertrude Chiltern, the Ideal Wife in my musical version of Wilde's *Ideal Husband*. We are making it a sort of family offering in honour of Her Majesty's coronation. I'm playing Sir Robert; but I don't know if you've met my son and daughter. Imogen is playing Mabel Chiltern, my ward, and Lysander is the Vicomte de Nanjac, an attaché at the French embassy.'

He led the children forward gracefully as he announced them and then explained Darcy's absence in America. 'However,' he added, 'this is a very special day for all of us. As you know, my father and mother parted some forty years ago. I was hardly three when my mother brought me back from Australia. You have all enjoyed Amanda Bollington's performances in countless roles since then. For *In Society*! she will be playing Lady Markby.'

Martyn extended a hand towards the prompt corner and beckoned Amanda on. She made a deep curtsey to the press and then turned to her son and gave him a peck on the cheek.

'For this special celebration I thought I would do something out of the ordinary. Since his work in the English theatre in the early years of the century, my father has had a distinguished career in theatre, films and radio in Australia. It has meant a great deal to me to be able to invite him back to the Old Country, to reunite him professionally and personally with me and my mother and to cast him as the Earl of Caversham. May I introduce my father, Maximilian Milman.'

This was a surprise for the assembled press corps and the cameras began to flash even before Max, who knew how to tease an entrance, emerged erect and smiling from the wings on the OP side.

Catching her first glimpse of him Amanda was amazed at how

little he seemed to have changed. Ignoring the cameras, he strolled straight towards her, bowed low and planted a kiss on her hand.

The family started a dutiful round of applause in which the journalists felt obliged to join. Meanwhile the cameras clicked away.

'Can we have a proper kiss?'

'This way, smile please! Give us a grin, Amanda!'

'Can't you look pleased to see him, Mrs Milman?' one photographer begged.

'I am not Mrs Milman,' said Amanda tersely.

Max smiled serenely and drew her to his side as the clamour died down.

'It is my misfortune,' he said, 'that I can no longer call Miss Bollington Mrs Milman. My misfortune – and my fault. However, we hope to have the happiest of professional relationships in our son's wonderful new show.'

'How many times have you been married, Mr Milman?' asked the *Sketch*.

'Before or after Amanda?' asked Max, innocently.

'Both.'

'Once before. I'm a bit vague about after.'

As they all laughed the *Sketch* persisted. 'Any chance of you getting together again?'

'That, of course, would be for the lady to decide.' He looked at Amanda. 'Besides, I'm not absolutely sure that I'm free . . .'

'How about you, Miss Bollington?'

'I think Maximilian is looking extremely well,' said Amanda, tight-lipped, 'after all these years – and after all he's been through.'

'We shall be coming into the stalls bar,' said Martyn, 'but first I should like to make two more important introductions. You all know that splendid show *Pennsylvania!* at the Scala. I'm delighted to say that Mr Louis Armbruster, who has brought so much to the London production, is going to choreograph and co-direct *In Society!* with me.'

Louis strode on, mildly annoyed that he received no applause. Martyn covered the silence: 'I know the casting of Mrs

Cheveley is not altogether a surprise to you, but I don't think you've had a chance yet to meet the delightful Miss Zelda Fane!'

He went to the wings and led Zelda on to another ripple of clapping from the stalls. 'We haven't played together since Gottfried Saxon's film of *Middlemarch* but we promised ourselves a return engagement – and this is it.'

'Do you have any romantic interests in Britain?' the *Mirror* called.

'Really, we are here to discuss the show, you know . . .' Martyn interrupted, but Zelda intervened happily.

'I have my eye on Martyn's father,' she said, smiling at Max, 'but I shall certainly check with Miss Bollington before I make a move.'

'Let's go through to the stalls bar,' said Violet hastily, 'then you can ask away as much as you like.'

In the bar Maximilian held court at one end, Zelda at the other. The family were isolated in the middle smiling with all the patient bravery of actors who realise that the press don't want to talk to them; nibbling on smoked salmon sandwiches and sipping champagne with fierce concentration to cover the undeniable fact that they were being ignored. Martyn, Maude and Amanda were old news – especially now that the story of a romance between Martyn and Zelda had been spiked. Lysander and Imogen would have to achieve something before the focus switched to them. Louis Armbruster hovered between Martyn and the posse surrounding Zelda; he was also fretting at the lack of attention he was receiving.

Max, champagne flute in hand, was thoroughly enjoying himself, romanticising his turn-of-the-century career in the English theatre and glamourising what had been a very up-and-down life in Australia. Gathering a bottle of champagne, he helped himself to another glass and waved the bottle in an expansive gesture in the direction of the red-nosed whisky-swigger he had not noticed before. 'Top up, old man,' he said.

'Chauncey Martin,' the red-nose introduced himself to Max. 'I'll stay with the scotch, thanks,' he said, 'kind of you, old darling.' He dangled his glass in front of the barmaid who gave him another generous double measure. 'I'm after a bit of period colour, Max,' he said, 'if I may call you Max.'

'What else?'

'Memories of old London. The old theatre. How it's changed. Forty years on. That sort of stuff. Care for a bite of lunch at the Wig and Pen?'

'I was going to lunch with the family,' said Max, 'but I suppose I can call this work.'

'I can guarantee you a decent spread in the mag,' Chauncey Martin reassured him. 'You're unique. All the others have been around for years. You've been Down Under.'

'You make me sound like a fucking fossil you've dug up,' said Max. 'Just when I was fancying my chances with Zelda there – still I suppose there'll be time to explore her on tour.'

The two elderly gentlemen drained their glasses and were tottering off towards the stairs when Violet pounced. 'Are you off, Mr Milman? Lots of people want to talk to you . . .' She looked suspiciously at Chauncey, unwilling to admit that she could not place him or remember inviting him.

'Taking Max off for a spot of lunch . . . Wig and Pen.'

'Will you be all right, Mr Milman? Would you prefer me to sit in on the interview?'

Max stopped and looked her up and down. 'My dear,' he said patiently, 'I'm not a damned debutante. We are going,' he twirled a hand, 'to rediscover the past. I don't think I need a chaperone. Anyway . . .' he leant over and placed a light kiss on her cheek, at the same time managing to squeeze her behind, ' . . . you're far too young.'

Violet retreated, while Lysander and Imogen, who had been gazing with fascination at their grandfather all morning and had missed nothing of this encounter, giggled. They caught Amanda's basilisk stare. She too had been privy to the incident. Her grandchildren went across to her. 'Come on, Amanda,' said Imo, 'it's our turn to lunch you. We know a dear little place – if you don't mind slumming.'

Happy behind a chop at the Wig and Pen at a table near a glowing fire, Max grew expansive.

'Touring days, Chauncey, touring days! The *Era*! The *Pink'un*! That was journalism, Chauncey. We go back, old boy, we go back!'

'We do indeed, Max; let me refill you.' He snapped his fingers to a waiter.

'Bloody hot in here,' said Max. 'Perhaps I could have a beer and a whisky chaser?'

'Good idea.'

Max was feeling that at last he had come home. The hours that he had spent since arriving at Tilbury had been strange. Meeting a whole new family. Meeting his grandchildren, delightful though they were. Meeting his daughter-in-law for the first time. Being installed in Darcy's old room with its big window overlooking the Royal Hospital. Coming to terms with Martyn was the strangest experience. The transformation of the toddling asthma victim he remembered, red-faced and whimpering, via the screen idol into the dignified theatrical knight who was employing him – it had all been a lot to take in. In a funny way, meeting Amanda had not been difficult. He had prepared himself for that, steeled himself to behave perfectly at the press call, and he had succeeded.

Max reckoned that he had come through the worst of his ordeal. He was sitting opposite a man who was roughly his contemporary in a restaurant which he could recognise as similar to the ones he had left behind. The brown windsor soup, the fatty meat, the soggy cabbage, the whisky, the bitter beer and the heat of the fire might have been found in a dozen chop-houses along the Strand when he was a call-boy at the Vaudeville in the nineties – though he would not have entered them. He warmed to the room and to Chauncey.

'By God, the Strand's changed,' he reflected. 'And not for the better. Poor old Tivoli a bloody picture palace! What would Marie Lloyd have said? Gaiety empty – what happened there?'

'Closed through the war,' said Chauncey, 'then Lupino Lane bought it in '45 but he's never done anything with it.'

'Shocking. And the Lyceum a dance hall! The Guv'nor must be turning in his grave!'

'Knew Irving well, did you?' the journalist fished.

Max was reluctant to disappoint his host. 'He was very kind to me,' he improvised. 'Said he saw me carrying on the flame. You know how fond he was of "Breezy Bill" Terris. He was inconsolable when Bill was shot down at the Adelphi stage door; but he used to say I had a bit of Bill's twinkle. Ellen confirmed it. Talked of reviving *The Vicar of Wakefield* with me as the Squire, you know. Very gracious Ellen Terry was. Knew her?'

'Only towards the end,' said Chauncey, 'when her mind was going. What an age of giants!'

Max nodded to a hovering waiter who refilled his whisky tumbler. 'Giants,' he said.

'They don't make actors like that any more.'

'What d'you think of my son?'

'Sir Martyn? Very good. Very stylish, very elegant. No fire in the belly though, Max. I saw his seasons at the Vic. Goodish Orlando, out of his depth in the Scottish piece. Princely Hamlet – but you remember Tree and Lewis Waller, Forbes Robertson, Martin Harvey . . .'

Max wiped away a tear with his large handkerchief. 'You played with them all?' Chauncey tempted.

'Played with them all,' Max lied.

'Will you be going down to St Austell?' the journalist asked casually.

Max looked puzzled. 'St Austell?'

'Where Nona went . . .'

'Nona?'

'Your first wife, Max. She moved to St Austell after the divorce. Married again.'

'My God!' Max was shocked, 'you know more about me than I know myself. To tell you the truth, I'd almost forgotten Nona.' He had not entirely forgotten thanks to the rich reminder from Mae Madely in the library back in Sydney. 'Married again, did she? I hope she's happy. And the boy . . .?'

Chauncey ignored the query and investigated further. 'You did a fair bit of remarrying Down Under, didn't you?'

'Three times after Ruby – Amanda, that is – or was it four? No, it should have been four but Dorothy's brother forbade it.'

'Dorothy?'

'You wouldn't have known Dorothy, would you? Dorothy Donaldson. Lovely girl. Impresario's sister.'

Max's voice began to slur. Woozy in the warmth, he felt a compulsion to oblige this strangely sympathetic listener who was paying such kind attention to his stories that he was actually taking notes.

'I think Ralph Donaldson might have let me marry her. He might have *made* me marry her if it hadn't been for that bloody brothel fire in Kalgoorlie. Of course, she was up the spout already . . .'

Dorothy? Ralph? Brothel fire? Kalgoorlie? Chauncey's old-fashioned shorthand flew across his notepad, peppered with proper names which he needed to identify. Max painstakingly fleshed out the story. The more questions the journalist asked, the more doggedly the old actor fished for the details long banished to the back of his mind.

Around six o'clock Max's head slumped on to the table. Chauncey assumed correctly that he had had his ration of information. Tucking his notes into his pocket he stopped a cab in Fleet Street, poured a bleary Max into it and gave Martyn's address in St Leonard's Terrace. He thrust a pound note into the driver's hand and asked him to make sure that Max reached the door which was where, fast asleep on the chill front step, Imogen found him when she came home.

Max awoke next morning with a splitting head, the winter sun piercing the room and a sympathetic Maude sitting beside his bed.

'How do you feel?' she enquired gently.

'Rotten,' he said. 'Am I in the doghouse?'

'I don't think Martyn was too pleased last night, but he's got other things to worry about this morning.'

'What's wrong?'

'There is almost nothing about our silly press conference in the papers.' She held up the *Daily Mail* for Max to see the headlines. The front page was awash with flood damage.

' "Coast of Kent and Lincolnshire devastated," ' she read.

' "Half of Canvey Island swept away. Nearly five hundred drowned." '

'I don't feel so good myself,' Max groaned.

After pointing out the one small picture of Zelda, tucked away after pages of devastated sea walls, rushing water, boats being rowed down village streets and lone survivors perched on their half-submerged rooftops, Maude returned to the subject of Max's health. He was suffering from more than a hangover and spent the next few days being nursed through a chill which turned to flu and might have worsened but for his strong constitution and the cosseting of his rediscovered family.

As Max awoke on the Sunday looking forward to a gentle recuperative day, Martyn burst into his room brandishing a copy of the *Sunday Digest*, a rag to which the Milmans did not subscribe but which was read devotedly downstairs by Tony and Grace. Martyn had received a panic call from Vi Redding at the crack of dawn alerting him to a damaging article. Rushing down to the kitchen he pounced on the offending newspaper as it lay unopened on the table.

Whatever misdemeanours the nation's scoutmasters had been up to that week were driven from the front page by large pictures of Max and Amanda taken at the press conference, coupled with fifty-year-old artistically posed portraits of both of them in the bloom of youth. Inset was a photograph of Martyn caught at his most theatrically noble. At the top ran the banner headline 'When did he last see his father?' and beneath it the by-line 'Sprauncey Chauncey – Man o' the Moment'.

With awful foreboding Max accepted the *Digest*'s invitation to turn to pages two, three, four and five. Chauncey Martin had failed to tell Max that one of his earliest jobs in journalism had been as the London stringer for *Truth*, a Melbourne paper. It was Chauncey who had supplied the report of Max's divorce proceedings which led to his long-ago dismissal by Miss Romany French. Taking that as a starting point the journalist rehashed the evidence of Nona, Max's first wife, and added the local Australian report of his lost legal battle with the Hannigans and his wild behaviour in the early hours in Collins Street. He followed up and fleshed out Max's vivid account of the *Ben Hur* tour and Dorothy's pregnancy. Max was again revealed as 'Fred', and Amanda as 'Ruby'. Her abandonment in Kalgoorlie was charted in detail. Sprauncey Chauncey quoted the local papers on the brothel fire. He had researched details of every nadir in Max's up-and-down career in Australia and his trail of broken marriages. Gleefully he printed Max's boasts of his close relationship with the great English actors of his youth and savaged their authenticity. Of his 'happy' reunion with Amanda he reported Max's scepticism about her ability as a comedian, dismissing her inability to play comedy in a phrase which, he said piously, was 'not suitable for reproduction in a family newspaper'.

He twisted the knife by commenting that the affairs of two such 'minor players long since past their prime and popularity' should not long have detained the discerning reader of the *Digest*. But he raked up the old Hollywood rumours of the affair between Zelda and Martyn, splattering the subtitles 'Happy Families?' and 'An Ideal Husband?' between the paragraphs. He stressed the point that 'this sordid and discredited crew has been gathered together by Sir Martyn to satisfy his own greed and passion for notoriety. Does he really propose to place this revival mess of tasteless no-talents cavorting to a tale by the Prince of Perverts before our young and innocent Queen as a celebration of her solemn coronation? 'Isn't this,' he thundered in conclusion, 'a dainty dish to set before a Queen?'

'How long have you known this Sprauncey Chauncey?' asked Martyn, enunciating the journalist's name with fastidious distaste.

'Met him at your press conference, Martyn,' Max said lamely. 'Seemed a pleasant enough old codger. Only person there who knew anything about me.'

'A damn sight too much,' snapped Martyn. 'He's obviously been lying in wait. Vi had never heard of him. She tells me she wanted to come with you to that disastrous lunch but you wouldn't let her.'

'Only trying to help, Martyn. You said you wanted publicity. And you haven't had much up until now, have you?' Max added a trifle uneasily.

'This sort of publicity I can do without!'

Max lay there wondering if it was all such a bad thing, in the long run. His life had never been a smooth, decorous affair. He had roughed it, toughed it out in difficult situations. Somehow he had survived. The only thing that really got to him was the exposure of his recent humiliation as a paid Tiresias in the company of a group of Sydney suburban amateurs. He could hear the telephones in the house ringing with unusual frequency for so early an hour on a Sunday morning. Still, he told himself, he had been in tougher corners than this.

Max Milman, ex-actor, dismissed by Ralph Donaldson at the end of the Kalgoorlie season with the traditional producer's threat that he would 'never work in this country again', sat on the veranda of the Railway Hotel at Oodnadatta blinking at the sunlight that shimmered to the horizon. The railway line which disappeared to the south, to Adelaide, seemed to shake like a brace of steel ribbons in an unsteady hand. In front of the hotel two billy-goats were settling a disagreement, raising a little cloud of dust and attracting onlookers with the clash of their horns. Desultory bets for drinks were laid on the results. Across the street a man hammered at a shop sign, screwing up his eyes against the sun, wiping his forehead with the back of a hairy hand, swearing at the flies which buzzed around him, and snatching longing glances at the pub. Down by the store a camel train was being loaded with the quarterly supplies for a station far out to the east.

A week or so before, back in Kalgoorlie, in the bar of the Exchange Hotel, Max had discussed his future with Ray Comstock. Donaldson had certainly queered his pitched with the major Australian managers and he had no great urge to return to England. The two actors were contemplating their dismal prospects when a stranger interrupted their conversation. Grizzled, with sharp eyes under bushy eyebrows, leather-faced, burnt nearly black, he looked as if he could chew nails without bothering to spit out the heads.

'You lads sound as though you could use an adventure,' he said. Max looked suspiciously at the stranger's glass but saw with some relief that it was nearly full. He emptied his own. The man nodded to the barman who drew refills for both actors. 'Joss Bimrose,' their benefactor introduced himself, 'prospector.'

Max took a deep swig and said; 'Cheers. Are you based in town?'

'Na,' said Bimrose. 'Just passin' through. I got a mind to sniff around the Arltunga fields up by Alice. Fancy coming along?'

'We're bloody actors,' said Max in disbelief.

'You look as though you could handle yourself – and from what I overheard you ain't got no place to act right now.'

Max looked at Comstock. 'What do you think, Ray?'

'I wasn't going anywhere, Max. Might as well go somewhere.'

The next morning Max set out to acquire his costume. He approached prospecting as he would a new role, starting with the clothes. He raided the Kalgoorlie thrift shops and came up with dungarees, a belt and a patched, grey, working flannel jacket. Satisfied that he looked the part he boarded the train at Kalgoorlie with his two companions, braced to experience once again the nothingness of the treeless Nullarbor Plain.

They waited five days in a flop-house in Adelaide before joining the little train which would crawl the seven hundred miles towards the centre. It was a fortnightly affair crowded with frontiersmen who, familiar with its rigours, soon made themselves comfortable. Cattlemen, government officials, prospectors, settlers, well-sinkers, sheepmen, carriers, 'roo shooters, linesmen, shearers, station hands and drovers made up the sparse population of the north. Amongst this motley bunch there was a mere handful of women. Max realised with a pang that one of his most important leisure activities was to be severely curtailed.

At every stop along the route Bimrose seemed to find someone to greet.

'Do you know everyone in this bloody country?' asked Max, increasingly aware of the unknown land ahead.

Bimrose scratched his face. Tongue-in-cheek, he waxed lyrical: 'I reckon I've covered the Territory,' he said. 'I know the man at the Ten Mile Tank on the South Australian border. I know the Afghan's dog at Angoranna and the boundary-rider west of Broken Hill.'

'We're in good hands,' joked Max.

'None better,' said Bimrose.

Finally, they drew into Oodnadatta, the railhead. Stepping from the train they were confronted by a handful of little houses with white roofs. 'And this,' said Bimrose, 'is the biggest town for two hundred and fifty miles to the south, five hundred to the east, fifty miles west and a thousand to the north.' Back down the track towards Adelaide the twin trails came together on the horizon. A cloud of dust sprang up from the trucking yards as a bawling herd of cattle was prodded forward by horsemen riding on its flanks. Driven a thousand miles from the direction of Queensland they were soon due to decorate the steak plates of Adelaide. In the midst of the arid countryside Oodnadatta was an oasis of green, watered by an artesian well which had set the hamlet firmly on its feet as a harbour for so much travelling stock. The trio of new arrivals sought the shade. Further progress would be more haphazard. The railway line had ended.

In the evening, pondering their next move, they chose the billiard room of the Railway Hotel as a debating chamber. The pub table was green in patches. 'Where do we go from here?' Max asked.

'North,' said Bimrose. 'We'll pick up pack horses tomorrow. Strike towards Alice and then off to Arltunga.'

A weatherbeaten man sitting across from their table intervened. 'I'm going north tomorrow,' he said. 'Care to ride alongside? Keep the distance from my camel's kicks and we'll get on fine.'

'Are you commercial?' asked Bimrose.

The man got up and came across to them. 'No, I'm a padre. John Flynn. I have a sort of roving commission from the inland mission. I try to touch on every scattered settlement. I'm heading for the North Territory.'

So, in the morning, with two pack horses and a wagon they joined Flynn's little caravan. From the plains they passed into sand ridges which stretched out towards the horizon like the vast waves of a petrified sea. Max marvelled at the change of scenery as they plodded on through jagged hills and among mis-shapen mountains. They camped at night by a waterhole and were serenaded by the ceaseless squabbling of wild fowl scudding across the giant water-lilies which coloured the pools red, pink and blue.

They parted from Flynn at Alice. The two actors stood together and watched as Flynn's three bad-tempered camels disappeared among the dusty mulga trees. Bimrose spurred the pack horses on their way and they set off for Arltunga.

It was a couple of days before they reached a rough mining camp. Sixty men and no women lived on a mountainside in sheds built of saplings. As they approached, Bimrose pointed out the smoke from their fires coiling lazily up amongst the bloodwoods; from down in the valley the bark of a dog echoed. The miners, a bearded, sun-tanned, self-reliant crowd, greeted them warmly. As darkness fell Bimrose explained the nature of their adventure. There was laughter at the thought of two actors turned pro-spectors. They joined a group around a steady fire where one of the miners boiled his quart pot and quietly cooked his flapjacks and shared them with the new arrivals. They slept under the stars.

In the morning they explored the site. Max's excitement grew as he felt he was near his goal. He stood on a hillock taking in the whole scene, watching Bimrose and Comstock picking their way through little sand hills dotted with lumps like ant-beds on a slope. He could see Bimrose puffing on his pipe, the smoke curling blue in the clear morning air. Suddenly, a patch of sand gave way under Bimrose and Max, aghast, saw him clutch at Comstock, wheeling wildly in a chute of sand which emptied into an old shaft at the foot of the hill. The two men careered and jolted down the shaft. Max pulled himself out of a horrified inertia and yelled for help. Miners snatched shovels and came running. The cries down the shaft grew more urgent. The trickle of sand was spreading to a flow, then an avalanche, pouring over Max's friends and beginning to bury them several feet down. Now the whole camp was racing towards the disaster.

They dug like madmen. Max, scratching in a frenzy with his borrowed shovel, saw Ray Comstock's unbelieving eyes disappear beneath the rush of sand. Bimrose's head had vanished already.

When they were finally dragged out, they were caked with sand: noses, ears, eyes were crammed with it. They were laid under a sapling of desert gum. Max watched as the miners covered the faces of his friends with rough blankets. Unprepared for the tragedy which left him in a state of shock, he sat mute under another tree as the miners began to dig again. This time their object was a shallow double grave. When it was ready, he stumbled to join the others as they lowered the sand-blasted corpses of Ray Comstock and Joss Bimrose beneath the surface. Hatless and solemn-faced, they stood around staring uneasily at their handiwork. Finally, the man who last night had shared his flapjacks with them, turned to Max.

'You want to say a few words, mate?'

Max shook his head. And walked slowly away from the group to where the pack horses and the wagon stood. Now they were his.

Max let the pack horses lead him for a day. That night he slept beneath the wagon. He knew he would not starve. The provisions that Bimrose had assembled for three would serve him for several days but he had no idea where he was.

The next day, after a biscuit breakfast, he proceeded in the direction in which the cart was pointed. That afternoon he spotted wheel tracks in the sand. He followed them and by sunset he lurched up before an old grey-stone homestead, its veranda screened by creepers which climbed up over the roof. Behind it stood a sturdy stable and beyond that a small stockyard. The saltbush plain in front was tipped with silver. The site, he reckoned, had been chosen because of the creek where the old white gums were alive with noisy parrots who had flown in for their evening drink. A few cattle and some horses were grazing amongst the shrubs. A dog ran out barking, setting off a cockerel's lusty crow.

Max saw a net curtain twitch as he surveyed the homestead. 'Anyone at home?' he tried.

'Who are you?' a woman's voice replied.

A shotgun appeared around the open doorway and Max raised his hands.

'I mean no harm. I'm trying to find Alice,' he said.

The gun was followed by a young woman dressed in a serviceable long black skirt and a black blouse. Her fair hair, pulled back from her fresh face, was secured under a black handkerchief. She looked at him. 'You're lost,' she said.

'Too right,' Max agreed.

'Better unhook your horses,' she said, standing her shotgun inside the doorway. She came forward to help him. Max eased himself stiffly off the wagon and together they led the horses down to the creek, disturbing a flock of wild duck.

The girl introduced herself, 'Esme Napier'.

Max felt that he would not need to do the same. He smiled graciously, waiting for her to recognise him. Was he not a star in Australia?

Not to Esme. 'What's yours?' she insisted.

'Max,' he said. 'Max Milman. Actor.'

'Actor?' The disbelief was written across her hitherto solemn face. Then it cracked, first into a smile. Then it relaxed into gales of laughter. Max shifted sheepishly from one foot to another.

Esme collected herself. 'I'm sorry,' she said, still stifling her giggles, 'I've never seen an actor before.'

Max made a low bow as if acknowledging applause.

'What are you doing here?' Esme enquired. 'You'll not find a theatre out this way.'

Max settled down on the grass as the horses quenched their thirst and told her the saga of the last few weeks. She listened with sympathy and became animated at the mention of John Flynn.

'A good man,' she said, pointing to a small mound some yards up from the creek. Max stared at it and the sad straggle of creepers which decorated it. 'He came by when Mungo was taken.'

She explained that she was a widow. Her young husband had fallen from Tucker, his favourite horse. 'Mungo was thrown against a gum like a sack. It took a long time but I got a board and I got him back to the house. He'd just recovered from a fever. I shouldn't have let him ride. He was faint with pain and still weak from the fever when John Flynn came by with his camel train. I was so glad to see him but there was little enough he could do. He gave Mungo morphine to ease the pain, but it wasn't long before I lost him.' Max sensed that she had not told enough people her sad tale to exorcise the memory. 'Flynn dug for me,' she looked again at the simple grave, 'and read the service.'

'He let you stay here alone?'

'I wouldn't go. Where could I have gone? I'm used to it here.'

The shadows had lengthened. The horses were no longer thirsty and munched the grasses around the creek. Esme got up to walk back to the neat homestead. The dark interior was cool. She lit a fire and produced a pan and two steaks.

They ate in silence.

Esme, watching him in the firelight, was intrigued by the idea of a strutting actor, no doubt used to a soft life, squatting by her fireside picking hungrily at the thick steak with his fingers.

'What sort of an actor are you?' she asked.

'I'm a good actor,' said Max. 'I do it all. Shakespeare, melo-drama, comedy, action, I can sing a song, you name it. Max Milman's game for anything.'

'I've never been to a play.'

'I'll give you a command performance after supper. What'll it be? What's your command, my lady?'

'Tell me some plays.'

'*Hamlet*, a bit heavy. *Ben Hur*, can't do justice to the chariot race. *Romeo and Juliet*?'

'I've heard of that,' said Esme, eagerly.

'I'll get the book,' said Max and went outside to rummage through his bags still not unloaded from the wagon. He found his worn and weather-beaten *Collected Shakespeare* at the bottom of a box.

'D'you want to read the girl's part?' Max asked.

'Oh no,' said Esme quickly and then paused. 'You see, I can't read.'

'Right,' Max said, covering her obvious embarrassment. 'It's a solo performance then.'

Max opened the book and became immediately involved in the prologue. It was some two years and more since he had played Shakespeare and his spirits rose as he faced the challenge of making the story real and vivid for the young girl who was hearing it for the first time. He discovered a new simplicity in the verse as it became increasingly important to him to carry her along as the plot unfolded.

Two households both alike in dignity.
In fair Verona where we lay our scene.
From ancient grudge break to new mutiny,
Where civil blood makes civil hands unclean . . .

Esme listened rapt. The beams of the storm lantern which lit the pages picked out Max's lively eyes. Such was his familiarity with the text that often he could raise them from the book and peer directly into hers as he winged home a point.

From forth the fatal loins of these two foes
A pair of star-crossed lovers take their life
Whose misadventured, piteous overthrows
Doth with their death bury their parent's strife.

Max's voice was low and conversational, coaxing Esme gently into the tale. She hung on every word of 'the fearsome passage of their death-marked love', laughing unreservedly when Max overacted the nurse's comedy, and weeping without restraint at Mercutio's death.

Max closed the book. 'It's getting late, little lady. I dare say you've work to do in the morning and I warrant it's after your usual bedtime.'

'It is that,' said Esme, 'but I was enjoying it. I really was.' She tried not to sound surprised.

'We'll finish it tomorrow night,' said Max.

'Are you going to stay on then?'

'Reckon I might make myself helpful?'

'I could use a hand with the cattle.'

'You get to learn about Shakespeare. I get a course in cattle care.'

'It's a deal,' said Esme, her eyes bright.

Her late night did not interfere with Esme's invariable habit of early rising. The smell and sizzle of frying bacon stirred Max. He plunged gratefully into the creek, ridding himself at last of days of desert dust, then stood over the bowl of hot water which she placed before a fragment of looking-glass propped up against his Shakespeare. Wielding his razor with care, he cut a swathe through the rough stubble which was threatening to become a beard. Pleased with what he saw, he stood back to admire his handiwork and smoothed his cheek with his fingers. In the cracked piece of mirror he could detect Esme, apparently concentrating on her frying pan, casting an occasional admiring glance in his direction. Got to be careful here, old man, he thought. He was surprised to find that he was more concerned with what might happen to Esme than how it would all end for him. Max Milman gets a conscience, he mused, must be getting old.

They followed a routine. By day, Esme taught Max her life's experience with cattle. After the sun went down, Max would read to her from his Shakespeare. Each night after the ritual reading they retired to their opposite corners of the room. After *Romeo and Juliet*, Max gave her *Macbeth*, *As You Like It* and *Julius Caesar*. He turned then to the sonnets. The words were a revelation to him. He read them directly to her, taking his time so that they could linger on the implications of the lines. Both of them sensed that the atmosphere in the room had changed. With the eighth sonnet, 'Music to hear, why hear'st thou music sadly? Sweets with sweets war not, joy delights in joy,' the mood grew more solemn. Max let the last couplet fall into silence: 'Whose speechless song being many, seeming one, sings this to thee. Thou single wilt prove none.' He looked up at her as he began sonnet nine. He saw she was already weeping, and wondered if he should go on. He looked down at the text and decided that it was all or nothing. 'Is it for fear to wet a widow's eye,' he read, 'That thou consum'st thyself in single life? Ah, if thou issueless shalt hap to die, the world will wail thee like a mateless wife . . .'

Esme, tears pouring down her face, fell into his arms. Max rocked her as her sobs subsided and then, gently lifting her face, brushed away the tears and kissed her. The weeks of self-denial were forgotten as they abandoned themselves with a passion in which Max lost himself with a commitment that he had never felt before.

When Esme knew that she was pregnant they sat down solemnly to discuss their future. Neither questioned that they would spend it together. They reckoned that Flynn would eventually pass back through the area, and planned a wedding on the grass that led down to the creek. 'Cockatoos for bridesmaids, prize pig for best man,' Max laughed.

One bright Saturday morning Esme started to do her week's washing. As she bent over the tub she felt a twinge of pain. Ignoring it she straightened her aching back and looked around. She could see Max chopping wood. An early-morning breeze sighed among the trees down by the creek. Ignoring her discomfort, Esme wrung out the clothes and lugged them across to the line. They felt uncommonly heavy. With a peg in her mouth she reached up, then gasped at a sudden, vicious pain. Max saw her fall from one corner of his eye, and came running over. She lay on the ground, writhing in agony. Blood seeped from beneath her skirts.

Max kept helpless vigil. Esme had miscarried. He had buried the baby near Mungo. He had cleared up the blood, the sweat, the tears. But he knew no way to save Esme, who went in and out of consciousness. Then, on a day when the sun was at its hottest, he heard in the distant silence the familiar sounds of John Flynn's approaching camels, grunting and snarling. Max rushed to meet them and Flynn, sensing the urgency, was inside the homestead within seconds.

Two days later a solemn procession set out for Birdsville. Flynn, asking no questions of Max, had honoured Esme's last wish and married them. Esme had died holding Max's hand. Another mound appeared next to Mungo's grave, and Flynn read the burial service. That evening the two men sat silently together, feeling keenly the emptiness of the homestead. At last Flynn broke the silence. 'You were the last man I expected to find here, Milman.'

Max nodded bleakly. 'I was in a play once,' he said. 'Mawkish stuff. They called it *The Love of a Good Woman*. I never thought

I'd come across it. Out here of all places, Flynn. Only the play ended differently. I was saved in the play. What's for me now?'

'There's a grand future in Australia.'

'I know.'

'You've got the cattle too. Esme had no relatives. It's a sizeable nest-egg she's left you.'

'She did me nothing but good; and all I could do was kill her.'

'Enough of that, Max.'

'I dare say,' said Max. 'I've learnt my lesson, Flynn. I've brought a load of bad luck with me out here. There's two men gone and a good woman – and the child. It's back on the boards for me. I may bore an audience – but I've never bored 'em to death.'

By the time Max awoke on the first day of rehearsal the headlines he had provoked were very much yesterday's news. Readers, who had eaten fish and chips out of the greasy remains of his reputation, were scanning new front pages for new sensations, weighing the merits of the Craig and Bentley murder case and arguing over Bentley's appeal against sentence for his part in Craig's killing of a Croydon policeman.

Max, who thought contemptuously that altogether too much attention was being paid to Spraunccy Chauncey's revelations, was relieved when he joined the family for breakfast to find that another topic was uppermost in their minds. A lightning strike had paralysed London traffic that morning. No one could be sure how the actors would get to the Dissenters' Hall in St John's Wood where they were due to rehearse at ten o'clock. The immediate family was not a problem. Tony would drive Max and Maude and the three children in the Rolls. It would be a squash but, with Max in front and the two boys on the jump seat, they could manage. Martyn and Louis Armbruster were to arrive together. A hire car had arrived at eight to collect Martyn in time to pick up Louis and the designer who was to show and explain his completed sets to the company before the formal read-through of the play. The only problem was Amanda, whose telephone rang unanswered.

Darcy

Darcy, who had only got back from the States the previous evening, joined the others at St Leonard's Terrace, bursting to tell of the wonders of New York. Even his first meeting with his long-lost grandfather took second place to his account of the Empire State building, the Staten Island ferry, dinner at Sardi's – 'with an old friend of Dad's . . . they actually have his caricature on the wall right over his favourite table!' – and visits to *Paint Your Wagon* (thumbs up), *Wish You Were Here* (thumbs down), the long-running *The King and I* (too late to see Gertrude Lawrence but bowled over by Yul Brynner) and *Two's Company* (just in time to catch Bette Davis's revue début).

Darcy was even looking forward to meeting Louis again. Two weeks in a strange, enticing town had, as so often, healed the wounds inflicted by passion on the very young. Besides, it was probably only to Louis that he could report his most amusing adventure. His plane had arrived in New York several hours late. The acquaintances who were there to welcome him had disappeared about their business leaving messages at the Algonquin that they would call in the morning.

Darcy decided to examine the hotel's facilities. First he treated himself to a Martini in the bar by the door and exchanged pleasantries with Harry at the newspaper kiosk. He made a new friend there when he was rumbled as Martyn's son. 'Sir Martyn always stays here, Mr Milman, pleased to have you with us.' Darcy gave himself dinner, opening an English paper which he had bought before realising that it was the one he had already read on the plane. He speculated on which of the many round tables was the famous one.

His next encounter was, of course, all the fault of Louis who had long since excited Darcy with a graphic account of the excitements to be found in New York bars. They sounded a tempting phenomenon, hugely different from the only English club of which he knew, the Rockingham, off Shaftesbury Avenue, which he understood to be a rallying point for discreet old queens. He had declined his one invitation there, fearing the faint chance that he might run into his father. Besides, he did not particularly like the old gentleman who had invited him. New York bars sounded altogether more alluring. One name, The Hat Bar, stuck in his mind. Pillaging his bedside cupboard he found the Manhattan phone book beneath the Gideon Bible and hunted for the address. There it was on the East Side, in the low thirties, some dozen or so blocks down from the Algonquin. He looked at his watch and saw that it was just after ten – probably too early from what he had gathered from Louis of young America's nocturnal habits – but he couldn't wait.

Fifteen minutes later he walked down the flight of stairs which led into a nearly empty semi-circular room with a bar curving around the wall which faced the entrance. Darcy chose a stool and, wishing to conform, after a glance at what the two or three other customers were drinking, he ordered a beer. None of his fellow-drinkers appealed to him, but his seat gave him a perfect position from which to inspect new arrivals. Watching the entrance he would see first the feet and then, as they descended, framed by the low ceiling, thighs and waist, torso and finally neck and head. He toyed with his beer as more customers arrived. None took his fancy, but as the night wore on he began to recognise a ritual. He saw the occasional man approach another and offer him a beer. Sometimes these offers were accepted. Later he watched one pair of new acquaintances leave The Hat Bar together.

It was after midnight and he was on his fourth drink when he felt his interest quicken for the first time. A pair of dark cowboy boots stood framed in the doorway and paused. Then, as they stepped down, two legs in a neat pair of pale, well-washed blue jeans came into view. Swiftly they were surmounted by a tight, plain white tee-shirt and a black leather jacket which covered a chest on which a great deal of loving physical attention had been lavished. A thick footballer's neck supported a strikingly handsome square-jawed face and then a neat crew-cut.

Darcy realised that he was looking straight at his all-American ideal of masculinity. He wondered if beginner's luck would be his. The man crossed casually to the other side of the bar. Darcy could not hear what he ordered, but the regulation beer appeared. Having carefully planned his opening line, Darcy realised with dismay that he could not use it until the stranger had drunk at least two thirds of his glass. What if a rival got to him first? He watched, on tenterhooks. The man seemed in no hurry. Indeed the rate of consumption in the bar had been so small all night that Darcy wondered how it could be made to pay. He practised sipping in time with his quarry. At last a respectable third remained in each glass. Oh hell, he thought, hoisting himself off his stool. It's now or never!

He crossed the bar. The man looked even more handsome at close quarters. Draining his own glass, Darcy indicated his fellow-drinker. 'Care for a beer?' he said as casually as he could.

The man turned and looked at him in amusement for several seconds. Finally he spoke dismissively in a high, lisping, suburban London accent; 'Dominick Dexter introduced us in Knightsbridge three years ago,' he said, 'but I wouldn't mind a beer, darling. How is dear old Dom?'

His American Dream shattered, Darcy bought the beer, and explained that Dominick, his father's old choreographer, had died some few months after the meeting that he had so completely and unfortunately forgotten; and that Vincent Nolan, Dominick's faithful, grief-stricken lover, had committed suicide soon afterwards. They fell silent for a few moments and then Darcy, anxious to extricate himself from an evening which had not turned out as he planned, pleaded jet-lag and an early start and made his way back to the Algonquin.

Zelda Fane's Daimler drew alongside the Dissenters' Hall in St John's Wood and Max, immediately spry, sprang to open the door for her. She rewarded him with a peck on the cheek and murmured, 'Who's been a naughty boy?' Emerging behind her were Harry Harmon and Braden Jefferson – Harry, nervous, voluble and excited; Braden, quietly correct, carrying her script.

Inside the hall the floor was chalked out in different colours to correspond with the ground plan for the various scenes. Louis fussed over the model as the designer unwrapped miniature pieces of the set. Martyn fussed over his mother.

'I've been phoning you all morning to arrange a car,' he said. 'How did you get here?'

'Walked,' said Amanda.

'Walked!'

'I often do,' she said. 'It clears my head and gets me going. Why were you worried? I could have caught a bus or telephoned for a taxi. I'm not completely helpless.'

'But there's a strike. No buses. No tubes.'

'Nobody tells me anything,' sniffed Amanda. 'I cut straight across the park, through Lancaster Gate and over the railway bridge by Royal Oak.'

'But that's miles.'

'Oh, stop fretting, Martyn. I'm in one piece. How's your father?'

'His tail's still somewhere between his legs.'

'Which is precisely where it should be! Let's hope his "gift for comedy" is intact,' Amanda added viciously, remembering Max's aspersions on her own skill in that department as reported by Sprauncey Chauncey.

The strike held up the cast and it was noon before they all found their way to the Dissenters' Hall. This gave those who got there on time an opportunity to consider potential friendships, liaisons, rivalries and touring romances.

Harry Harmon always employed an efficient production team and prided himself on the gentility of his regime. Coffee, china tea and biscuits appeared as the cast filtered in. Martyn's Pensioners were dressed rather self-consciously for the occasion. Rehearsals for Sir Martyn's shows had always been sedate, decorous affairs. Adela Skelton, sipping her tea alongside Maude and Amanda, stared disapprovingly as Louis Armbruster's dancers turned up in a motley collection of casual clothes, dance outfits, headbands and pumps. 'Really,' she hissed. 'What have they come as? Gypsies?'

'That's what we call them back home,' Zelda intervened. She was making the rounds of the hall introducing herself to everyone and dispensing gracious concern.

'My late husband was a great fan of yours, Zelda,' Amanda said sweetly. 'He loved your pictures.'

'Your late husband . . .?' Zelda asked, puzzled.

'There was life after Max Milman, you know, dear. You don't imagine that I've been pining alone for forty years, do you?'

Amanda

Amanda had not had an easy ride on her return from Australia. Although Aubrey Desborough honoured his promise to find her a place in his company when he took *Improper Peter* out on tour, it was not an engagement she enjoyed.

They arrived in Newcastle on a bitterly cold winter Sunday. The recommended digs had all been taken by the large cast of a tour which was playing its second week in the city. The endless tramp through the streets, dragging Martyn, who was swathed in an overcoat two sizes too big for him, convinced Amanda that this was no way to bring up a child. When they finally found a friendly pub which offered a bed they fell gratefully into it, oblivious of the din which swelled up to them from the noisy rooms below. Martyn slept immediately while Amanda lay awake wondering how to solve the problem of her son's future.

The decision was soon taken out of her hands. Keeping his company going for more than a few weeks was beyond Aubrey Desborough's already over-extended finances. After two Sunday train calls for which Amanda dressed to the nines hoping that some bright manager would spot her as they changed trains at Crewe, disaster hit the company at Liverpool. Attendances throughout the week were sparse, but Desborough calculated that the weekend houses would tide him over. When audiences inconveniently stayed away he called his dispirited band together and explained that the curtain had fallen on *Improper Peter* for the last time. He produced enough money to pay their fares back to London but not to cover the week's wages. The sorry caravan of Evadne Rivers, Gerald the juvenile and Amanda with Martyn and their bits and pieces dragged their feet to Lime Street station.

The Desboroughs stayed behind to save what they could from the wreckage and settle with the theatre.

'We bounce back,' were the last words Amanda heard from him, spoken with less conviction than usual.

Installed in Mrs Crowther's theatrical lodgings in Kennington, Amanda decided to make her assault on the West End. She selected her targets carefully, scanning the theatrical papers for plays about to go into production and storing every piece of theatrical gossip which came her way. Her first attack was on a producer's office in John Street. A man called Masterson was said to be casting a new play, *The Bloom on the Peach*.

An actor must always call on reserves of optimism and courage before an interview. Amanda needed a double helping of both. She had already been refused an appointment and was bluffing her way in. In the outer office she found two secretaries behind a glass screen marked 'Enquiries' bashing away at their typewriters. Steeling herself, she knocked. One secretary ceased tapping and pushed open the glass panel. She uttered an uninterested, 'Yes?'

'I have come to see Mr Masterson.'

'Have you an appointment? He is exceedingly busy this morning.'

'I have no actual appointment, but it is a matter of very great importance.'

'It's not just an audition, is it?'

Amanda did not reply.

'It's not just an audition, is it?' the girl insisted.

'Would you kindly take my name up? It is a matter of very great importance.' Amanda laid heavy emphasis on 'importance'. She held her breath as she awaited the result. It worked. The girl made a note of her name, emerged from behind the glass panel and walked stiffly out of the ante-room. She returned almost immediately and, holding the door open, said, 'Mr Masterson will see you now.'

Amanda climbed a flight of stairs. The office she entered was long and dark, its walls covered with framed play-bills. At its end sat a severe-looking man who glanced up from a script which lay on top of a rubble of other scripts, files, letters and two telephones which were almost submerged under the debris. He put the script he was reading to one side and looked at Amanda coldly.

'I am told you have something of great importance to discuss with me?'

Amanda had prepared herself for the question. 'It may not be important to you, Mr Masterson, but it is of great importance to me. I want a job.'

'But my secretary told me . . .'

'Don't you see, it *is* important, Mr Masterson? It is *very* important. I want to act for you. I want a role in *The Bloom on the Peach*. May I not show you?'

Masterson allowed the words to fall into silence, then he stood up and, skirting his desk, crossed the room to the door. He opened it, bowed slightly and stood waiting for her to leave. She hesitated for a moment, cast him one despairing look and walked from the room defeated.

Descending the staircase she saw the two secretaries smile at each other. She hurried blindly into the street. Stifling a sob she was disconcerted to find herself stumbling into the arms of an equally surprised Archie Durrant.

'Well, well, little lady,' he said predictably, 'why are you weeping?' But before Amanda could begin her litany of disappointments he had a solution. 'Spot of lunch, my dear. Simpson's, just along the way, upstairs. Roast beef of old England. That sort of thing. Buck you up no end.'

These staccato sentences, which were very much Archie's usual style, neatly punctuated Amanda's grateful sobs. Tactfully he did not press her for the reason for her grief.

By the time they reached the restaurant Amanda had pulled herself together sufficiently to be grateful that she had taken some care to look her best for Mr Masterson. Archie was now to get the benefit. 'Looking corking,' he said, after the waiter had settled her in her chair. She had repaired her face in the ladies' powder room.

'Oh, it *is* good to see you,' she said.

'Tour over?'

'Yes. It was not the triumph Mr Desborough had hoped for. Liverpool liked it even less than Perth.'

'How's the little lad?'

'I shall have to send him to my family in Somerset. I am resolved to try my luck in the West End of London.'

'I should like that,' said Archie simply. 'Not keen on you trudging about the country.'

'Of course my parents will say told you so.'

'What else are parents for?' said Archie tolerantly. 'Sure the fellow's given you enough beef?'

At the end of the meal they agreed to meet again the next evening. Archie specified the Café Royal, and pressed a generous five shillings into Amanda's hand to cover the taxi fare.

The tide, Amanda told her patient landlady, was changing. Next morning there was confirmation. Of the many letters Amanda had written to managers, one elicited a reply. Coming down to breakfast with Martyn she found the envelope proudly displayed, propped up by her tea-cup. Tearing it open in the fierce certainty that it contained good news, she felt her heart leap when she saw that the stationery was H B Irving's.

'You see, dear,' said the landlady, peering over her shoulder as she poured tea, 'it's always the best ones who take the trouble to reply.'

The offer from Irving's son was to read for a small part in *The Arch Pretender*, a play he was presenting at the Savoy Theatre. The fortunate applicant would also be required to understudy the leading lady – Mrs Irving.

Kitted out in one of her stage frocks for dinner at the Café Royal, Amanda could barely wait to tell Archie the good news. It is an actor's privilege to count a part as good as hers until she fails to get it. She was bubbling with optimism as Archie led her to their table.

'Here's a changed girl,' he said, 'a chap might think you'd had some good news.'

'I have! I have!' said Amanda.

'But I haven't told you yet.'

'Told me what?'

'Fellow at the club. Old friend, went to school together. Man called Masterson. Looking for a pretty girl for his new play *The Bloom on the Peach*. Wants to see you tomorrow afternoon. Ambassadors Theatre, four o'clock.' Amanda burst into tears.

Archie knew that actresses were queer cattle. He took a large white handkerchief from his pocket and handed it to her.

'I'm so sorry,' Amanda said. 'What will people think?'

'Oh, I expect they see pretty women crying every day in a place like this,' said Archie helpfully.

Promptly at noon Amanda presented herself at the stage door of the Savoy. She was the last actress to be auditioned. She read the role for Irving and his wife, Dorothea Baird, who were sitting in the stalls. There was a short pause. Then they summoned her to join them and announced that they were delighted that she was to join their company. Irving, whose ascetic face reminded her vividly of his father whom she had once seen as Cardinal Richelieu, indicated that his manager would settle terms. Amanda hesitated. Now she did not want *The Arch Pretender*. At least, she wanted it only if she failed to get the new part in *The Bloom on the Peach* that afternoon. She tried to temporise.

'Mr Irving – could this offer remain open until tomorrow morning?'

Irving stiffened. 'But why, my dear?'

'Mr Irving, I'm . . . I don't actually know whether I shall be free.'

'Why might you not be free?'

'Because I am going this afternoon to the Ambassadors Theatre to read a part in Mr Masterson's new play with Miss Olga Nethersole.'

Irving bristled at this. 'And if you get it you will have no use for us?'

'Well, I . . . I . . .'

'And if you are not successful you will condescend to return. Is that it?'

'Well . . .'

'Miss Bollington, you have just taken up my time and Mrs Irving's time. You wrote to me to ask to be considered for this role. We have paid you the compliment of choosing you among several aspiring actresses – some of whom have considerable experience in the West End. Now you want us to wait on your good or ill fortune.'

Amanda could not ignore the anger in his voice but she was determined to win him over. 'I know you must think that I am behaving very badly, Mr Irving. You have indeed paid me a huge compliment. I do not wish to seem graceless or ungrateful; but the other role is a new part in a new play. *The Arch Pretender* has long been a success. Who will return to see a new girl in one short scene? Mr Masterson's play would be a great chance for me to be noticed. I had to ask you, but, of course, I understand if you decide that you cannot, that you are unable . . .'

Having exhausted her excuses Amanda tailed off into embarrassment. There was silence. When she looked up she saw that Mrs Irving's hand lay gently on her husband's wrist.

'Miss Bollington,' he said, 'I am an actor too. We are both actors.' He took his wife's hand. 'Go to the Ambassadors and read for Mr Masterson and Miss Nethersole. We wish you luck – and if you do not succeed we will welcome you back.'

'Capital, girlie,' Archie said. 'Now for old Masterson. He's going to love you.'

When she arrived at the stage door of the Ambassadors, Amanda discovered that *The Bloom on the Peach* had already been in rehearsal for a week. Neither Miss Nethersole nor the author was happy with the juvenile, who had been 'released'.

'I'm surprised they put up with her for so long,' said the confiding stage manager as he handed her the 'sides', the miserable little typescripts which were called 'parts', and which contained only the last few words of each cue before Amanda's own lines. Of the rest of the play she had no idea.

Amanda had gone to some trouble to dress completely differently from the way she had presented herself to Mr Masterson at their too recent, uncomfortable meeting. Then her braided cloth jacket, her white tucked blouse and fluted skirt had, she hoped, made her look both attractive and purposeful. With her limited wardrobe it had not been easy, but the other girls in the digs had rallied round. Blue bows and filmy flounces gave her a different look, topped with a pale-blue hat with a ribbon bow, a cheeky up-turned brim and a spotted veil. It came from Berwick Market and the whole thing had cost her seven shillings. She stood in the wings, heard her first cue and, conquering her nerves, strode on and spoke her first line.

There was a significant pause and then she saw Miss Nethersole turn away and address the stalls. 'Mr Masterson,' she enquired, 'need she speak her line the instant she appears? Surely there is "a situation" here – or am I mistaken?'

Amanda heard Masterson's voice from the stalls, warmer, more involved than it had sounded in his office. 'Yes, my dear,' he called out as he got up from his seat on the aisle and approached the stage. 'She won't speak as soon as she comes on. Of course there *is* a situation. Miss Bollington, may I present you to Miss Nethersole?'

'Bollington?' said Olga Nethersole. 'What an odd name!'

Amanda smiled modestly, stifling the urge to remark that Nethersole was not unduly mellifluous.

'That's what I thought,' said Masterson. 'I was sure I had heard it before, but I can't for the life of me recall where.'

'It's a good job you don't have to remember lines,' said Olga Nethersole amiably. 'Come on, Miss Bollington, let's get on with it.'

The audition went smoothly and, when it ended, Amanda was told that she had got the role.

Martyn

Hanna, who was one of the late arrivals at the Dissenters' Hall, made immediately for Maude in a flurry of apologies. She had not known about the strike and had waited alone at a bus stop for what seemed like hours before giving up and trudging to the underground. There she heard about the disruption and realised that she would have to walk; but first she had to hurry home to warn her son, so that he wouldn't be late for his lectures. Now she was exhausted.

'Sit down, dear,' said Maude, 'have a cup of tea. You're not by any means the last.'

No sooner had Hanna settled herself by Maude's side and dipped a Marie biscuit in her tea than Martyn arrived to introduce her to Zelda. Hanna, rising in haste to show proper concern for the star she was to understudy, spilt her tea, biscuit, cup and saucer over the floor and Zelda's immaculate court shoes. Before she could be restrained, she was down on her knees dabbing away rigorously with her handkerchief in an attempt to remove the stains. Zelda leant down gracefully to help her to her feet.

'Now you don't need to bother with that, honey,' she said. 'I'm sure we're going to be great friends. Martyn tells me you were with Brecht before the war in Germany.'

'Oh yes,' Hanna said, pleased that Martyn had pointed it out. 'In *Dreigroschenoper*.'

'I worked with the old fiend once in LA,' said Zelda, 'when he and Laughton staged *Galileo* in the forties. Not a barrel of laughs, Bert, was he?'

For Hanna, who had for years kept hope alive by reminiscing with awe on her association with the great man, this was a difficult pill to swallow. However, she was determined not to upset this exotic creature at their first meeting and contented herself with saying 'He was very serious'.

When the last straggler had surfaced, Martyn summoned the company to the semi-circle of chairs and trestle tables which had been arranged at one end of the large hall. In front of them his production staff had placed another table on which stood the model of the set. By its side was an upright piano at which Freda August had already installed herself. Martyn, Louis and the young designer took their places by the model. Stage management sat in a row behind them. The rest of the company sorted themselves out in the semi-circle. Adrian Arbuthnot, who had been chattering to Maude, shepherded her and Amanda to their seats. Adela Skelton joined them. Zelda encouraged Hanna to sit with her. Max found himself a chair on her other side as far away from Amanda as possible. The three Milman children formed a companionable balance in the centre of the semi-circle, along with the butlers and footmen. Behind Freda's piano a dozen chairs housed the still-chattering gypsies. Behind Zelda, discreetly alert, was Braden Jefferson who handed her the script as Martyn rose and called for silence.

'Ladies and gentlemen,' he said. 'Thank you all for getting here. No thanks to London Transport! Now we must make up for lost time so I don't propose to make a long speech. Many of you are old friends and colleagues but I'm delighted to welcome some new members to our family. Zelda Fane is of course playing Mrs Cheveley. I know we have all long been admirers of Miss Fane on the screen, and I'm sure you are looking forward to working with her for the first time as much as I am for the second.'

Maude started a little ripple of applause which was enthusiastically taken up by the rest of the company.

'I don't think I need say anything about my father, Max Milman. You will have read more than you need to know about him in the newspapers.'

This time the reaction was laughter, led by Max.

'He and my mother are playing Lady Markby and the Earl of

Caversham. They will be acting together for the first time in some forty years. I'm sure they will strike sparks off each other.'

It was Amanda's turn to lead the laughter with a diplomatic chuckle.

'Since the last time most of us worked alongside, two important things have happened. One very sad and one very exciting. The sadness which many of us share is for the passing of our old friend Dominick Dexter who has staged the musical numbers and the dances so beautifully for all my entertainments since the very first, *The Pink Princess*.'

'A lovely show,' breathed Adela Skelton.

'Thank you, Adela. But that brings me to the *exciting* turn of events. Since the war we have become aware of a new and vibrant form of musical play which has come to us from America and blown away some of the cobwebs with which the old shows were festooned. *Oklahoma!* blazed a trail and we have also been swept along on a tide of energy and enthusiasm by *Annie Get Your Gun*, *Carousel* and others. At this moment *Pennsylvania!* is packing them in at the Scala and the man responsible for recreating Don Ericson's vital choreography over here is Louis Armbruster who, I am delighted to say, is going to stage the dances for *In Society!*.'

At the mention of Armbruster's name the little band of dancers, who owed their jobs to him, whooped and clapped.

Now it was time for them to gather round the model as Tom Tanqueray, known to his friends as The Second Mrs, demonstrated its virtues. Tanqueray had replaced the long-serving Cedric, who, accepting his demotion to dress designer with ill-grace, had chosen not to be present. The gypsies squatted on the floor in front of the model. The older actors peered from their chairs – in Adela's case through an impressive lorgnette.

Martyn had anticipated large, built scenes to convey the opulence of the Chilterns' impressive staircase and their fine ballroom, as well as Lord Goring's well-heeled bachelor rooms. He would accommodate lengthy scene changes with ballads and point numbers played well down-stage, a method he had previously perfected in his Ruritanian spectacles. 'We can do it in One,' had been his constant plea. This had been invariably countered by

Louis who had insisted: 'You can do fuck-all in One, Martyn, except stop the show stone dead. This is 1953, they won't sit through some old bag like Adela Skelton simpering a soprano nothing, however far down-stage the cow wanders.'

Louis had advocated a swiftly moving series of light screens giving an almost filmic fluidity to the action. To this solution Martyn had objected that there was no space for the *fin de siècle* extravagance which the play demanded. 'Shifting screens may be all right for *Madam Butterfly*, Louis. I mean I used them myself years ago at Covent Garden when I staged it for Beecham, but it won't do for Wilde.'

It was here that the young designer justified his promotion with a series of elaborate *trompe l'œil* decorations on Louis's mobile screens which, while they could be changed swiftly, at the same time conveyed the sense of wealth and opulence for which Martyn yearned. In addition, Tanqueray solved the problem of bringing on and off sufficient heavy furniture to meet the demands of the melodramatic plot: a near railway siding of turntables, tracks and trucks wheeled on love-seats for love scenes, desks in which incriminating letters could be discovered, and sliding walls behind which scheming adventuresses could conceal themselves.

Louis had thrown one more tantrum when he demanded to know how his dancers were to negotiate this stage machinery without breaking their legs or their necks. The young designer had contrived to find enough space for them to dance up a storm.

Now, the Dissenters' Hall was invaded by the happiness which is felt by actors only amidst the high optimism of the first day of rehearsals when the set is revealed and the prospect of a long run, secure employment, accommodated mortgages, paid-up school fees and settled debts stretches before them.

Martyn smiled contentedly at the model as he dismissed the company for lunch. He was not even mildly irritated when Adela Skelton sidled up to him and suggested that Lady Basildon surely needed 'a teeny-weeny little numberette' if her character was to pull its weight in the show. 'Not for me, you understand, Martyn, dear. For the play.'

Martyn merely nodded vaguely and pushed a tiny, meticulously painted *boulle* desk across the model stage one way and propelled a miniature sofa, its cover intricately decorated with cabbage roses, slowly back on its tracks in the opposite direction.

Martyn

Martyn had been exiled to Highbridge, a little town in Somerset, while Amanda pursued her career as a West End actress and Archie slowly and devotedly pursued her.

Here, Martyn's model theatre was a rough affair improvised from boxes begged from Thomas Knight's boot and shoe shop in Church Street and Robert Knight's central supply stores in Market Street. He entered this fantasy world when he could escape from chores on the farm.

The Great War had started, and Amanda felt more secure in the knowledge that her son would be out of London and living with her family. She had taken him part of the way, but left him alone in a carriage on the little Somerset and Dorset Joint Railway, with a label tied securely to his jacket. It corresponded exactly to the one attached to his trunk. Both read 'Martyn Milman c/o Bollington, Church Farm, Highbridge'. Amanda kissed him goodbye, told him to be brave, and waved farewell as the dirty yellow and chocolate carriages pulled out of the station in the direction of the moorland and the Somerset levels. Then she turned and waited for the train which would get her back to London in time for the theatre. Neither wept. Amanda, who grew daily more practical as she became more independent, simply told herself that it was the sensible thing to do. It was the end of the intimacy that they had shared as they bucketed around Australia and the English provinces.

For Martyn it was a new adventure. At five he was not sure what life in the country would be like. The idea of the railway journey on his own made him feel immensely grown-up in spite of his betraying short trousers. His mother had given the conductor two shillings and sixpence to put him on the platform at Highbridge and, as the train had no corridor, he could come to little harm. At each station the kindly man checked that he was all right and in between Martyn gazed at the unfolding, unfamiliar landscape of moorland broken by little ditches, withy beds and stacks of neatly-cut peat.

A pony-trap full of smiling Bollingtons was waiting at Highbridge as the train drew in. One firm pair of avuncular Bollington arms picked Martyn up and placed him on the front of the trap. Another Bollington brother made equally light work of his trunk and, by the time the train had pulled away and the level-crossing gates swung open, Martyn was enveloped in Bollington good humour as the pony and trap spun along to Church Farm under Brent Knoll where his grandparents were waiting to inspect him.

From his easy familiarity with theatrical digs; from a bedroom shared with his mother and from the sound of the landlady's maid's feet pounding upstairs with breakfast for two; from hours spent backstage in his mother's dressing-room surrounded by women with brightly-painted faces in various, unconcerned stages of undress; from complimentary seats in stage boxes at matinées perched on an extra hassock provided by a sympathetic programme-seller so that he might better peer over the polished railing to view the action; from all these urban and theatrical delights Martyn was removed to the regular, dawn-to-dusk hard work of the small farm.

At the beginning, he waited each morning for the arrival of the postman, Puddy, in case there was a card from his mother; his wait was rarely rewarded more than once a week and as the months went by the letters meant less to him. Entertainment dwindled into an occasional chance to watch a march past by the visiting Barry Dock Salvation Army Band ferried over from Cardiff on the packet steamship *Waverley*, or a rare visit to the Manor Gardens Theatre in Burnham to listen to Madam Poppy Watson's Ladies Orchestra. His grandparents had never understood why Ruby had wanted to go on the stage. Nor how she had managed it. They were concerned to keep such nonsense out of her son's head.

Martyn did not dislike the open-air life of the farm. Two of his amiable uncles made it seem fun. Although the right age for military service, they were both exempt. A third, who had an instinct for engineering, and had branched out with the Brent Knoll cycle works and joined the Territorials, was fighting in France. Martyn's waggish old grandfather teased him that he too was destined to be a farmer. 'No,' he would shout petulantly, 'I'm going to be an actor. Like Mummy . . . and Daddy,' he would add defiantly. Then he noticed that his grandparents would catch each other's eyes. He would run off across the cool stone flags and up the stairs to his room, slam the door and chatter to the cut-out characters he nudged about on his cardboard stage.

Max was enrolled at Highbridge Elementary, walking willingly to school in the mornings and back home less willingly at the end of the day to help with haymaking. Riding on a load of hay snuggled up close to Percy York, a farm labourer's son slightly older than he, was the only part of the ritual which he enjoyed. He did not know why. Otherwise his enthusiasm for farm work was limited to collecting eggs from the Light Sussex and Rhode Island Reds which clucked and crowed their way about the farmyard. He liked the excitement of harvesting when, as a field was shorn and the corn dwindled down to a few square yards, there were terrified rabbits to be chased and captured. And there was the ritual of cider-making. He would watch eagerly as baskets of apples were tipped into a vast metal hopper and crushed ready for the presses. He ran to round up any fruit which bounced away and fell on the floor. Then, as the residue was transferred to the press and placed in layers alternating with clean wheat straw, he would wait until the huge, heavy oak beam at the top of the pile was screwed tight, crushing what lay beneath it into a solid, sweating 'cheese'. As the sweet apple juice ran down its sides into a waiting wooden trough he would catch a mugful and retire to a shady spot to enjoy it.

At school, Martyn was an immediate success. The large classroom was open for morning assembly and could then be divided into three as the staff pulled great screens across. As he progressed up through the school he became top, without apparent effort, of each class he entered. He enjoyed the extra attention of the teachers which excellence attracts. School plays became his passion and Bollington neighbours would nod their heads and murmur that there was no doubt that he was 'Ruby's son'. The headmistress, frustrated by the lack of challenge in her curriculum, kept him behind for piano lessons and here too he excelled.

When his mother came to stay at Christmas she monitored his progress and congratulated him warmly on his playing. The slight west country burr which had crept into his voice disturbed her but she told herself that it would easily be eradicated.

Such was the placid, rural routine of Martyn's days. The war ended, but that made little difference to Highbridge. The dead were mourned and collections for a war memorial began. The survivors were welcomed home, Uncle Bob Bollington among them. As the Brent Knoll cycle enterprise had failed, Bob found employment at the Somerset and Devon Joint Railway works. Life on the farm went on unruffled.

Martyn's destiny lay elsewhere. His mother came, not to visit, but to take him back to London.

'Are we going back to Mrs Crowther's?' Martyn asked, naming the last theatrical digs in which they had stayed. He could just remember it.

'Oh no, dear,' said Amanda, but she would not reveal their precise destination. 'It's a surprise,' was all she would say.

At Paddington he was bemused by the crowds thronging the platform. It seemed extraordinary that in such a mass of people a man in uniform with tall polished boots and a peaked cap was able to spot him and his mother and to retrieve their bags from the train. Then this stranger led the way to a gleaming motor car and held open the door so that they could enter. After that he stowed the luggage in the boot. Of course Martyn had seen cars before but he had never ridden in one, and he remained open-eyed as the driver negotiated his way through streets infinitely more crowded than those of Highbridge on the busiest market day – and no cows nor sheep in sight. This bewitching journey ended in Kensington when the car drew up outside a tall house in Roland Gardens. Standing on the steps in the open doorway was a young woman in a black dress with a starched white apron and a stiff white cap.

'I'll give you a hand, Bill,' she said to the driver, running down to the car as he held open the door for Amanda and Martyn.

When travellers and luggage were safely inside, Amanda said: 'Annie will take you up to your room,' and leant down to plant a kiss on his forehead.

'Is all this yours?' Martyn asked, unable to take in the change in the family fortunes.

'It is our home,' said Amanda, simply.

Annie and Martyn followed Bill up the stairs; through an open door he could see a grand piano.

'You'll be able to play on that, Master Martyn,' said Annie. It was the first time anyone had called him Master Martyn. He did not fail to notice it and stiffened his back.

'It's a big one,' he said politely.

'Yes, it's a grand piano.'

'Grand's the word for it,' said Martyn who had only played on, or indeed heard of, an upright until then.

'We'll just go through the nursery,' said Annie as they followed Bill into a brightly painted, airy room and then to another smaller one where he was setting down the trunk.

'This is your room, Master Martyn,' said Bill, taking off his cap and wiping his forehead with his other hand, 'I hope you'll be very happy here with us.' He turned to Annie. 'I'll put the car away, love,' he said.

Martyn surveyed his territory. It was a small room but it did not seem so to him. There was a brand-new bed, a bedside table, two chairs and a bright rug on the polished boards. Annie watched, amused, as he took it all in and then, smiling, led him down to the drawing-room where his mother was standing by the grand piano, back-lit by tall windows.

Gathering Martyn to her, Amanda led him to the large sofa and sat him down.

'Do you remember Archie, darling?' she enquired. 'Archie Durrant?'

Martyn tried to remember. He was afraid, with some odd childish instinct, that if he did not remember he might be denied possession of this splendid new kingdom which he appeared to be about to inherit.

'Did we know him in Australia?' he asked.

'Not quite as long ago as that, darling,' said Amanda, quickly. Her voice was soft and encouraging. Martyn was reassured. He was not going to be tricked out of his new possessions. 'Do you remember the ship?'

'Was he on that?' Martyn tried even harder to remember. 'Was he the funny man with the white hat?'

Archie's solar topee had stuck in his mind.

'Yes!' said Amanda, delighted. 'Yes, that man was Archie! He is such a good man. A fine man. A man on whom you can rely, Martyn.' She paused in her parade of Archie's virtues, afraid perhaps of overdoing it and broke the news. 'Archie and I are married. Archie Durrant is my husband.'

Martyn remembered that years ago in a bedroom of some theatrical digs she had told him that Max, his father, was staying in Australia. He knew intuitively that he must not ask about him at this moment. He tried to think of a suitable question. 'Will your stage name be Amanda Durrant now?' he asked.

Amanda laughed. 'No, darling, I shall still be Amanda Bollington – but I don't think I shall be acting quite as much.'

'Why not?'

'I must spend a lot of my time looking after Archie.'

'Shall I have to call him daddy?' he said, still taking refuge in practical questions while he waited to discover if this dramatic change meant anything to him apart from a great deal of creature comforts.

'It would be very nice if you did, darling,' said Amanda. 'Go downstairs and knock on the big door to the right, that is his study.'

Sensing the importance of getting away to a good start with a brand-new father, Martyn set off. There was one moment of hesitation half-way down the stairs when he wondered if he would recognise Archie without his white hat. Then he reminded himself that as he would almost certainly be the only person in the room it would not be a problem. He knocked on the door and immediately a gruff but kindly voice said 'Enter'.

He opened the door and saw a man he dimly remembered sitting in an armchair and smiling at him. When he crossed to

Archie, his hand was shaken and he was given a polite kiss on his forehead, a kiss scented with tobacco from the neat moustache.

'Good afternoon, Daddy,' he said. 'Have you still got your white hat?'

'By jove, Martyn, I believe I have,' said Archie, taking the question as evidence of Martyn's total recall of their previous association. 'If I'm not very much mistaken it's in the wardrobe upstairs. We'll get it out one day – not that there's much occasion for it in this deuced climate,' he added regretfully.

The idyll in Kensington was not to be everlasting. Martyn was sent away to school. He was entered for Clevedon, his father's old college – not Max's of course. As Amanda pointed out when she and Archie were discussing the matter, Max had been educated at the University of Life – and much good it had done him.

Clevedon, perched on rocks which look over the Bristol Channel, had an admirable prep school, and when the new term began Archie and Amanda, with Bill at the wheel, took Martyn down.

Unlike the traditional trunks of the other new arrivals, Martyn's belongings were stowed in a theatrical skip. Amanda, who grew more practical as her contours thickened comfortably, had no intention of returning to life as a touring player and saw no use for the skip as a West End actress or as a Kensington hostess.

Martyn looked forward to life at Clevedon with no apprehension; Archie had painted a rosy picture of his own years there. He fitted easily and happily into the routine. He continued to play the piano. He acted in junior plays and acquitted himself well enough in school sports not to incur the contempt reserved for small boys who showed no skill at all on the playing fields. Two years later he was admitted to Brock's House as a senior.

Coldstream seduced Martyn during a rehearsal for the school play.

Martyn's delicate looks and his mother's career as an actress made him an automatic candidate for a leading role. Blakiston, his housemaster, had even seen Max touring in Shakespeare in the early years of the century.

'Pity your father didn't stick at it, Milman – an excellent Petruchio, a fine Mercutio – a great shame that he devoted himself to that fustian Roman nonsense.'

'I can't remember him,' said Martyn.

'Do you think you might go on the stage yourself, Milman?'

'My step-father is very much against it, sir.' Archie's unvaried attitude to actors was that it was no life for a man. 'I don't think my mother minds either way; but she points out the disappointments and the long periods out of work.'

Blakiston nodded. 'Very wise, I dare say; but we don't have to worry about unemployment at Clevedon, do we?' They laughed conspiratorially.

Martyn wanted badly to be in the play. Blakiston was an inspiring teacher, a cricket and rugger blue and an ex-president of the Oxford University Dramatic Society who delighted in leading the boys in his house by example. A muscular Christian, he had survived the war with distinction and a handful of medals. He had returned to Clevedon, it was whispered, as a stepping-stone to a bishopric.

'We're giving *Richard III* this year, Milman,' he told Martyn. 'Coldstream is treating us to his Crookback. I want you to take on the Lady Anne. You know: "Was ever woman in this humour woo'd? Was ever woman in this humour won?" ' Martyn did not know and said so.

'It's a difficult scene. Gloucester has killed your father and your husband; but in about five minutes he twists you round his little finger.'

'Sounds a tall order, sir,' said Martyn. But he was excited at the prospect of acting with Coldstream – one of those charismatic schoolboys, captain of everything there was to be captain of, summer and winter – games teams, cadet corps, house and school. His progress around Clevedon's Victorian buildings was royal in its swagger. A Hamlet, a hat-trick, a hundred – all were easily achieved by Coldstream and served to mesmerise the junior boys. Academic achievement required no effort on his part and he mocked those who needed to study. He patronised masters less glamorous than Blakiston and waited impatiently for the day when he could leave school and run the world, or at least the Empire.

206

After Blakiston and the two boys had blocked out their scene in rehearsal Martyn was flattered when Coldstream took him to one side. 'Well done, Milman. Jolly good first effort. Come to my study after prep and we'll run it through a couple of times.'

Coldstream's room was the most comfortable in Brock's. A fire burnt brightly in the grate. A plate of water biscuits spread with Gentleman's Relish awaited Martyn on a side-table. The captain of the house sprawled in his armchair idly studying the text of Act I scene II.

'Take a biccy, sonny,' he said magnanimously, indicating the plate, 'and pour me a glass of sherry, will you? It's out of sight behind the desk.'

Martyn founded the hidden sherry bottle and filled a glass.

'Have a drop yourself,' Coldstream encouraged him. 'Take a pew.' He pointed to the chair on the other side of the fireplace. Martyn glowed with pride at these special signs of favour and sipped happily at the unaccustomed sherry. This was the life! 'Shall we read it again and then put it on its feet?' said Coldstream. 'You first.'

Martyn launched into Lady Anne's opening soliloquy, her lament for the dead and her curse on their murderer.

'Good,' said Coldstream, before reading Richard's instruction to the bearers of the coffin. 'Stay, you that bear the corse and set it down.'

They read the scene through. 'That struck a few more sparks,' said Coldstream, rising languidly from his chair. 'Now, young Milman, let's see if we can get some real electricity into it. Give me my cue.'

Martyn spoke the last line of Anne's soliloquy again: 'Rest you, whiles I lament King Henry's corse.' Coldstream indicated that his desk would represent the bier and began to circle it as he read his lines, making reference to the text before each short speech and then lifting his eyes to look deeply into Martyn's as he spoke. Martyn found himself backing instinctively away, frightened but fascinated, as the older boy stalked him. 'And thou unfit for *any* place but hell,' he shouted.

Coldstream lowered his measured, mature voice: 'Yes, one place else if you will hear me name it.'

Martyn caught the quieter, more intense tone. 'Some dungeon,' he replied, flouncing his head.

Both boys had stopped moving.

'Your bed chamber,' said Coldstream without needing to refer to his text.

Martyn looked down at the book. 'Ill rest betide the chamber where thou liest!'

Coldstream's gaze held steady as he advanced on Martyn. 'So, will it, Madam, till I lie with you.'

He put a hand on Martyn's neck.

'I hope so,' breathed Martyn.

'I know so,' said Coldstream.

Throwing the playscript aside, he slowly undressed Martyn as, with great pauses, he spoke the lines,

> But gentle Lady Anne,
> To leave this keen encounter of our wits,
> And fall somewhat into a slower method . . .

Stroking the already excited Martyn, he lowered him to the rug beside the fire.

'That was quick, young Milman,' he said, looking down as Martyn lost control. 'We'll have to teach you to go slower.'

Coldstream's increased pleasure as he taught his young partner more variations on the themes they rehearsed and re-rehearsed led him to become more daring. He began to visit Martyn in his dormitory long after lights out. Martyn lay awake, vowing that he would send him away: but he found himself unable to do so when Coldstream padded silently to his bedside and lowered his athletic body firmly over him.

When the play was performed at the end of term, Amanda and Archie came down to monitor Martyn's performance.

Sitting with them in the echoing auditorium as the final applause died away, Blakiston bubbled with enthusiasm. 'Won't he make a fine little actor, Miss Bollington?'

Amanda, who had been surprised, and in a way on which she could not exactly put her finger disturbed, by Martyn's performance, said, 'He was very good . . . but so was the other boy, the Richard.'

'It's no life for a man,' muttered Archie predictably. 'I can never make out how the beggars can remember all those lines.'

The performance was repeated three times. On the last night there was a grand party in the senior dormitory. Sentries were posted to monitor the staircase to Blakiston's part of the house. Wine and cider were smuggled in. Flickering candles lent a romantic, conspiratorial atmosphere.

Blakiston, who knew exactly what was afoot, indulged the boys and did not emerge from his rooms until the revellers had lurched to their beds. Seeing that the sentry had been withdrawn, he considered it safe to patrol his house to make sure that no boy was suffering severe after-effects.

Entering the junior dormitory he was dismayed to come upon Coldstream embracing Martyn – their figures entangled on Martyn's bed, brightly lit by the full moon which streamed through the windows.

'Coldstream,' he said sharply. 'Go to your dormitory. Report to me at nine in the morning.' Sheepishly Coldstream pulled up his pyjamas and slouched guiltily past the housemaster who sat down on the side of Martyn's bed. 'Cover yourself, boy,' he said. 'Am I to understand that this is an isolated incident prompted by the carousing in the senior dorm?'

Martyn's lips tried to form the lie but Blakiston saw that it stuck in his throat.

'So,' he continued, 'your silence answers for you. How long have you indulged in this behaviour?'

Martyn started to weep.

Blakiston was remorseless. 'How long?'

'Since . . . since . . .'

'Since rehearsals started?'

Martyn tried to say yes.

'Speak up.'

'Yes, sir.'

When he knocked on Blakiston's door in the morning, Coldstream heard with trepidation the stern 'Come'.

He was not invited to sit.

'How long have you been tampering with this child, Coldstream?'

Coldstream saw a way out. 'It was just a silly drunken prank, sir, after the party.'

'You had never visited him in this way before?'

'Oh no, sir. Certainly not.'

'Then I am afraid, boy, that you have compounded your sexual offence with a lie. I have ascertained that you have been paying regular visits to Milman after lights out. I shall ask your parents to remove you from Clevedon at once. I shall tell them why. And I shall admit no appeal.'

Blakiston took a softer line with Martyn, emphasising the seriousness of his offence and the repugnance with which Clevedon in general and the housemaster in particular viewed it. The worst punishment was that his parents would be informed. As Martyn left Blakiston's study, he passed Coldstream, who said bitterly: 'I'll get you for this, you little squealer.'

Entracte

At the Dissenters' Hall the company were half-way into the first stagger through of *In Society!*. In the two weeks of rehearsal which lay behind them they had seen precious little of one another's work. Principals played their scenes under Martyn's direction in the main hall. The dancers were dismissed to another large room where Louis harried, harangued and inspired them, building a series of vital dances which sent them scattering into huddles of excited discussion whenever he broke them for coffee. In a smaller room upstairs, off the gallery which surrounded the old hall, Freda August patiently banged out the tunes for the soloists, thumping them into their heads whenever she could grab them from Martyn's book rehearsals. Occasionally she looked in on Louis's sessions, shuddering at what he, the dance arranger and a young rehearsal pianist were doing to Martyn's stately rhythms. She voiced her doubts to Martyn but he frowned and brushed aside her objections. 'Got to move with the times, Freda darling.'

In the second week the production team began to dovetail some of the varied elements. Songs, hitherto rehearsed at the piano, were put on their feet in the context of the scenes from which they sprang; chorus dancers were integrated into the routines devised for the principals; chorus singers mingled with the dancers, learning less demanding movements. However it was not until the stagger that the entire company gathered in the large space. The principals marvelled at the energy of the dancers. The dancers laughed at the jokes delivered by the principals. Zelda's provocative songs, invariably backed by a group of elegant boys, burst on the others, increasing the feeling of confidence which was building among the company. Darcy and Imogen's light, affectionate duets won applause. Maude's more solemn songs urging her husband to be true to his ideals were greeted with respect. Anthony Arbuthnot tried enthusiastically to fan respect into applause. Maude, in her turn, led the laughter as Arbuthnot confidently, almost negligently, delivered his silly-ass song.

Viewing his investment in context for the first time, Harry Harmon lit another cigar and puffed contentedly on it. 'Going well, Martyn,' he said as his star emerged from a huddled conversation with Armbruster, the young designer and his stage manager.

'Louis's work is dynamite, isn't it?' Martyn agreed proprietorially. 'We made the right decision there,' he added, as though Harry might have had some hand in it.

'Certainly did,' puffed Harmon, patting Louis on his shoulder. 'Well done, boy.'

Louis smiled at Martyn. 'Quite a team,' he said. 'Wait till he sees the ballet in Act Two. Whad'ya say, Martyn?'

'It's going to stop the show,' said Martyn confidently. 'Let's hope the aged parents are up to following it.'

As it happened, the second act ballet went off at half-cock. It required more rehearsal and produced only a splatter of applause from the company and a storm of expletives from Louis as he cursed his dancers.

Apparently oblivious, Amanda and Max sailed effortlessly through their duet, earning the encores which the company instinctively demanded from them. For all their combined years of experience, the song was a departure for both of them. They had been nervous about unveiling it for the first time. Amanda surprised herself by blushing at the applause while Max hurrumphed and coughed his way out of his happy embarrassment.

As Martyn began to play his next scene he saw with some amusement that his parents were sitting together at the side of the room.

'You haven't seen my flat, Max,' Amanda said. 'Would you care to come to dinner tonight?'

'Can't, my dear,' whispered Max, keeping one eye on the next scene. 'More's the pity. We ought to celebrate now we've got that out of the way; but I'm afraid I've got a date.'

'Oh?' said Amanda quizzically. 'And who with?'

'Our famous film star,' said Max, 'Madame Fane. I'm taking her to the Café Royal. She opened her violet eyes and asked me if I didn't think that, as she was in an Oscar Wilde play, she ought not to see the old place?'

'I suppose she called it "research"?' Amanda was amused. 'In depth, I have no doubt,' she said. 'Never mind, there's plenty of time before we move to Bristol.'

All London played host to the cast of *In Society!* that evening. Dancers must eat; and chorus girls rehearsing dance routines for a show which might run for a year or fold in a week; and an old actor stiff in his joints but holding himself like a duke in order to hang on to his role as a butler in an Oscar Wilde musical. Even he must live on something more than his magnified memories. At the Minestrone, an actors' haunt in Old Compton Street, they could dine alongside a comedian fresh from failing to make Skegness laugh; singers living on Masonic guineas; would-be dress-designers, scene-shifters, aspiring agents, ladies who earned their spaghetti by hanging upside down on trapezes and others on the midwifery side of the theatre. The smell of fried onions and ground coffee floated over the hoping-to-be-blasé babble at the marble-topped tables and reached the hungry nostrils of the tight little chorus group from *In Society!* who had been in work for a fortnight. Slowly they were making inroads into the high piles of bills on skewers which they had run up in the past and which were Madame Minestrone's only method of accountancy. Sitting at the *caisse* inside the entrance, Madame Minestrone was a generous, black-clad island, framed by the bill mountains. She watched indulgently as every now and then a favourite would pay off a few bills, after which credit would continue to climb ceilingwards.

Handing out the food was the job of her son, Andy, waiter and uncrowned king of the Minestrone, whose smiling, round, tawny face assured both the welcome and the credit. His hoarse whisper confirmed whether the dancer who must eat should be given a steak or condemned to a pile of pasta which soon wore off and left the stomach clamouring for more.

In spite of their present financial stability and the euphoria of a promising run-through, the chorus of *In Society!* were still cautious in making their orders. 'Escalope de veau?' Andy suggested in his most avuncular tones. 'For all of you?'

They looked at one another. 'I'll have spaghetti,' said one.

'So will I,' said another.

'Roll and butter and a cup of coffee,' said a third.

'You will all have an escalope,' said Andy firmly. 'You are young and clever people. I have confidence in you. You need energy. Escalope with spaghetti,' he emphasised. 'Pappa,' he yelled to his father, whose spluttering frying-pan was responsible for the comforting fried-onion smell wafting from the kitchen at the back. 'Eight nice escalopes. And sudden.' He turned to the eight open mouths. 'You pay me later,' he said. His eyes travelled to the skewers of bills surrounding his mother. 'Later,' he repeated a little sadly. Dancers must eat.

The dancers settled down to speculate on how hard Louis would work them tomorrow.

Maude

Not far away, across Soho at the Moulin d'Or, Maude Milman was dining with Adrian Arbuthnot. She was fussed over by George and Ernest, while their mother complained to her about vegetable marrows which stubbornly refused to pollinate.

''omosexual,' she said dismissively and moved on to welcome another couple who had just arrived.

'You were awfully good today,' Maude said girlishly. 'Everybody thought so.'

'Did Sir Martyn like it?'

'I haven't seen him since we broke – but I'm sure he did. He's in meetings with Louis most of the time.'

'They make a very close team,' Adrian fished.

Maude lost her patience prettily. 'Oh really, Adrian,' she said tartly. 'Are you pretending to be stupid or is it a natural talent?'

Adrian stopped picking at his smoked salmon and spluttered. It was the first time that Maude had been remotely critical of him.

'You know perfectly well that Martyn is, how shall I put it, a naughty boy on occasions. No, don't protest! Everybody in the theatre knows it. The public, of course, don't. He's very discreet, and he's very careful not to embarrass me. I know he wouldn't think of leaving me. We have, in a way which we have defined to our own satisfaction, a happy marriage. We married when we were very young, very much in love and very optimistic. Martyn had the usual run-ins with other boys at school; but, when he left, one of his mother's friends took him in hand and seduced him, rather pleasantly, I understand. He assumed that he was "cured" – ridiculous word to use in these circumstances. He was horrified when he found out that he had a relapse. And very secretive. By then we had the children. I still had no idea. I was wildly jealous if he looked at another girl – especially if I was at home and he was thrown together with someone tempting on stage or in a film. Men as rivals never occurred to me. I didn't find out until he came back from Hollywood.'

Maude sipped her wine.

'How did you discover it?'

'It was odd. There'd been a silly Hollywood rumour about Zelda Fane and Martyn when they were making *Middlemarch*. I stayed in London with the kids. Martyn explained over the phone that it was all a studio publicity stunt and we laughed it off; but a few days after he got home he came to me with a hang-dog face . . . It was extremely unpleasant. I had to go and see a doctor and have some injections. I demanded to know who she was – someone on the liner on the way home, I assumed. At first he wouldn't tell me: but after I'd shrieked "Who was she?" half a dozen times like a third-rate melodrama queen he lost his patience and told me it was a man. One of the crew on the ship apparently.'

'How awful for you!'

'No, it wasn't really. Once I got used to the idea I found I rather preferred it. It was so different from what I had feared. It seemed to be part of another Martyn altogether. Besides we had the family. We never thought of breaking up. It works.'

After a silence while their plates were cleared and more wine was poured Maude changed tack.

'Where are you staying in Bristol?' she asked.

'I haven't decided yet,' said Adrian. 'I only just got the digs list.'

'I'm staying in a pretty little village just outside, in the Mendips,' Maude offered. 'Martyn will be so busy. Why don't you stay with me?'

Adrian gulped.

'Martyn suggested it,' Maude said airily. 'He thought it would be perfect for us.'

Darcy

Darcy meanwhile was furthering his recent fascination with all things American by getting to know Braden Jefferson.

During the tea-break he had seized the opportunity to ask Brad if he was enjoying London.

'What I've seen of it.'

'Are you star-minding this evening?'

'No,' said Brad, 'your grandfather's in the chair.'

'Care to have dinner?'

'Why not? Where?'

'Jardin des Gourmets.'

Brad played it very straight. 'Hey, is that a good idea?'

'Why not?'

'One of Zelda's friends – some guy in the front office at Columbia Pictures – says it's okay for lunch; but, I quote, "In the evening it is a notorious haunt for homosexuals."'

'Does that worry you?'

'I've never met one.'

Brad's straight face confused Darcy, but he ploughed on. 'How about eight o'clock? It's in Greek Street.'

'I'll see you there,' said Brad, acknowledging Zelda's beckoning finger from across the room.

Now they settled themselves side by side on a banquette and stared at the menu with artificial concentration.

'What did you play in Dad's movie?' asked Darcy to break the awkward silence. 'In *Middlemarch*? I've seen it three or four times but I can't remember you.'

'You must have blinked. I had two lines as the coachman in the opening sequence – pre-credits. "Whoa!" and "Gee-up". They left in the "Whoa!". "Gee-up" got lost in the cutting-room.' Brad looked at Darcy with a broad smile. 'Pity! It was a great line!'

They both laughed.

In the decade and a half since the film, Brad had developed a smooth, sociable veneer but somehow had preserved the simplicity he had brought to Hollywood in the first place. He was enjoying keeping Darcy guessing.

'When did you give up acting?' the younger man asked.

'Pretty soon afterwards. Keate Watershed took me on as a sort of gopher for a bit. Nice guy. Straight in every sense of the word; but when he went back to Westerns I was kind of out of place on the range. I worked for a couple of decorators. Then there was a war – remember? I was an airman. I ran into Zelda at the Stage Door Canteen. She told me to look her up when I came out. So I did. She's easy. We get on well. It's better than working.' Having given his resumé, Brad reassumed the dead-pan face he had put on when he had been invited to dinner. 'I don't see any of these faggots they talked about.'

Darcy's eyes ranged the length of the restaurant. He could see at least three tables occupied by carefully groomed middle-aged men leaning forward in animated conversation with younger monosyllabic companions. 'There's a fair chance those three couples are thinking about it,' he said.

'Really!' Brad sounded thoughtfully surprised. 'God, how strange! I would never have known. Shall we order?'

Darcy was nonplussed. Certain that he stood more than a chance with Brad, he could not fathom the apparent naivety. Brad, who was enjoying himself and liked Darcy's puppyish puzzlement, kept the conversation firmly to the subject of the show and the London theatrical scene.

'How did you enjoy the run-through?' he asked.

'I was amazed how it all came together. I think it's really got a chance.'

'Second act ballet was a bit of a fuck-up.'

'Louis will sort that out with some kicking and screaming.'

'Your father puts a lot of trust in him.'

Darcy said nothing for a moment. By now the steak Diane they had both ordered was flaming at the side of their table. 'Playing with fire,' murmured Brad.

Darcy, uncertain whether he was referring to the steak or his father, turned towards him. He was about to ask a question. Then he thought better of it. He picked up a fork and pushed his spinach around in the brown juices. The meal was not going according to plan. He withdrew into what he considered a sophisticated appraisal of the restaurant's celebrated wine list, muttering something he had heard a friend of his father say about the Beychevelle.

'What was Dad like in those days?'

'He was very like you. Good-looking. Very serious. Of course he was older than you are now. He'd done more. He was very much the visiting classical star. I was in awe of him.'

'We always wondered why he never went back. The film was quite a hit over here.'

'It was a hit at home too. It still is in art houses.'

'Did he and old Zelda really have a fling? Ma swears it was a studio publicity thing.'

'Not so much of the *old* Zelda! But I think your mother is right. I've been with her three years now and she always talks of him as a friend.'

They spoke of Zelda's films, of Martyn's theatrical successes and his wartime propaganda movies. Darcy enthused about his visit to New York. He hoped to interest Brad in his nocturnal activities but his guest kept refusing the bait and turning the conversation back to the theatre. Frustrated but afraid to make a false move, Darcy ordered another bottle of wine with a view to loosening Brad's tongue. In the event it was his own which began to chatter.

Later, as he was leaving with his older companion, one of the young men who had been dining further along the room stopped at the table to enquire how rehearsals were going.

'Fine,' said Darcy. 'We had a run-through today. It went awfully well. There are more laughs than usual in Dad's things. That's the Oscar Wilde influence, I suppose. Oh, this is Braden Jefferson, Zelda Fane's manager.' He indicated Brad with a proudly proprietorial gesture. 'We were just saying how it was all fitting into place.'

The young man ignored Brad apart from a nod. 'How are your friend Louis's dances?' A note of acid crept into his voice. He had been rejected at the final audition.

'Great, but there's a lot of work to do.'

'I thought you said it would be a cinch,' the young man said waspishly. 'Darcy was going to put in a word for me, Mr Jefferson.' He flashed a smile at Brad. 'His influence on Louis Armbruster must be on the wane,' he added knowingly and rejoined his host who was waiting impatiently at the door. 'Sorry, I just had to find out who Darcy's new beau is,' he explained, loudly enough to be overheard. 'He's dotty about him.'

'You don't have to tell me that,' said the older man as he opened the door. 'Mum's got eyes on stalks.'

'What was all that about?' asked Brad.

'It's a bit embarrassing,' Darcy said. 'I introduced Louis to Dad. You wouldn't understand this, but he and I had a bit of a fling.'

'You were lovers?'

'Well, yes.'

'What's wrong with that?'

'You said . . .'

'That was just a game. I wanted to see just how much you'd believe. How simple you thought I was.'

'Bastard,' said Darcy, more in relief than anger. 'So you know the whole set-up?'

'Of course. Louis came round and dished with Zelda as soon as we arrived. It's a dangerous dance you Milmans are treading with Mr Armbruster.'

Darcy looked worried. 'There's something destructive about Louis,' he said. 'D'you think Dad's going to be all right? Will he just make a fool of himself?'

Brad's reply was equally serious. 'I hope that's all,' he said. 'Louis is very ambitious. But you know that already. I wouldn't like Martyn to get hurt. I was very fond of him.'

'Oh, *no*!' Darcy took the hint. 'I see what you mean about a dangerous dance. What's the next step?'

'A taxi home, I should think,' said Brad. 'We don't need Louis to arrange that. As soon as you've paid the bill,' he added.

They kissed in the cab on the way to the studio flat.

'How was that?' Darcy asked foolishly.

'A chip off the old block,' said Brad.

In Hollywood Road Louis Armbruster was loosening the ropes with which he had trussed Martyn. As he massaged the older man's stiffened muscles, Martyn groaned and Louis launched into his familiar litany of complaint about the unadventurousness of the British in bed in general and Martyn in particular. 'I've half a mind to leave you tied up here while I go get something to eat,' he threatened, flexing his naked torso in the firelight.

'But I promised to take you to the Grill,' Martyn reminded him.

'I could take myself.'

'You won't get such a good table.'

'That's easy. I book it in your name and turn up without you.'

'For God's sake, Louis, get me out of this harness.'

With a couple of deft flicks Armbruster released him and Martyn stood and stretched. 'Let's get dressed,' he said, 'I'll ring for the car.'

In spite of, or because of – he no longer knew which – the humiliations to which Louis subjected him in their private meetings, Martyn found him ever more difficult to resist. Louis, on the other hand, played him with easy detachment, never granting a favour without claiming a concession. On this occasion the failure of his second act ballet to live up to expectations had put him in a bad mood and he enjoyed taking out his frustrations on Martyn, confident that the severity of his love-making would only increase the actor's dependence on him.

His mission accomplished, he allowed Martyn the luxury of buying him a lavish dinner at the Savoy with only the merest flirtation with a waiter to keep him in thrall.

'Do you have to tie me up?' Martyn asked plaintively over coffee.

'Christ!' said Louis. 'I have to get *some* fun out of it.'

Lysander

In a dark cellar in Earl's Court, Lysander Milman sat next to an attractive young Australian girl whom he had only just met. Mae Madeley was on her first visit to Britain. She had taken a long leave from her Sydney library and arrived in London courtesy of the *Sunday Digest*. When Sprauncey Chauncey's revelations about Max were reported in the Australian press Mae, seeing a chance at last to establish that Max was indeed her grandfather, promptly wrote to the journalist. Within days she was on her way and set up in a small bedsitter in Earl's Court, paid for by the newspaper. She shed her trim librarian image and kitted herself out in long black skirts and sweaters. Her dark hair hung straight down on to her shoulders, severely framing her face which had a fashionable Grecoesque pallor. Briefed by Chauncey on the Milman family, she acquired Lysander by the simple device of waiting outside the Dissenters' Hall and asking him for his autograph. It was the first time that this had happened to Lysander and he reacted like so many young actors with a flustered, 'Surely you don't want mine . . .?'

'Oh, but I do, please, Mr Milman.'

'But I'm not . . .' Pleasure outweighed modesty and Lysander took her pen and asked, 'Who shall I make it out to?'

'For me, Mae, Mae Madeley,' she said 'and would you put the date, please? Then when you are really famous I can show people I spotted you first.'

Finding that she had just come to London and knew very few people, Lysander suggested dinner, which is how they came to be sitting in the Blondel, the popular new cellar café where the young flocked to drink espresso coffee, eat nut cutlets and listen to mournful troubadour guitarists. Mae decided that her easy assumption of her bohemian character was a fine piece of acting, which only increased her conviction that she was indeed a Milman.

'Did you know my grandfather spent most of his life in Australia?' Lysander asked.

'Oh yes,' said Mae guardedly.

'Did you ever see him?'

She evaded the point of the question. 'I certainly heard him. He was on the radio a lot.'

'Was he really?' Lysander was excited and then embarrassed. 'He seems to have been a bit of an old reprobate . . .' he said, with a hint of approval.

'He certainly had a reputation.'

'He doesn't give up. He's taken Zelda Fane to the Café Royal tonight. Not a bad catch for a seventy-three-year-old.' Mae smiled and Lysander remembered his own date. 'Not that his grandson's doing too badly either,' he added.

They clinked glasses of viscous red plonk and despatched their tasteless, sauce sogged vegetarian food with every appearance of relish.

It was a short walk to Mae's bedsitter. Lysander surveyed the small bare room, the poster of Bondi Beach stuck to the wall, and the dishevelled sheets on the mattress which lay on the floor.

'I'm afraid it's a bit untidy,' Mae apologised. 'Percy and I only just moved in.'

'Percy?' Lysander queried with a guilty start.

Mae laughed. 'Don't worry, Percy's just a friend.'

Lysander still sounded disappointed. 'What time does he get back?' he asked.

'He's here already,' said Mae. 'Mind you don't step on him.' Lysander looked even more puzzled. 'Percy's my hamster. I got him as soon as I arrived. I have to have someone to talk to.'

'You've got me now,' said Lysander proprietorially, as they settled down on the mattress united in the innocence of two cups of cocoa.

Imogen

At Calettas in the King's Road the *tête-à-tête* pair were Imogen and Kurt Kornfeld, Hanna's son. It had been Imogen's suggestion that they should meet there when Kurt nervously issued his invitation. She had heard her mother say that it was the cheapest, friendliest restaurant in Chelsea. 'Cheap and cheerful and just a touch of Bohemia,' was what Maude had said. A thoughtful girl, Imogen knew that Kurt was unlikely to be flush. Indeed she was surprised that he was in a position to ask her out at all.

As she entered the long, narrow room she scanned it for Kurt. She stood awkwardly for a moment and then a kindly, crumbling waiter approached her. He reminded her of the old man in *You Never Can Tell*. She had just appeared in the play at RADA as one of the irrepressible twins. However, as he greeted her she realised that he was Italian.

'Will you be alone, my lady?' he asked.

'Oh no, I'm meeting a friend. I think he may have booked.'

Bending painstakingly close over the list of reservations at the desk, the waiter found the booking at last, triumphantly squatting his thumb on the hieroglyphics which represented it. 'Kornfeld!' he cried. 'Follow me, my lady. I sit you here and you will be able to see the young man when he enters – and he will be able to see you.' In a masterly mixture of the paternal and the deferential he settled Imogen in her chair, brought her bread and butter and asked if she would like a drink.

'Oh, no,' said Imogen, conscious of her suitor's budget, 'thank you, just water.'

As the old man creaked off to fetch her carafe Imogen surveyed the restaurant. Some sketchy murals, long smothered in the daily accretion of smoke and steam from the kitchen, had mellowed into a pale beige monochrome. She wondered which Chelsea artist had subsidised his daily meals back in the thirties by decorating the room in which he ate them. Pale little lamps twinkled on the tables. A handful were occupied by couples – young men in cords with patched sports coats over fair isle sweaters; fresh-faced girls, simply dressed in blouse and skirt, like Imogen. In opposite corners sat two pairs of older diners. Two matrons she placed from Cadogan Square as they picked at their dover sole and sipped from glasses of white wine. Across the room a short-cropped, forceful woman harangued her pallid companion, who nervously fingered her loose bun as she nodded enthusiastically in cringing agreement. Imogen wondered if Kurt would not find it too quiet, too dull; but she had underestimated his excitement at asking her out for the first time.

He erupted in the doorway in a flurry of eagerness and anxiety, brushing his long, dark hair from his eyes and throwing off his threadbare overcoat into the arms of the old waiter. 'Mr Kornfeld!' the man guessed correctly. 'The signorina is there. She is waiting,' he added in mild reproof. But by that time Kurt was beside Imogen.

'Can you forgive me, Imo? Those stupid doctors would not let me go. Chop! Chop! Chop! Cutting up people. Dead people!' He sank into his chair and turned to find the waiter solicitously at his elbow. 'Champagne!' he commanded. 'For the most beautiful girl in the world.' Imogen blushed. 'And for me,' Kurt beat his chest and flashed a big smile at Imogen and a brief but confident one at the waiter who padded off happily, nodding and smiling at the diners he passed on his way to the kitchen. All eyes were now riveted on the table where the big boy with long hair lunged forward and gazed into the eyes of the young girl opposite.

'Champagne?' she queried. Not wishing to hurt his feelings she sought to find a reason for refusing it which would not touch on his celebrated poverty. 'What will happen if you have to do an operation tomorrow and your hand is not steady?'

The mercurial Kurt switched his moods to extreme seriousness. 'Imo, no one is going to ask me to operate on anybody tomorrow. You forget I am not yet a doctor. I am a medical student. Three times I have failed my finals. Who will let me near a body which is alive? You think I cannot afford this champagne . . .'

'No, no,' Imogen protested politely and then capitulated. 'Well, it does seem extravagant.'

'The family of Kornfeld has had a bit of luck. It is what you call a windfall.' Although Kurt had been brought up in England since he was six, his vocabulary retained traces of an awkward formality. 'So, we celebrate!' He smiled broadly again. Imogen did not like to spoil his happiness and smiled back. Kurt's high spirits remained buoyant as the old waiter opened the champagne and filled their glasses. Bowing discreetly, he backed away to greet another group of arrivals as the two youngsters raised their glasses to each other.

'Tell me about your good luck,' Imogen said.

'No, no. It is a family secret. Tell me about your play. My mother says it will be a big success.'

'Oh, I do hope so,' said Imogen. 'I've never known Daddy so highly strung. Some parts of it are frightfully good. Indeed most of it is – but some bits don't seem to belong on the same stage. This American choreographer . . .'

'Has he been rude to you?' Kurt jumped in, bristling.

'Oh no! Quite the reverse. It's just that his dancers are so frightfully energetic they don't seem to fit in with Daddy's songs and scenes which are so elegant and witty.'

'You have spoken of this to your father?'

'Goodness, no! He thinks Louis is perfect. I think he also trusts him to know what's up to date.'

'How did your song go?'

'Good – I think. At least I didn't forget my words. And it's fun doing it with Darcy, although it makes me giggle to think of him as my fiancé.'

Kurt downed the last of his champagne. His voice getting louder, he called for the waiter, who pottered patiently across to them and took their order. Kurt chose a bottle of wine and then turned his eyes earnestly on Imogen. 'How would you think of your fiancé?' he said.

'How do you mean?'

'What would he be like?'

Imogen giggled. 'Short and fat and blond,' she said.

'Now you make a joke.'

'Only a little joke, Kurt. I've never really given it much thought. Cary Grant, Gary Cooper, Errol Flynn . . .'

'These are old men.' He dismissed them.

Blessed by the benign attentions of the waiter; warmed by some indefinable, thick creamy soup which needed infinite additions of salt and pepper to lend its anonymity some taste; excited by the wine and by each other's carefree company, the time sped by. At eleven they realised that but for them the restaurant was empty, and the old man, his head bent, snoozed patiently by the door. Kurt proudly paid the bill and carefully wrapped Imo's coat around her, letting his arms linger over her in an embrace before he followed her out into the cold night air.

They sang and skipped their way down Smith Street and turned into St Leonard's Terrace, where Kurt was allowed a peck on the check at the top of the steps before he rolled off into the night following the route his mother had trod an hour or so earlier.

Hanna

Hanna had spent a cosy evening below stairs enjoying a kitchen supper with Tony and Grace. Although she shared the windfall of which Kurt had spoken to Imo, she was troubled about its provenance. She had given up her part-time menial jobs when she started to work as Zelda's understudy – all but one. She continued, one night a week, to care for an incontinent nonagenarian on her regular nurse's night off. Rehearsals the next day inevitably took their toll, but she could not give up her duties until the cast of *In Society!* left London for the tour.

However, it was not her demanding patient who occupied her mind this evening. She unburdened herself to her two friends. 'Kurt,' she told them, 'has been earning a bit of extra money in the evenings.'

'About time he started helping his mother,' Grace chipped in tartly.

'He is a good boy. And his studies are so hard for him,' Hanna defended her son stoutly, 'but we need extra money for his fees.'

'What's he been doing?' Tony asked.

'He gets sometimes a job as a waiter or barman. It is for functions. It makes for him a long day after his studies but he does it. He is a good boy,' she repeated, as if to convince herself as much as the others.

'Something's worrying you, Hanna,' said Grace sympathetically. 'You can tell us.'

'The other night he was working at Albert Hall.' Hanna looked from one to the other suspiciously. She conquered her doubts and ploughed on. 'It was big gala of ballet – Grand Ballet Marquis de Cuevas. Star was Dourakova, Russian who jumped over Iron

228

Curtain and now she is the toast of two continents. How I wish I was ballerina not actress so my stupid accent would not matter. But this is another tragedy. It is not relevant. I am sorry,' she apologised to her sympathetic audience.

'Don't worry, dear,' soothed Grace.

'Go on, love,' encouraged Tony.

'My Kurt, he is earning the money as a waiter. There is a big buffet after the performance and Kurt is handing out salmon with mayonnaise. It is a very responsible position,' Hanna said proudly. 'He leave the salad and cold potatoes to those who are not so good. This Dourakova is a greedy girl and when Kurt give her the salmon she lean forward and grab the plate and help herself to much more. Then she goes away and puts a pile of potato on the plate and a big mountain of salad. Kurt, he stares at her in disgust. It is not until she has gone to sit with the other ballet snobs that he look down and see something shining in the mayonnaise. It is an ear-ring.'

'*Her* ear-ring?' said Grace.

'This he does not know. Maybe it is nothing. Just a bauble. Costume rubbish. So he put it in a paper napkin. This goes into his pocket.'

'Risky,' said Tony.

'He does not know what to do so he brings it home to his mother. He awoke me at twelve o'clock. I was half-asleep and he holds it under my face. "See what I have brought you," he says "What is this?" I said. "It is an ear-ring," he says. "This I know. Whose ear-ring?" "I do not know. I found it, Mama," he says proudly. "It is for you." By now I am a little more awake. "Where did you find it?" I ask him. "On the way home?" Now I take a good look, I say, "These, I think, are diamonds." "We can sell it," Kurt said. "Who will want one ear-ring?" I asked him. "They can take apart the design and use only the stone," he explained. "Perhaps we had better to give it to the police and there may be an award."

' "A *reward*," he corrects me. "And what if there is not? What if it was dropped by the greedy Dourakova? Great ballerina! From what I have seen of her generosity a reward would be peanuts." '

'What did you do?' Grace asked.

'I took it to a little man who has a shop off Kensington High Street. I take it the very next morning and I show it to him. He does not hit around the bushes. He tells me these are very good diamonds as he looks at them through his glass. Then he looks very hard at me. I tell him it is of my family. He asks me where is the other of the pair. I say I have sold it some time ago when life is hard. "And now life is hard again?" he asked me. "Yes," I tell him, and about how Kurt must one day soon become a doctor but we cannot wait. He looks very kind at me and says if I have already sold the other I must know how much it is worth and I pretend to nod, very wise. He give me one thousand pounds in notes of fifty pounds each. Never have I seen so much money, so I gather it up and I take it home to Kurt and we are happy because now we can pay the fees and the rent.'

The words poured out of Hanna in a rueful confession. 'But next day I see in the *Evening News* that the great ballerina Dourakova has lost her diamond ear-ring and she is *distraught*. I wonder what the man in the jeweller's shop will say. And then I see story is in *Standard* and *Star* and again the next day it is in the morning papers; but by now we have spent some of the money and we cannot give it back. And every day I am thinking that police will come.'

Hanna's confession tailed off. Grace and Tony let it sink in.

'There's no doubt you did wrong, dear,' said Grace.

'But I'm not sure I shouldn't have done the same,' said Tony.

'That dancer sounds like a right old cow and you certainly need it more than her.'

'It's really Kurt who stole it,' said Grace, thinking it through.

'Oh no,' protested Hanna. 'He simply brought it home to his mother to ask her what he should do. He is a good boy. If there is a criminal it is me.'

'How long ago was all this?' Tony asked.

'It is nearly two weeks now. Every day I am afraid the police will come.'

'But they haven't, dear, have they?' said Tony. 'Maybe they won't.'

'Considerin' what you've been through, dear,' said Grace, 'I think you deserve a bit of good luck. You forget about the law. Tony,' she ordered, 'get the brandy. Hanna looks all shook up, poor darling. Give 'er a good old-fashioned tot before she goes out into that shivering cold.'

Max

The waiters at the Café Royal were unusually solicitous when they saw the dignified old gentleman escort Zelda Fane into the Grill Room. Max was explaining that in the old days the marble-topped tables and sand-floored open rooms had been the gathering place for Wilde and his cronies. 'Not that I got in with that lot,' he said dismissively. He pointed out gallantly that the Grill Room was an altogether more appropriate setting for a beautiful woman. Relishing her reflection from a bewildering number of angles, Zelda happily agreed, settling herself on a ruby banquette to admire the neo-rococo splendour, the wayward frescos on the ceiling and the pouting caryatids on the walls garlanded with wreaths.

'What do you make of this dance chappie?' Max asked after they had ordered. 'You've known him longer than the rest of us. Bit of a holy terror, ain't he?'

Zelda smiled. 'Louis is very ambitious,' she said, 'and ruthless. I hope Martyn isn't trusting him too much.'

Max gave her a suspicious glance. He wanted very much to find out more about his son; but through the days of rehearsal he had become concerned about just how much he might discover. Nor was Zelda anxious to gossip about Martyn's predicament with Max in the same detail with which she had examined it with Braden.

She chose the easy way out, turning her violet eyes up at Max and asking him about himself.

For Zelda, Max relived his arrival in Australia, passing swiftly over the débâcle in Melbourne on his first tour and dwelling at much greater length on his triumphant return as *Ben Hur*. He hammed up the mining disaster and told the story of the death of Esme in the outback as sentimentally as Dickens despatching Little Nell. Zelda egged him on to describe his efforts to re-establish himself in the theatre. Donaldson's attempt to freeze him out was only partially successful. His ability to learn quickly landed him a job with Gregan McMahon – the director who had walked away from *Ben Hur* in the early stages of rehearsal. McMahon went on to set up an avant-garde repertory company in Melbourne. Max, looking for anything to tide him over, found himself playing Ibsen's John Gabriel Borkman.

Chatting with McMahon after his Repertory Players had given a passable performance of a double bill of Sheridan's *The Critic* and St John Hankins's *The Two Mr Wetherbys*, Max quickly realised the director's obsession with Shaw and the Royal Court Theatre in London. He carelessly dropped the names of Shaw, Hauptmann, Granville Barker and Yeats as though his appearance in the fustian *Ben Hur* had been but a temporary aberration.

McMahon responded enthusiastically. 'I am interested, Mr Milman, in plays which illustrate an ideal, whether it be social, moral, poetic, fantastic, or even utilitarian.' McMahon, filled with passion, harangued him into the night. Max, soberly sipping at his pint, nodded wisely. 'I envisage a drama in which the characters are true to life instead of to the idiosyncrasies of individual actors.'

'My view exactly,' Max lied.

'I see the way of the future in ensemble acting, co-ordinated and guided by a regisseur. I see the death of the star-virtuoso system now so much in vogue.'

Max picked up his cue. 'I said as much to Harley and GBS five years ago, Mr McMahon. They had very kindly invited me to the dress of one of Maeterlinck's little numbers. "Harley," I said, "Harley, old man, you've got a winner here." He was childishly grateful. And GBS, I can see him now, tapping on his nose and pulling at that straggly beige beard, GBS said: "Harley," he said, "Harley, if old Max tells you you've got a winner, you can take it you've won." Wonderful way with words, Shaw's got, y'know.'

'But why did you come out here with that ridiculous *Hur* play, Mr Milman?'

'Temporary aberration, Mr McMahon, may I call you Gregan? No, you see, Greg, I'd been doing a bit of Ibsen here and a bit of Shaw there and, I, well, to tell you the truth, that winter was damned inclement, so when Donaldson called upon me and made such a generous offer and painted such a picture of sun and sand and surf, I'm afraid I forgot my art for a moment and settled for the sunshine. I've always regretted it.' Max put on his penitent face, and McMahon mentioned that his Borkman had just had a heart attack. He feared he must postpone. Suddenly the idea which Max had been hoping to implant in his mind occurred to him.

'Are you a quick study, Mr Milman?'

'Photographic, Greg. Show me the sides and I've mastered 'em.'

'I wonder. I just wonder . . .'

'Wonder what?'

'If I should consider asking you to take on Borkman for me.'

'It would be the fulfilment of my dearest wish.' Max launched into another flight of self-promotion fantasy. 'How amused Harley will be when he gets to hear about it. Y'see, he wanted me to do it at the Court, but I'd already signed for Donaldson and I felt I couldn't let the boy down. Max Milman's word is his bond. And now here you are offering me the very same role with your fine company.'

McMahon, who had not yet made the offer concrete, found himself in the awkward position of being unable to withdraw it. Max clasped his hand, and shook it firmly.

'Max Milman's word is his bond,' he repeated, and kept shaking.

'Of course, I can't pay much at the Repertory Theatre . . .' said the producer. 'The Turn Verein Hall doesn't seat that many and Australia has yet to embrace Henrik Ibsen wholeheartedly.'

'Don't think of it,' said Max. 'If I'm playing in a fine ensemble I expect to be paid what my colleagues are paid. Like you I abhor the star system. Let me be a team player.' Max could barely believe what he heard himself saying; but he knew that to re-establish himself he must be seen. He knew no more of John

Gabriel Borkman than the title, and that he had just heard for the first time from McMahon's lips. However, he reckoned that as it was the title role he was bound to be noticed and he firmly intended to make sure that he was.

'When can you start?' asked McMahon.

'No time like the present,' said Max. 'I'll take the book home tonight and I shall present myself to your company on the morrow.'

Max fitted in surprisingly well as Borkman. The role is a dominating one and Max's long absence from the stage found him fresh and keen to master the great speeches. There was no chance that he would be lost among the ensemble players. Gregan McMahon was delighted with Max's strong performance. He was less pleased when he discovered that his new leading man's word was not as binding as he had suggested.

McMahon was standing at the stage door of the Turn Verein Hall on the second night, scratching the bald, high-domed head which made him look a little like Humpty-Dumpty. His blue eyes twinkled happily at the memory of the first performance which had gone better than he had dared to hope. The *Argus* praised his production, enthused about Max, and had even given Ibsen a cautious welcome.

Max sauntered through the stage door and greeted him.

'Excellent notices, Max,' said McMahon.

'Good, are they? Never read 'em myself,' Max replied untruthfully. 'Tell me, Greg, how long d'you reckon we'll run?'

'Through the season, I should hope,' said McMahon. 'I'll be adding to the repertory, of course, but I'll hope to find a couple of juicy roles for you. Which of your friend Shaw's plays do you fancy?'

'Aah!' said Max sharply. 'Bit of a catch there. I thought you were giving it a shot while it took the fancy of the town and then I'd be pushing along.'

'Pushing along! But in rehearsal you said you were looking forward to fresh challenges.'

'Yes and no,' said Max. 'I was having a nip in the bar at the Bendigo before lunch when this chap approached me. Apparently he was in last night and mighty impressed by what he saw. Anyway, to cut a long story short he's a film-maker. Owns a few picture palaces and now he wants to make his own moving pictures. Real Australian subjects. Open-air stuff. Stirring, building-a-young-country-sort-of-thing. Ned Kelly. Eureka Stockade. Genuine home-grown adventure.'

The twinkle died in McMahon's eyes. 'Are you telling me you're quitting, Milman? Giving in your notice before the play's even up and running?'

'Steady on, Greg,' Max cautioned him. 'I'm saying nothing of the sort. I came to help you out of a hole playing old John Gabriel. I'll let you have a month or whatever; but I can't get involved in the repertory. I've given the lad my word that I'll start with him when he's ready to shoot. It's some epic. He's planning to proceed up Sydney way – by the Parramatta. I've said I'll be there and,' Max added rashly, 'Max Milman's word is his bond.'

Gregan McMahon said nothing but turned and walked unhappily towards his office.

'Don't worry, Greg,' Max called after him. 'I'll play out the run here. Cooper don't need me till next month – and that's more than you'll get out of Henrik in East Melbourne.'

Beaumont Cooper – whose name Max had dropped casually – was a sort of Australian Barnum who had presented his rowdy company of cowboys, Indians, sharpshooters and horses for several years of intermittent performances at his three thousand-seater Hippodrome Tent Theatre in Sydney. Besides his cowboy and bushranger spectacles he also staged stock melodramas such as *Uncle Tom's Cabin* and *East Lynne*. Advertisements proclaimed that Cooper had collected priceless mementoes, like the gold escort coach robbed by the notorious Frank Gardener and his gang, and prominently featured in a melodrama based on Gardener's exploits. A less lucky purchase was the rope which hanged Ned Kelly. Beaumont Cooper's plans to put Kelly's last stand on stage had been scuppered years before by Ralph Donaldson's more ambitious production.

Although Donaldson was contemptuous of Cooper's rough and ready dramas, Cooper was bitterly jealous of Donaldson's more genteel organisation. He remembered the impact that Max had made in his two spectacular appearances. It mattered little to him that Max's career had been in eclipse for a few years. He had heard the gossip about Dorothy but, as he watched Max dominating the stage as Borkman, he saw his chance to add some authority to his film ambitions.

The two men met again at Max's hotel, the Bendigo, after the second night of the play. With a thick steak on his plate and a pint of beer beside it, Max listened happily to Cooper's plans for him.

'I've gone as far as I can in the tenting biz,' said Cooper who had already signalled his intention of moving from plays to film by donning riding boots and breeches and affecting a whip which he cracked against his boots when he wished to emphasise a point. 'Film is the coming thing, Max, and Beaumont Cooper has never been behind the times. Besides, I've done all I can on the stage. I've got my tent in Sydney. I've set up a second Hippodrome down here in Melbourne and I'm tired of taking the company on tour.'

'You travel in some style, I hear.'

'Horse-drawn caravans and specially-hired trains,' said Cooper. 'My lady, Lottie – Lottie Lovely – my leading actress, has seen enough of the old country, I reckon. Oh, she travels in luxury. I had two beautiful boudoir cars run up for her. The bigger one is nine metres long and two-and-a-half wide.' Beaumont Cooper liked talking of the comfort he lavished on his young wife. 'I furnished it in polished cedar and the upholstery is gold and red velvet. There's a plate-glass sliding panel dividing it into two rooms. The finest paintings hang on the walls. A plush velvet sofa unrolls to make a bed at night. Oh yes, my Lottie travels in style; but it's time the travelling days were over. That's the beauty of the moving picture, Max. A couple of weeks of hard work in the studio and on the lot and then you send the celluloid out to do the job for you. I can rig up a screen in my tent and sit at home with Lottie and collect. Ever done pictures, Max?'

'Can't say I have,' Max confessed. 'But,' he said, denying his career so far, 'I've always thought my modern, understated acting was just the thing for the screen. None of that exaggerated mugging.'

'My point exactly,' Cooper agreed. 'Lottie is a wonderful little performer but she's used to semaphoring to the back of a tent holding three thousand. I want to pair her with an actor who can bring her down a bit.'

'Impart a little subtlety.'

'Spot on! I think you'll make a great team.'

'I look forward to it,' said Max enthusiastically. He had already seen Lottie's pictures plastered all over Melbourne. 'Are you directing personally?'

'God, no! I know better than to risk my cash on a beginner. I'm bringing in a crack Yank. I'm not saying I won't direct later when I've got the hang of it. But for my first picture I want the best – and everybody says that Vivian Van Dawn is the best money can buy. He's crazy about the script.'

'What's it called?' Max asked.

'*The Bondage of the Bush*. Great title, don't you think?' Beaumont Cooper gave Max no time to reply before charging enthusiastically into a summary of the plot. 'You are Dan Romer. You're a boundary rider. You have a faithful black, Gee-bung, who works for you. You also have a spoilt wife, played by Lottie. She's unfaithful to you with a travelling salesman. You kill her . . .'

'A bit soon to get rid of your leading lady,' Max interrupted.

'Wait!' commanded Cooper. 'You're arrested. You're tried and convicted. The judge is sympathetic. He recommends a reprieve. The home secretary, a cold and stubborn man, refuses. You are due to hang. You lead a prison break-out. Great scene, five hundred extras. Gee-bung is waiting with your favourite steed. You're off into the bush. Spectacular scenery, a flock of real sheep, a shearing contest. You win. Lottie now plays a squatter's daughter – a hard horse-riding heroine. We'll have to use a double, Lottie don't like the gee-gees. When you see her you can't believe your eyes – she looks so like your dead wife, but nice with it and brave. Great lines for the captions. "You forget, Dan, that I am an Australian girl. I've been accustomed to station life from childhood and when I am thrown upon my own resources

you will find me quite capable of managing my own affairs."
Magnificent dialogue, eh?'

Max nodded.

'She takes you in. She believes your story. She's doubtful about
Gee-bung but you persuade her he's an okay bloke. "I shall always
stick up for the Aboriginal people," you say. "We have taken this
country away from them. The least we can do is treat them with
justice and humanity." Powerful stuff! Advanced!' Cooper looked
at Max for confirmation.

'Packs a punch,' Max agreed. He could see he was being offered
a meaty role.

'But there is danger. Lottie has rejected a suave and evil bushranger called Ben Hall. He penetrates your disguise. He reports
back to Sydney. There is a manhunt. Eventually you are caught.
Lottie pleads for your reprieve – and here's the twist. Meanwhile,
the home secretary mistakenly believes that his own wife is
unfaithful. He realises how easy it might have been for him to
kill her in his fury. Chastened by this revelation he grants Romer
– that's you – a reprieve and resolves to show his wife more
affection. You get to marry Lottie and together you ride off into
a nice old Australian sunset. How does that take you, Max?'

'Great!' said Max. 'I can't wait to start. When?'

'Van Dawn ships in at the end of the month. We agree the
locations and the rest of the casting and then it's go!'

Max had despatched his steak and called for a bottle of champagne. 'To *The Bondage of the Bush*,' he said, raising his glass.

'*The Bondage of the Bush*!' toasted Beaumont Cooper.

'And Lottie!' added Max.

Vivian Van Dawn stood on the banks of the Parramatta River at
Dundas, near Ryde, New South Wales. It was a fine day and the
sun was hot and high in the sky. He was wearing boots and
breeches and carrying a whip, and wore a monocle precariously
perched over his right eye. Van Dawn was blind in the eye but
he always used the trick to impress the crew on the first day. He
sent an assistant away to correct a detail in an extra's costume,
having first made sure it was out of place. Now he was marshal-
ling his crew, his actors and an impressive crowd to stage the

prison break-out for *The Bondage of the Bush* and at the same time giving a publicity interview to a lad called Fred L Curtis, the young and impressionable reporter of *Everyone's*.

'I told Bluey on Saturday,' he said, pointing to a harassed, leather-skinned man who was barking orders as he hurried up and down the river banks. 'I told him I wanted five hundred supers on Tuesday, to play the convicts. Well, it's Tuesday and there they are.'

'That's a tall order.' The reporter was impressed.

Van Dawn's chest puffed out. 'Biggest crowd of supers ever drafted into one scene in a native Australian movie,' he said. 'You see, Bluey couldn't advertise. He wouldn't have time to weed out the right types from among the thousands of unemployed who would have turned up to answer the ad.'

'Still, five hundred's a lot of men to round up.'

'Bush telegraph: Bluey put the word around in the right places and at eight this morning there were five hundred guys waiting at Fort Macquarie. We checked 'em off as they got on to the ferry and handed each man his costume. By the time the boat got to Dundas every extra was dressed and ready to go on set. That's time-saving.'

'What about the stars?'

'You don't put film stars in a cattle boat,' Van Dawn laughed, 'even if they ain't stars yet. If you want to make a star you gotta treat the guy like a star. Now Max Milman is not yet a star of motion pictures, but he has potential. The camera loves him. I predict great things. And he can act.'

'What about Lottie Lovely?' the reporter asked.

'Lovely by name and lovely by looks. But she hasn't the same track record as Max. You should hear him talk of his days with Irving, Beerbohm Tree, Shaw. He's worked with the best in the theatre and he still looks gorgeous.' Van Dawn slowed down so that the reporter could get his fast-flowing pen around the adjective for which he did not have the shorthand. 'Max is working very intimately with Lottie. There is a chemistry between them. They are making motion picture magic on screen.'

'How about off-screen?' asked Fred L Curtis inquisitively.

'That will do for now,' said Van Dawn brusquely, and walked

away to check the positions of the six cameramen who were to cover the break-out. The reporter turned his attention to the harassed Bluey – which meant firing his questions from the hip as he pantingly pursued his quarry.

'Biggest bloody mob scene ever taken in Australia,' confirmed the first assistant.

'What do you pay the supers?'

'A pound for a seven-hour day. You see that lot over there?' Bluey pointed to a crowd of about a hundred men who were lolling on the ground by a mud swamp. 'They get an extra five bob to go into the water and work on the prop logs. Dirty work manoeuvering those logs. They weigh a ton and they got real bark on 'em. They gotta pilot them through the mangroves and roll 'em through the mud of the Parramatta. Max is going to skip across 'em after the break-out – that's how he escapes.'

'An agent I know said one of his artists is on a twelve-week contract at forty quid a week and yet he's down here picking up his pound a day, doing extra work.'

'Times is hard,' said Bluey. 'But you won't catch Max Milman doing that. He's the star.'

'And he's in nearly every scene, isn't he?'

'Good as.' Bluey had lost interest in the reporter's questions. He was checking the twenty carpenters who were finishing off the prison stockade, the arrival of two pontoons towed from Glebe Point to Dundas laden with props and the six elevated platforms which were to support the six cameras.

'Why is Lottie Lovely here?' the reporter enquired. 'Surely she's not in the break-out?'

'God no! But everywhere Max goes, she comes along,' said the distracted Bluey. 'She says she's learning film technique from Max. Judging by the time she spends in that little caravan it ain't only film technique he's teaching her.'

'Where's Mr Beaumont Cooper?' Curtis asked.

'Rustling up some more bloody cash, I shouldn't wonder,' said Bluey, stepping into one of the two motor launches he had hired so that he and Van Dawn could speed up and down the river barking orders. 'Mr Van Dawn has already spent the forty thousand pounds we budgeted. If Cooper don't top it up we'll be suspending after today.'

The boat moved away leaving Curtis on the bank elated by the scope of the whole operation. He stopped to listen to Van Dawn's voice bawling instructions. They were carried over an area of about a square mile by loudspeakers hung from the branches of the gum trees. As he followed the action he saw that he was approaching the caravan which Bluey had indicated had been provided for Max.

'Mr Milman, please, Mr Milman on set, please,' Van Dawn's instructions echoed across the river. Leaning against a gum tree Curtis watched the door of the caravan open. He saw Max pulling on a pair of rough convict trousers. Then he saw of a pair of white arms slipping the convict jacket over his shoulders. Max turned to thank his helper, bending down to embrace her tiny figure. Fred L Curtis was not surprised to see that it was Lottie Lovely in a kimono, which he rightly deduced to be no part of her wardrobe for the film.

By twelve o'clock Van Dawn was happy with his seven takes of the water scenes and Max's daring dash across the floating logs. The five hundred extras were lined up in long queues, marched past a table, and each handed a paper bag containing thick chunks of bread and cheese and a cup of tea. Van Dawn lunched with Max and Lottie at a small table laid outside Max's caravan. Lottie had replaced her kimono with a sensible skirt and blouse as she presided over the table.

Promptly at one o'clock Van Dawn sprang from the table and summoned his five hundred supers for the big riot scene. Max followed, giving Lottie a discreet peck on the cheek and a whispered promise.

Max was to lead the crowd of malcontents to storm the recently completed prison gates and attack the warders. In the elaborately planned action the jailers were grabbed by the convicts and thrown into a shallow well of stagnant water. As they attempted to scramble out the triumphant convicts kicked at their knuckles and forced them back down into the mud. Meanwhile Max was to leap clear and make for the logs to complete his escape – the sequence which had already been shot that morning.

Spurred on by Van Dawn's exhortations, the five hundred routed the warders seven times, clean uniforms replacing those muddied in earlier takes. All in all, two men fainted, one narrowly escaped drowning and another was stunned as he fell heavily to the ground. By four o'clock Van Dawn declared himself satisfied. 'We've got quality in these cans, Max,' he confided to his leading man. 'You were sensational. This is going to make you an international star.'

'You think so?' said Max. He was happy as always to receive praise: but he was also anxious to return to Lottie who was waiting in his caravan. Van Dawn was not keen to let him go. 'I shot two hundred foot of film today, Max, that's going to show you at your most heroic. The girls back home are going to buy that bare chest of yours in a big way. That's why I spent well past twelve hundred pounds on today's shoot. It's the action climax.'

'I'd better get out of this gear,' said Max.

'Van Dawn said this movie is going to make us international stars,' Max told Lottie as he embraced her in the caravan. 'California here we come!'

'Oh, Max, d'you really think so? Both of us?'

'I'm not going without you, baby.'

'When shall we break the news to Beaumont?'

'We'd better get the movie made first,' Max counselled. 'He doesn't suspect anything, does he?'

'He's too busy raising money,' said Lottie. 'Van Dawn's turned out to be a lot more pricey than he bargained for. Beaumont spends most of his days with the banks. I've never known him so stretched. It's all right being a rich man's wife but it ain't much fun when he spends most of his time trying to stay rich.'

'While the cat's away . . .' breathed Max, easing her down on to the flimsy couch in the corner of the caravan. 'How do you like my bare chest?' he joked. 'Van Dawn says American women will be fighting over it . . .'

'They'll have to fight me first.'

'He said today's work will be the movie's action climax.'

Lottie lay back voluptuously. 'And you certainly know about an action climax,' she breathed.

They were still wrapped round each other on the couch when Bluey knocked on the door. 'All paid off,' he shouted, knowing better than to enter. 'Your car's ready for you, Mr Milman.'

'Coming, Bluey,' Max called back.

The pay car had arrived promptly at four with a substantial police escort. Bluey, along with his other chores, supervised the erection of a box-like office barricaded off with just sufficient room to allow one person at a time to approach the window, sign his receipt, and pass on to the second window and collect his pay. With rigorous efficiency he had the five hundred extras washed and changed, paid and on board the ferry for their return to Sydney in less than three quarters of an hour.

'Five hundred quid I paid those extras, Max,' he said, when the two stars emerged from the caravan fully clothed and wearing their most innocent expressions. 'We're well over the forty thousand budget, y'know,' he confided. 'Is Mr Cooper worried?' he asked Lottie.

'Beaumont will provide,' she said confidently. 'He promised me in his marriage vows.'

But Beaumont was not able to provide. He had exhausted his credit. The all-important bush sequence with Lottie and the faithful Gee-bong had still to be shot. Without that the film would make no sense. In desperation Beaumont humbled himself and applied to his old enemy Ralph Donaldson for funds to complete his movie. Donaldson chose to receive him in the panelled splendours of Stowey.

'So you're in trouble, Cooper, are you?'

'Temporary, purely temporary,' Beaumont Cooper blustered. 'Van Dawn says the movie has incredible international potential.'

'It'll be the first Aussie movie that has,' said Donaldson sceptically. 'Who's starring in it – your wife, of course – but who else?'

'A fine actor,' said Cooper tentatively, 'Max Milman. It's his first film . . . but . . .'

'But it will also be his last,' Donaldson butted in.

'I don't understand . . .'

'Some years ago I told that bastard that he would never work again in this country. You've given him a break. I intend to stop him in his tracks.'

'But . . .'

'No buts, Cooper. How much do you need to finish the film?'

'Twenty thousand, I reckon.'

'I'll advance you the twenty thousand on condition you never employ Max Milman again, in films, in theatre, even in your ridiculous circus tents.'

'I've given him a three-picture deal.'

'Break it. I dare say the options are all on your side.'

'He's got great potential . . .'

'That's what I'm out to put a stop to. Do you agree?'

Donaldson had done his homework. Now he watched Beaumont Cooper closely over his desk and played his trump card. 'Of course,' he said, 'you know he's screwing your wife?'

Some months later, at the Premier Picture Garden, an open-air cinema in the suburbs of Adelaide, a humbled Max Milman managed to find the sixpence required to gain entry to a showing of *The Bondage of the Bush*. He could not afford the shilling which would have admitted him to the Reserved Lawn.

'They could really freeze you out like that?' an amazed Zelda Fane asked Max. 'It's worse than a studio suspension in Hollywood.'

'It finished me for ten years,' said Max. 'I'd burnt my boats with Gregan McMahon – mind you, I don't think I could have stuck that po-faced regime for long. Donaldson had me by the balls as far as the rest of the legit work was concerned. Nobody would touch me. All the big promoters were warned off and so were the movie chains. I couldn't get arrested. Actually that wasn't strictly true. I got arrested a few times. Mainly vagrancy and drink. In the end I fetched up in a vineyard in the Barrossa. Nobody knew me up there, it was a cosy little property, a dozen hectares or so. Nice people – struggling to make ends meet on a rough and rugged site. I was taken on as a general labourer. They tried anything to keep going: vines, mines, cattle, sheep. I didn't get much more than food and keep.'

'I didn't even know they made wine in Australia,' Zelda confessed.

'The main trade was the fortified,' Max explained. 'Ports and sherries: but they had all the right grapes: shiraz, cabernet sauvignon, riesling and verdelho. There's going to be a market for Australian wine one day. I had a happy time licking my wounds up Yalumba way. That's an abo word. Just means, "all the country around". Then I got a bit above meself. Worked at a winery. German chap called Henschke took me on as a cellarman. It was a big operation. They had about five hundred hectares and they used to buy the grapes as well. The guy who ran it was engineer, inventor, chemist and salesman all rolled into one. A pioneer genius. It was like a little town, his operation – laboratory, winery, cellars, distillery, vinegar works, cooperage, blacksmith's shop, piggery. He didn't even waste the grape skins. Fed 'em to the porkers. Produced some very special bacon. It was all built around a sort of chateau – French-style – made up out of Barrossa Bluestone. The cellars were quarried out of the side of a hill. I can still taste the lunches we used to stop for, bread and cheese or a ham sandwich washed down with a tumbler of iced claret.'

Max smacked his lips and breathed in the scent of the brandy which he had been warming in his hands as he reminisced. 'Good days,' he sighed. 'I was there five years or so. Good times.'

'What happened?' asked Zelda.

'Usual thing.'

'Wife? Daughter?'

'Both on that occasion,' Max confessed ruefully. 'Not together, of course. They used to feed me. The wife's speciality was barbecued kangaroo with a plum sauce. The daughter went in for seafood, yabbies, crayfish, green-lipped mussels. But they both found out. Christ! Was I putting on weight!' He smiled. 'They weren't impressed. Of course they couldn't tell old man Henschke, but they made it pretty clear to me that they weren't amused and I'd better move along. The Kraut couldn't believe it when I gave in my notice. Said he was grooming me for wine stardom – head cellarman at least. I said it was wanderlust. He said he under-

246

stood. Lovely place. Lovely names! Jacob's Creek, Orlando, Coonawarra. We'll all be drinkin' 'em one day – if I live that long. I'd put money on it.'

'And you were still persona non grata in the theatre?'

'Come again?'

'Blacklisted.'

'Oh yes. I drifted back to Melbourne and lay low.'

'How did you survive?'

'His Britannic Maj looked after me for a bit.'

'In the slammer? What for?'

'Good acting.'

Max's hunt for digs when he arrived back in Melbourne, tired, dirty and skint, had not been immediately successful. Eventually he came across an advertisement in an old newspaper for a room in a suburb, Tallangatta. Summoning up his optimism like an actor setting out for a hopeless audition he shouldered his bags and took the bus. After two changes and diligent enquiry he arrived in front of a tall, slatted gate on which the words *Non-Pareil* were scrawled. Scrawny geraniums and limp fuchsias slumbered in the dusty garden as he pushed open the gate. He banged the door and sent the birds perched on the fence shrieking into the sky. There was a wooden slatted house raised on stilts to lift it beyond the danger of snakes. The skins of their dead relatives, captured and killed, decorated the fence which surrounded the gloomy property. Two steps led up to a wooden veranda. On a rail around it a praying mantis swayed. Underneath the boards a tarantula was weaving its web.

Max knocked on the door which was already ajar and stood there as it swung open. 'Anyone at home?' he called. When no one replied he put down his case in the hall and explored the house. A corridor, which ran the length of it, led to a staircase oddly climbing up from the back. To Max's right was a door marked private. On his left another door was open. Peering in, Max saw that it too ran the length of the building. Through the rear window he could see a peach tree blooming tentatively in the back yard. Stepping cautiously along the passage Max took a couple of steps up the stairs, enough to see that several more doors gave off another corridor. Most of them were open and revealed rooms in various states of disarray. He helped himself to a glass of water in the small kitchen and returned to sit in the sun on the rocking-chair which was the sole piece of shaded furniture on the baking veranda. Before long he rocked himself into a deep sleep from which he was awoken when the tenants returned. He did not hear the latch lift on the gate and was unaware of them until a pointed cough aroused him. He saw a scrawny washed-out woman in a dirty, pastel dress and a cloche hat standing over him. Beside her loomed a large florid man who was covered in a voluminous cloak and a black sombrero. Max rubbed his eyes and remembered where he was and why he was there.

'I came in answer to the ad,' he said.

The man and the woman looked at each other, puzzled.

'It was a rather old paper,' Max apologised. 'I found it in a bin at the bus station when I came into town.'

'We have only just taken this property,' intoned the man whose cloak parted so that Max saw how enormously fat he was. 'The advertisement to which you refer must have been placed by the previous tenant.' He stroked his paunch. 'We had not intended to share our abode, had we, my love?' He turned to his wife for confirmation.

'Indeed no, Horatio,' she agreed.

'I have not introduced myself,' the man said sonorously, taking off his sombrero and patting a greasy black curl down on his broad, pasty forehead. 'Horatio Lightbeam. You may have heard of me.'

Max cudgelled his brain, wondering from the man's manner if he was an actor. 'The name does ring a bell,' he said.

'Theosophist, Spiritualist, Chairman of the Antipodean New Thought Alliance, and Medium,' Mr Lightbeam informed him. 'And this is Mrs Lightbeam. The Lightbeam of my life, my wife, my friend and an expert performer upon the guitar, piano accordion and harmonium.'

'A multitude of accomplishments,' said Max.

'And you, sir?'

'I am an actor,' said Max, 'Max Milman.'

'Can't say I know the name,' said Lightbeam. Max was not sure whether to be disappointed or relieved. 'Mrs Lightbeam and I rarely attend the theatre, still less the cinema. Our evenings are occupied with meetings, lectures, theosophical discussion and, of course, my seances.'

'A roaring trade.' Max wondered if he had been too flippant; but he judged correctly that neither of the Lightbeams was blessed with a sense of irony.

'The gift does demand constant exploration,' said Lightbeam.

'And it is very taxing,' said his wife in a voice as thin as his was rounded.

'It is principally trumpet mediumship that I practise. Direct voice sittings. I sometimes accommodate as many as twenty-five or thirty people.'

'It is very exhausting,' said Mrs Lightbeam.

'Such numbers are a dangerous strain on the medium.'

'Do you charge?' asked Max.

'That would never do,' said Lightbeam firmly. 'It would be a misuse of the gift.'

'No fee is specified,' Mrs Lightbeam elaborated, 'but a brass bowl is put out for donations. People are very generous.'

'It must be gratifying to be able to provide comfort from beyond the grave.' Max found himself being drawn into the mad world which his hosts inhabited with such conviction.

'We employ three aluminium trumpets,' said the medium. 'An Irish voice, "Danny", invariably acts as a sort of master of cere-monies. He introduces other visitors from across the divide, Irish voices, Cockney voices, the voices of American Indians, Chinese, Eskimos and Hindus have all visited our gatherings, speaking always in their quaintly accented English.'

'Mr Lightbeam has many testimonials to the accuracy of the information he elicits from those who have passed over.'

'Sometimes I am in great pain. Occasionally I actually pass blood. That frightens me.'

'With good reason,' agreed Max. 'So I suppose there is no chance of a room?'

'Have we said that, my love?' Mr Lightbeam turned to his wife.

'Have we rejected Mr . . . ah, Mr . . .?'

'Milman.'

'Certainly not, dearest,' said Mrs Lightbeam quickly, 'I find him remarkably sympathetic.'

'You are right, my love. He has an aura. I begin to feel that he may have been sent.'

'How much are you asking?' Max enquired.

'What can you afford?'

'Precious little – until something turns up.'

'Yours is a precarious profession, I understand,' said Lightbeam. 'You must wait upon an offer. I wait upon the spirits. Perhaps we could find some humble mode in which you could assist us. In that way we could arrive at an accommodation to our mutual benefit.'

'How do you mean?' said Max, sensing a chance of getting away with free board and lodging.

'You are an actor.' Mr Lightbeam looked him up and down. 'Do you include among your talents the art of throwing your voice?'

'Venting?' asked Max, beginning to see what the man was driving at. 'As a matter of fact I did pick a bit up from a colleague on the halls early on.' In fact Max had acquired a rudimentary skill picked up in a pub in Bradford on a Monday night over a drink.

'It is because of the strain,' said Horatio Lightbeam. 'It takes so much out of me. Often when I have established contact I am too weak to continue. It is very frustrating and deeply disappointing for my flock.'

'They ain't so keen to fill the brass bowl?'

'Precisely. You take my meaning.'

'What are you suggesting, Horatio?' asked Mrs Lightbeam nervously.

'My love, I am proposing that Mr Milman observe several of our seances and then – should my powers fail – he would be available to throw his voice through the trumpet so that our dear friends would not depart disappointed.'

'Very generous,' his wife agreed. 'Inspired is, I think, the word.'

'Perhaps,' ventured Horatio Lightbeam, 'divinely inspired?'

Max's apprenticeship was short and intensive. In the evenings he sat hidden in an alcove in the long, darkened room, observing a circle of some twenty to thirty of the faithful as they held hands and waited to hear news of the departed transmitted in the variety of voices which Horatio Lightbeam conjured up. By day Horatio helped the actor improve his voice-throwing skills and let him into the secrets of leading the congregation. He had perfected ways of exacting information which gave the news imparted by his voices the effect of stunning revelation. With Mrs Lightbeam, he also did conscientious research into the background of the seance sitters, all of whom came by appointment.

Max no longer knew where a genuine manifestation stopped and charlatanry began. However throwing his voice and conjuring up various fake messages was no burden. Although the lifestyle of the Lightbeams was not lavish, he was happy to take advantage of it for the time being.

As his hosts trusted him more, so he discovered that Mr Lightbeam had a fondness for the bottle and a wandering eye which was gratified in frequent flirtations with the decidedly unhealthy-looking women who made up the bulk of the flock. Max observed these fledgling romances with amusement and no envy. However, he noticed that Mrs Lightbeam watched with some pain.

The Lightbeams, having recently arrived in Melbourne, were a novelty. Business was brisk. They came from Sydney and there was some mystery surrounding their departure. Max wondered idly if they had left in a hurry: but he stopped short of asking Horatio, even after one particularly tiring session when the medium revived his spirits with liberal helpings of whisky and grew garrulous.

'Time we put you to work, Max, old fellow,' he slurred as he sprawled in an armchair which barely contained his bulk. 'My powers are overstrained: but I cannot disappoint the people.'

'Business is booming.'

'Never business, Max. Never. We minister, we bring comfort. We accept the gratitude of the faithful.' He hiccuped. 'Humbly.'

A couple of days elapsed before the next seance. Max wondered how he had allowed himself to become involved in the ludicrous pantomime. But the actor in him looked forward to his performance. 'Keeping the curtain up,' he justified it to himself.

Mrs Lightbeam admitted the faithful and settled them in their chairs. Horatio was the dominating presence in the circle. Max was concealed behind a heavy velvet curtain. As Mrs Lightbeam removed the lamps Max felt a slight tremor of first-night nerves.

Horatio opened the proceedings and quickly made contact with Danny, his master of ceremonies. It soon became clear that Danny was not performing up to his usual standard. The rapt circle stirred uneasily at this unexpected development until Max took up the cue he had agreed with Lightbeam, a repeated 'to be sure, to be sure' from Danny. He introduced himself as Paddy, Danny's brother, embroidering his entrance with the information that he had died in the great potato famine. 'Terrible day. Terrible days!' Growing in confidence, Max followed the routine he had observed. A succession of ghostly voices emanated from the trumpets. Departed relatives and friends were conjured up, articles of furniture rattled as Mrs Lightbeam tugged on pieces of string or tapped gently on selected hands around the circle.

Just as Max was beginning to relish his performance a light flashed across the room. The walls and timbers shook, chairs rattled and the three trumpets crashed to the floor. The circle broke up in confusion. 'Return the lamps!' shouted an authoritative voice. Mrs Lightbeam scuttled into the hall and returned with one in each hand. From his curtained hiding-place Max saw that three men were standing amidst an astonished group of women. Horatio Lightbeam slumped in his chair.

'Police! Nobody move!' said the tallest of the three men. 'Acting on information received from Mr Johnson here of *Smith's Weekly*,' Max recognised a thin, sandy-haired young man whom he had seen at a seance some days earlier, 'we have reason to believe that a fraudulent attempt to extract money has been practised on these premises. I am also accompanied by Mr Pinkerton Frond, a spiritualist sponsored by Sir Arthur Conan Doyle, a Fellow of the Royal Geographical Society, who practises as a legitimate clairvoyant, psychometrist and healer.'

Mr Frond, a tall, thin, sallow fellow clad in black, took over. 'I have recently arrived in this country having travelled the world widely, interviewed many mediums and striven manfully to root out frauds. It is I who, in the city of Sydney, recently exposed Frank Adams. He produced live fish and birds at his seances. Palming an eighteen-inch, shovel-nosed shark to impress his patrons was a fish too far. I am happy to say that he now languishes in jail.'

He indicated that the policeman could take statements from Lightbeam's parishioners while he conducted a search of the premises. 'It will not serve for any accomplice to cut and run,' he said threateningly, pointing his remarks to the alcove which concealed Max. 'Members of the constabulary have been posted outside.'

The curtain was torn back and Max was exposed.

'How did you wriggle out of it, Max?' asked Zelda. 'I'm fascinated.'

'Long and the short of it is, I didn't,' said Max. 'Caught red-handed. Open and shut case. I felt sorry for old Lightbeam. I don't think he started out crook. Probably had a bit of a gift. Went to his head. It finished him. He died in prison. I got four years. They wouldn't believe it was my first performance. Apparently I impressed Mr Pinkerton Frond so much he reckoned I'd been doing it for ever. Only time I've been sent to jail for giving too convincing a performance. They let me out after two for good behaviour. Another first!'

'Whatever did you do when you were released?'

'Kept out of trouble.' Max grimaced. 'Almost. I nearly got nicked back in Sydney. Picked up a girl who must have been twenty if she was a day. Turned out to be a fourteen-year-old from Fort Street Girls High School. I'll never know how I got off that. Good brief, I suppose. Young guy called Henry Minogue – I came out of it smelling of roses.'

'But work?' asked Zelda. 'Were you still blacklisted?'

'Not in radio. Wireless was the new thing. It didn't pay a fortune but they'd just cottoned on to daily soaps. I was nursing a beer one night in the Assembly Hotel. Passed for bohemia in Sydney at that time. Some poofter radio producer was crying into his gin about how was he going to cast this plum part. "Got nobody here with class," he was moaning to the roster of old deadbeats. I perked up and said, "I reckon I got some class." "Who are you?" says he. "Max Milman," says I. He looked like he's seen a ghost. "My God," he says, "I saw you as Ben Hur when I was a nipper. I can still remember those thighs!" They all laughed at that. "Where've you bin?" one of 'em asks. "Resting," I say. They all look sympathetic and next thing I know I'm in. And I mean in everything!

'There were Aussie versions of *Superman* and *Tarzan*. Kids' stuff, *The Search for the Golden Boomerang* was one. I did a lift from some English books. *The Air Adventures of Biggles*. They went mad for cockney shows too. God knows why! *Mrs 'Olmes and Mrs H'entwhistle* was big. Then there was *Dad and Dave* later in the thirties. *Martin's Corner* in the forties. There was a cracker called *First Light Fraser*. Thursday night it went out. It was set, they used to say, in war-torn Europe. Always a big cliff-hanger at the end of each episode. They're still doing it. Same crew. Same hacks turning up as doctors in the outback, venerable family solicitors, handsome young wastrels. They look like a row of old walnuts. God knows what'll happen to 'em when television gets going. There's going to be some shattered illusions on the sheep stations when the shearers get to see the faces attached to the sexy voices they've been having the hots for over twenty years.'

'Why did you give it up?' asked Zelda.

'Usual thing. It gave me up.'

'A woman again?'

'Right first time. Wife of a station head. Made another bloody mistake. I married her. Not for long.'

'I've lost count,' said Zelda.

'So 'ave I.'

'And now you're back with number one?'

Zelda gave the old man a long searching look.

Max pondered her suggestion. 'You might just be right,' he agreed. 'At my time of life there's something to be said for coming home and settling down. Besides, I like Martyn's kids. They don't tie you down so much. They kind of moor you.' He changed tack. 'What about you?' he said to Zelda. 'I've talked about me all night. How many Mr Fanes have there been?'

'None at all. Not even a near thing. Same girlfriend. House in the hills. Works in real estate. End of story. Very boring.'

'Didn't those studios try to make you marry?'

'Oh yes, but I got away with a couple of walk-outs. As long as the columns said you and some guy were an item every now and again, it was okay. The only time I nearly got involved was with Keate. Keate Watershed.'

'The cowboy?'

'Don't look so surprised. He's a nice guy. He's coming over for the opening.'

'Not your girlfriend?'

'No. Laura's coming over quietly later on.'

Zelda

Zelda wondered how much of her life she should unveil for Max. Her early years in Texas? The name she bore before she changed it – Fanny Crumb? Her French, Irish and Cherokee ancestors? The dancing lessons she took at five to rectify rickets, engagements when she was fourteen, preening and prancing for five dollars a night for Rotarians, Elks and Shriners? (Her mother told them she was eighteen and they believed her.) Her first, unsuccessful attack on Hollywood when she got no further than the line-up of female dancers at the Frisby Pom Pom Club in a revue called *Glorifying Hollywood's Most Beautiful Girls*, where she first realised she preferred women as lovers? Her defeated move to New York and a period of poverty so intense that she hung around the back of theatres where she could just about hear parts of the shows she could not afford to see?

No. Zelda decided to pick up her story at the time she met Mercedes de Acosta.

'Who?' asked Max.

'She was extraordinary,' Zelda told him, 'she still is. She knew everybody in New York. She wasn't beautiful. Dark hair, brown eyes, about five feet four. She was like a little black bird. She always wore black or white or a mixture of the two – cloaks, well-cut jackets, tricorn hats. There was a husband somewhere, but he wasn't allowed to get in the way. It was the twenties, Mercedes loved the speakeasies and the louche drag clubs. That's where I met her. I was doing a top-hat and tails number. She was round to the dressing-room like a bullet. Next day the little cold water walk-up I shared with two other girls was buried under champagne and lilies and caviar. No half-measures for Mercedes.

When she called to see how I liked the presents she was amazed. "Darling," she said, "I'm getting you out of here." She put me in the Algonquin. That's how I started to get noticed. Mercedes was on the rebound from Eva La Gallienne. She'd written a play for Eva, *Joan of Arc* I think, some crap. Anyway, it was no good and Eva went off to try out Ibsen on Chicago. I must have wavered a bit because she put her hands on her hips and made her famous boast, "I can get any woman away from any man."

' "But Mercedes," I said, "I'm not with any man."

'Life opened up for me at the Algonquin. There were chorus bits and then understudying Ruby Keeler. By the time Mercedes shot off to Hollywood in pursuit of Garbo I was beginning to do all right.'

'Shot off after Garbo . . .?' Max's mouth dropped open.

'Oh, yes, didn't you know?'

'Didn't get to hear too much of that Down Under.' Max tried not to look shocked.

Zelda piled on the evidence. 'Garbo and I weren't the only ones,' she said. 'There was Eleanor Duse and Karsavina and Isadora Duncan and Nazimova and Ona Munsen and Dietrich, of course.'

'*Marlene* Dietrich?'

'Know any other Dietrichs? Why not, Max? I had a fling with Marlene when I got back to Hollywood.'

'My God! That I envy you,' said Max.

' "In Europe," Dietrich used to tell them, "it doesn't matter if you're a man or a woman; we make love to anyone we find attractive." I met her at a dance show. I'd gone with Mercedes, just for old times sake, but I must have been looking good. It was one of my white nights – white slacks, white turtleneck, white top coat. There in front of us was Marlene. Mercedes introduced me and I didn't really think more of it. But next day my maid comes in with this damn great bunch of white roses and says there's a Miss Dietrich in the hall. She looked kinda shy and clicked her heels and took my hand very formal, very German and shook it. "I brought you the flowers," she said, very soft, "white flowers because you looked like a prince last night." I wanted to talk about her movies. It was all new to me but she wouldn't have it. "No more talk," she said. "I am lonely. That is why I came to you. You are the person to whom I have felt drawn. I want to ask if you will let me cook for you." '

Max laughed.

'She loved cooking. And she was good at it. Cooking, cleaning, all that *hausfrau* stuff. And she bombarded me with flowers. After the roses it was tulips. Then more roses. Dozens of them. Then carnations. Sometimes they came twice a day. One day she sent ten dozen rare orchids from San Francisco. The maid went insane. She couldn't find enough vases. Talk about a bower. I was walking on flowers, falling over flowers, sleeping on flowers. Finally I got mad at her. I called my car, told the maid to stuff every flower in the back and take 'em off to the hospital. Every damn flower in the house. Then I rang her. "Marlene," I told her, "one more flower and I'll drown you in your own pool." Know what the idiot woman did? She changed gifts. Next it was Lalique, then boxes from Bullock's Wilshire Boulevard with dressing-gowns, scarves, pyjamas, slacks, sweaters, lamps, lampshades. I sent 'em all back. In the end she laughed. We got to be friends as well as lovers. She even started sending me things from the men's department at Bullock's.'

'Maybe it's a good job I didn't make it to Hollywood,' said Max. 'I'm not sure I'd have fitted in.'

'You know what de Mille said?'

'No.'

'An actress is something more than a woman. An actor is something less than a man.'

'Not Max Milman,' said the old actor. 'Not me.'

'Going around with Marlene got me noticed. In Tinseltown you have to draw attention to yourself. There are always fifty other girls trying to get parts in pictures. Producers don't know one pretty face from another – unless, say, you got cheekbones like Kate Hepburn.' Zelda paused and appeared to be visualising the Hepburn face. 'Greatest calcium deposit since the white cliffs of Dover,' she mused dramatically.

Max laughed.

So did Zelda. 'I didn't say it,' she confessed. 'That was Art Buchwald.'

'Did you ever work with Hepburn?' Max asked.

'No, I thought I was going to in *Stage Door* but they gave it to Annie Miller. *Society Scandals* was my big break. *Middlemarch* was my chance to go legit, but people still saw me as a musical girl. I never quite cracked the label. By the late forties the high-kicking parts were getting fewer. That's when I started touring. I started with *Anything Goes*. I've been more or less on the road ever since.' Zelda looked around the room. 'My God, Max, they'll be stacking the tables in a minute!'

'I'll drop you off,' said Max gallantly. 'Your secretary guy having a night off, is he?'

'He needs one,' said Zelda. 'He's had his hands full. I've no idea where he is tonight,' she lied.

Chauncey

It was a late spring Sunday afternoon when the cast and crew of *In Society!* left London for Bristol. The giant pantechnicons carrying the scenery, the heavy, intricate stage machinery, the carefully stowed props and the baskets of costumes had pulled out from the south London sheds of the set-builders the day before.

The get-in at the Hippodrome was not likely to be a quick one. Tommy Tanqueray's brainchild had been carefully packed in a hundred cardboard frames and now carpenters, electricians, stage-hands and stage managers tried, with the young designer, to make sense of his blueprint and the carefully labelled individual pieces. As the first actors left London the crew members were still scratching their heads over the puzzle.

Maude chose to drive herself down to Chewton Mendip. This enabled her to pick up Adrian Arbuthnot at his Chiswick flat on the way. Grace was joining the others on the train, and Tony drove Martyn and Louis in the Rolls. They left early, anxious to walk the stage and see how the set looked. Harry Harmon, who knew he ought to be there to make sure that things were going smoothly, had not been able to resist Zelda's invitation to ride down with her and Braden Jefferson in the Daimler he had found for her.

Max and Amanda opted to take the train.

'Just like old days,' he said as he gallantly doffed his hat when he called to pick her up from Kinnerton Street.

'Just a short run,' she said. 'Not cross-country.'

'Shan't be wavin' to old pals on another platform at Crewe,' Max agreed.

At Paddington they joined the other senior members of the

company in their first-class seats, and waved and smiled at the young dancers and actors who were gathering on the platform with their bags and grips and arguing happily about who would sit with whom in which cheaper coach. In a rare gesture of democracy Martyn had insisted that his three children should travel with the other youngsters and not be cosseted with the old-stagers.

Kurt Kornfeld came to see Hanna off; but his mother was well aware that he was using her as an excuse to say goodbye to Imogen and extract a kiss. As soon as he had seated Hanna and stowed her dilapidated bags on the rack above, he made for the barrier through which Imo and Lysander were passing. Mae Madely hung from Lysander's arm. As they passed the carriage in which Amanda and Max had taken window seats the little group waved. Max took a second look at Mae's pretty, dramatically white face framed by long, severe, black hair.

'Young Lysander's struck lucky,' he said, feeling that there was something uncomfortably familiar about the girl's face.

'My dear, she's an autograph hunter!' Amanda said. 'She'd have stayed a perfectly good fan: but he had to run after her. I don't know what the theatre's coming to!'

'Boys will be boys,' said Max, indulgently. He watched Mac's behind undulate up the platform.

'And men will be men,' snapped Amanda. 'Certainly Milman men!'

Kurt and Mae saw Imogen and Lysander into their compartments and waited at the corridor windows for a farewell embrace before the train began slowly to gather speed. It left behind a gaggle of waving friends and lovers, all making promises to come to Bristol for the first performance.

Inside the crowded coaches the atmosphere was jovial and excited. Several of the chorus boys were passing around copies of the *Sunday Digest*. It was the second week of publication of a series of sensational articles called 'Wicked Men', an exposé of homosexual vice in the capital. The more camp dancers flitted from one compartment to another reading out the most lurid extracts.

'Who wrote that rubbish?' One of the dancers waving the

Digest reached the compartment in which the three Milman children had gathered. They were sharing it with a boy and a girl from the chorus and an old gentleman who was hidden behind the *Sunday Times*. Darcy had asked the question. The dancer turned to the front page to see who was credited.

'By Chauncey Martin,' he read.

The Milmans looked at one another.

'That old bastard,' said Darcy.

The old gentleman behind the *Sunday Times* said nothing, but the chorus boy beside him spoke up for the first time.

'Bitter old queen, that Miss Martin,' he said. 'A bloke I know's had her. She's only got one arm. Sad case, she is. Has to pay for it. That's why she's doin' this.'

Chauncey Martin's eyebrows shot up behind the *Sunday Times*. He knew better than anyone that the allegation was not true, but he was as fascinated by the details as he was proud of the effect his series was causing. He did, in fact, possess two arms but one was somewhat shorter than the other. He meditated on how a rumour could grow from a grain of truth sown in a fertile field of gossip. He was still working on his series for the *Digest* and he had decided that it was time to look at 'Wicked Men' outside London. Naturally his readers expected the capital to be a sink of iniquity and vice. He reckoned he would provoke even more outrage if he invaded the provinces. He decided to hit Bristol first so that he could monitor Max's first appearance in *In Society!* at the same time. He had not quite done with the Milman clan. Somewhere on the horizon he could envisage a tearful reunion between Max and Mae Madely, whose rent the *Digest* was still paying. Max might deny grandparentage, but Chauncey was sure that he had gleaned enough circumstantial evidence from his Australian investigators to make the charge stick. Another large photo-spread looked a distinct possibility. For once he was relieved that the *Digest* had chosen not to print a photograph of him beside his by-line. Max was the only Milman who would be likely to recognise him. As extra precaution he had grown a trim little moustache. Chauncey put down his paper, folded it and pretended to sleep.

The Milmans chattered on. The journalist heard that Mae was

coming down to stay with Lysander on the first night. This was a titillating development of which he had not been informed. Imogen was looking forward to seeing someone called Kurt. They discussed their mother's hotel in Chewton Mendip. From what was said and what was not said, Chauncey deduced that Maude was staying with another young actor in the company. He caught only his first name. Adrian. Martyn was staying at the Grand, sharing a suite with the choreographer, an American. A foreign woman came into the compartment briefly and fussed over the Milman children. Old nanny, he wondered? No, she was too theatrical. Under the cheap clothes there was an attractive woman. More like an actress. As she talked of 'my Kurt' he saw Imogen brighten. For one optimistic moment of melodramatic speculation Chauncey wondered if the foreign woman could be a spy. He reminded himself that he already had a handful of 'Wicked Men' on the go; but the prospect of the reunion of a fornicating septuagenarian and the daughter of his long-lost illegitimate child, coupled with the hope of finding a spy ring in Bristol was pushing even his luck.

Hanna returned to her seat cheered by the sight of Imogen's face at the mention of Kurt. Her son had been so much happier since their windfall. His furrowed face had become carefree. He had taken Imogen out and lavished presents on her. His medical work had improved. She still blamed herself for the poverty to which she had brought him, no matter how often she told herself that his prospects in Germany would have been infinitely worse. The job of understudying Zelda provided her with more funds than she had seen for some time. However, the ear-ring money was running out. How could she prolong her son's brief encounter with happiness?

Martyn and Louis instructed Tony to drive straight to the Hippo-drome stage door. The alley behind the theatre was damp and dark. Louis recognised the familiar smell of piss. The business of unloading through the huge open scene dock-doors was continu-ing. This was not a good sign. It should have been long done. Martyn tightened the belt of his neat Burberry and strode through the stage door, barely acknowledging Ronald, the stage door keeper. Louis, less familiar with the layout, lagged behind.

'Christ, sir's in an hurry,' said Ronald over his hatch. 'I've got his fan-mail here.'

'Any for me?' Louis asked.

'Name?'

'Louis Armbruster – choreographer,' Louis said importantly.

'No, sir, nobody loves you.'

Louis caught up with Martyn, who was fretting at the side of the stage. Alongside stood the pale, tense figure of Tommy Tanqueray, and the enormous production manager who was scratching a bald head with one hand and simultaneously picking the remains of his lunch out of his teeth with the other. Across the floor of the stage an intricate lattice of rails and cables was confusingly assembled. Through the dock-doors Louis saw the piles of boards which would constitute the floor of the set. Martyn knew that they could not be laid until the machinery had been installed and tested to ensure that it was working. In another van were stacked Tanqueray's delicately detailed *trompe l'œil* screens. They were neatly packed in precise positions in which they would stay until they could be moved inside and hung. A massive stair-case which was to be flown in from the flys was similarly abandoned in its vehicle as the army of stage-hands, carpenters and electricians clambered carefully over the train-set they were trying to coax into working order.

'When do we open?' Louis asked Martyn.

'You tell him, Reg.' Martyn passed the buck to the production manager, who removed his left hand from his teeth. 'Very difficult question to answer, Mr Armbruster,' he said, after a moment's thought. 'We was goin' to focus an' light tomorrow; stagger a tech Tuesday an' then 'ave a dress on Wednesday. Two if we could make it. But the schedule's all gone to buggery.'

'Why, Tommy?' Louis turned on the designer.

'I can't understand it, Louis. We assembled it all on the floor of the shed back in the Walworth Road. It worked like a dream.'

Martyn snapped: 'Has Mr Harmon arrived yet, Reg?'

'I think 'e's seeing Miss Fane into the Grand, sir.'

'Well, get him over here. This is just what we didn't need. He should be here.' He hurried tetchily away to the phone by the stage door.

Louis turned to survey the brightly lit auditorium. The first thing he always did on arriving in a new theatre was to stand on the stage and look out at the challenging cavern that stood before him. If he was performing he would imagine himself bringing those rows of people in the mezzanine, the overflowing boxes and the packed stalls together in an intimacy created by his performing personality. He saw himself, single-handed, turning the vast arc into his own little space. As choreographer he made a further leap of the imagination and saw himself out in front holding his breath in admiration at the intricate patterns of the spectacle he had created. Lost for a moment, he could visualise the swiftly sliding panels which he had helped to devise. There was the ballroom scene that he had choreographed. Another set of panels moved past in his mind's eye, revealing the spirited Rotten Row ballet against a gorgeous green background. He almost applauded another impeccable set change, and then there was Zelda, swishing the scarlet skirt under her exquisite bustle, as four boys propelled her to and fro across the wide stage. Louis was lost in admiration for what he had created, when his optimistic fantasy was broken.

'Give us an 'and, love,' said a light, no-nonsense voice behind him.

Before he knew what he was doing, he found himself helping a heavy middle-aged man hump a large hamper overflowing with clothes. With some difficulty they manoeuvred it down a set of temporary steps from the stage into the stalls. The basket landed with a thud in one of the aisles. 'Thanks, dear,' said the wardrobe man. 'Could've broken your mother's back, that lot.'

Louis grunted.

'You with the show?'

'Let's put it this way, I'm not against it,' said Louis grouchily. 'I choreographed it.'

'You're American!'

'Very smart!'

'I used to be a dancer,' said the wardrobe man. 'Nothing big, you know. Touring musicals an' that. And panto. One show ran out of steam here in Bristol an' as I'd found true love the night before I decided to hang up me pumps. Been here ever since. True love only lasted a month.' He shrugged.

'What sort of dump is it?'

'All right when you get to know it. Where you staying?'

'Sir Martyn and I are at the Grand.'

'There's posh! Mind you, there's not much night-life there.'

'There's not much night-life in London,' said Louis.

'Bristol's not so bad if you know where to look.'

Louis perked up. 'And where might that be?'

'There's a coffee bar just opened – you know that new espresso stuff. It's called the Peccadillo. It's on the way up the hill towards Clifton – just behind the shops on the right.' The wardrobe man looked quizzically at Louis. 'You get some what you might call artistic types in there of an evening. And one or two down from the BBC up Whiteladies Road.'

'And that's night-life?'

'There's a couple of pubs. One towards the Docks, Avonmouth way. Sailors, mostly,' he leered. 'Oh, and there's the Two Cabots – they were famous sailors too, local boys, I understand, long ago. It's in Castle Alley. They have quite a varied clientele,' he added primly, 'especially in the back bar.' The wardrobe man bent over to start sorting the bundles of costumes. 'Nice talking to you,' he said. 'Hope the show goes well.'

'Thanks,' Louis replied, taking a pen from his pocket and noting the addresses he had been given, 'it looks as if we may have time on our hands while they sort this lot out.'

In the wings Martyn conducted a crisis conference with a flustered Harry Harmon, a near-tearful Tommy Tanqueray, a phlegmatic Reg, and Robert Caswell, the stage manager.

'There is no way we are going to open on Thursday, Harry,' he was saying. 'You'll be lucky if we can get the curtain up on Saturday.'

'But we've sold four houses this week, Martyn.'

'Stuff four houses. I'm not getting up on that fucking Hornby set until I know it's working. I'm not having my play ruined by incompetence back-stage. We've got the cast here. Find a rehearsal room. Find two. We can all put in some more work. You can use the time, can't you, Louis?'

'I'll say.'

'Find somewhere to band call, Harry, I don't like the acoustics in the bar. We used it for *April in Provence* and I nearly cut two numbers. They sounded so dreadful until I got the orchestra into the pit. Try the Colston Hall. We can't let the momentum go now they're all teed up.'

'How long is it going to take to sort this out?' Harry turned despairingly to Tommy and Reg. They shrugged.

'I think there's a couple of major components missing,' said Reg, portentously.

'Maybe they got left behind,' said Tommy. 'It's not my fault.'

'I don't care whose fault it is,' shouted Martyn, so loudly that the stage army stopped work and stared at him.

'Just a suggestion,' offered Harry timidly, 'but couldn't we open with cloths and . . . and blacks . . . and then put in the whole shooting match when we've got it sorted?'

'No, we could not, Harry! Don't be so bloody stupid! Now get on with building bloody Clapham Junction! I'm going to the hotel and I'm going to have some dinner. Come on, Louis.'

Louis, who had become used to programming Martyn's every response over the rehearsal period, was surprised to find him so fired up. However, as they got into the car, Martyn flopped into the backseat with a weary sigh. 'What do you think?'

'It's a mess,' said Louis.

'I'm not opening until I'm happy it works. I've told Robert Caswell to call the company for eleven in the morning. By then I hope to know what rehearsal space Harry's got for us.' Suddenly Martyn realised that the car had not moved. The driver was waiting for instructions. 'Sorry, Tony. Hotel. Bloody mess.'

'Sounds like it, sir. Remember *Wonderful Moonlight*?'

'Don't remind me! This is worse! I'm going to have a bath and a good dinner and I'm going to sleep.'

'You don't fancy a bit of night-life? A guy in the stalls told me about a couple of dives.'

'I'm diving into bed. You please yourself.'

In the lobby of the Grand the old man hiding behind the newspaper near the desk noticed that Sir Martyn and his younger companion took a single key. He made a note of the number in his pad and then watched Tony struggle after them with an assortment of cases.

Chauncey made for the dining-room, demolished a steak, put away a couple of whiskies and studied the information he had been given before leaving London. He was to meet a friend of his principal London informant at a place called the Peccadillo. He reckoned information in Bristol would come cheaper than in London and had budgeted a modest fifty pounds. His rendezvous was for eight thirty and as he entered the bare little bar with half a dozen formica-topped tables and clusters of wicker chairs he reckoned that it would not detain him long. He spotted his contact, a pale youth, clutching, by arrangement, a day-old copy of the *Bristol Evening Post* and sitting under a gaudy poster of the south of France. Collecting an espresso, Chauncey made his way over.

'You must be Colin?' he said.

'Yes, Mr Martin,' said the youth, blushing nearly as red as the two shiny elastoplast spots carefully applied to cover minor blemishes on his cheeks.

'Don't be shy, lad,' said Chauncey benignly, adding, 'don't call me Mr Martin. I'm Mr Appleby while I'm on this job. Appleby, got it?'

'Yes, Mr Martin.'

'Appleby!'

'Appleby.'

'Good lad. So the Peccadillo isn't where the action is tonight?'

'It might liven up.'

'It'll have to be quick. What time does the Two Cabots close?'

'Ten o'clock on a Sunday, sir.'

'And don't call me sir. It won't hurt if they think I'm a punter. That's how your friend Keith and I worked it. I want to get in a good hour at the pub. We'll give it ten minutes here. Get yourself another coffee, son. Here's a tenner. It's an advance. You'll get the rest when I get some information.'

'Thank you, Mr . . . Appleby.'

Colin dutifully returned with his coffee, having parried jokes from the man behind the machine about the provenance of his recently acquired ten-pound note and the identity of the stranger. Apart from a sandalled, corduroy-trousered, fair-isle-sweatered pair whom they could just hear talking BBC wireless shop in a far corner, no one entered the bar.

Chauncey finished taking desultory notes of Colin's scanty information on the Bristol scene and got up. 'Come on, son. Time to wet your whistle,' and together they left the bright bar and padded down a dimly-lit backstreet. It led to a steep hill with shuttered antique shops on either side.

'How far is it, Colin?'

'Not far, Mr Appleby,' Colin replied. 'See, I got the name first time.'

'Well done,' grunted Chauncey, puffing a little, although it was a downhill trek.

'You're not a wicked man yourself, Mr Appleby, are you?' asked Colin, staring at the old boy's florid face and new moustache.

'Good God, no!'

'Only a chap at work said something about you only having one arm an' that. An' you couldn't get any. But you got two, 'aven't you? I've seen 'em.'

'Yes, Colin, I have two. So I am definitely not a queer. Happy?'

'Here's Castle Alley,' Colin said. 'It's just at the end.'

They plodded along a narrow waterfront to a small riverside pub. Rosy lights shone from the windows and an inn sign, with an old sea-dog portrayed on either side, creaked as it swayed in the breeze.

'Auntie's bar is in the back,' said Colin, about to open the door.

'We'll get a drink in here and take it through,' Chauncey told him.

'It'll look better if you buy it,' said Colin, 'you bein' a bit older,' he added flatteringly to the reporter who could give him fifty years and more.

Chauncey surveyed the public bar with disgust while the barman poured him a triple scotch. He added a splash of soda.

'Lager and lime, please,' Colin requested.

A sprinkling of men chatted at tables around the bar. Another couple stood talking to a blowsy woman who laughed too readily at their jokes. Could be a pro, Chauncey decided. Not a bad sign sometimes in the provinces.

They went through to the back room. The lights were a little dimmer there, housed in coy pink shades. The barmaid was a stout seventy-something, bleached and bosomy. On the walls of her bar Chauncey noticed theatre bills for the Empire, the Little Theatre, the Theatre Royal and, occupying pride of place, the fancy art nouveau design which Martyn had approved for *In Society!*.

'Evenin', Colin,' she greeted the boy. 'Who's your friend?'

'This is Mr Appleby, Auntie. He's down to see that musical at the Hippo.'

'Evenin',' said Auntie. 'Bit of trouble there, I hear.'

'Oh, where did you hear that?' asked Chauncey.

'Friend of mine. Works in wardrobe. In here lunchtime. He says it's an 'ell of a mess. That won't please Dame Martyn. You in the theatre, love?'

'Only as an aficionado,' the phrase rolled off Chauncey's tongue.

'Better watch out then – that Chauncey Martin's after folks like that!' Auntie let out a peal of laughter. Her chins wobbled and her breasts heaved. Colin glanced nervously at Chauncey but saw that he was laughing just as uproariously. Quickly, Colin joined in.

'I can tell you had a theatrical past,' said the reporter, 'Auntie, is it?'

'T'is 'ere. But I used to be Rowena. I was the Hoopla Girl with a Dog Act,' said Auntie proudly. 'You know – every time one of my partner Superbo's dogs brought off a trick I'd strike a pose and say, "Hoopla!" It was to draw the applause,' she added. 'Of course I was thinner then.'

'Where did you play?'

'All over. But we was most proud of the Palladium. We was on the second-ever bill in Argyll Street. Course it was still Ringler's Circus in them days. 1902!'

'Fifty-one years ago,' enthused Chauncey. 'Have a drink, my dear. Not champagne, I think, not even out of your slipper!' Auntie went off into more peals of laughter. 'What'll it be?'

'Drop of gin, dear. Thanks very much.'

'You'd better fill us up again, too, before the rush starts,' said Chauncey as two young men pushed their way through the doors.

'You be nice to Colin,' Auntie simpered. 'He's my favourite.'

'I'll bet you say that to all the boys,' Chauncey countered.

He and Colin took their drinks into a corner and discreetly raised them to Auntie as she served the newcomers.

'This looks more promising, Colin,' said Chauncey, happy to slip into observant obscurity. 'Let's watch an' wait.'

'That's two army blokes,' his companion informed him. 'They've been in a couple of times. They hitches lifts from over Larkhill an' 'ope they get picked up. I'm not sayin' they're on the game exactly; but I never seen 'em say no to a hand-out.'

The two soldiers, both in civilian clothes, sipped their half-pints of beer at the bar, engaged Auntie in a little banter and inspected the room. They showed some interest in Chauncey but were warned off by Colin's fiercely proprietorial stare.

At about half past nine Chauncey was ready to return to the hotel when he heard a car pull up outside. An American voice said; 'Hang on here, Tony. I'll just get a night-cap.'

'We'll give it another couple of minutes,' said Chauncey to the faithful Colin, who had become less coherent after a couple of refills. Suddenly the doors of the back bar were thrown open and a slightly swaying Louis Armbruster stood in the doorway. Smartly dressed in a cashmere coat and a red silk scarf, he made a vivid contrast to the drab occupants of the room. He strolled to the bar, happily aware of the effect he was creating, perched on a stool, and flashed a row of perfect teeth at a fascinated Auntie. 'I hear your English bitter beer is excellent,' he said. 'May I try it?'

'I should have put you down as a Bourbon man,' said Auntie, dimpling in every fold. 'But suit yourself. I'd say you was a Yank.'

'How did you guess?'

'Are you with the show?'

'Let's say I'm not against it,' said Louis, smiling at his own much repeated joke.

Auntie giggled. 'I hear it's going to be really good,' she said diplomatically. That Sir Martyn always puts on a good show. I was in show-business myself once, you know.'

Louis lost marks by not picking up his cue. 'We're having a spot of technical trouble,' he confessed. 'It's a very ambitious set. I doubt if Bristol has ever seen anything like it. We may not open on Thursday.'

'But they've sent me my tickets!' cried Auntie. 'Don't tell me it's off!'

'I think it's gotta be postponed,' said Louis, 'but don't you worry, darling, whenever it opens I'll see you get in. I'm the choreographer,' he explained airily.

'Who's that?' asked one of the soldiers. Both had been edging nearer to the conversation from the moment they saw the thickness of the wallet Louis pulled out when he paid for his drink.

'He does the dances, silly,' said Auntie.

'You a dancer then?' asked one.

'Like Fred Astaire?' said the other.

'I kinda invent them now. I used to be a dancer. Now I'm in charge of the dancers.'

'D'you know that Zelda Fane, then?'

'Of course.'

'Good legs! I could give 'er one if I was that way inclined.'

'Can you get us tickets too?' asked the bolder of the two men.

'Why not? When do you want to see it?'

The soldiers looked at each other, unsure.

'Have a drink?' Louis invited, pulling his stool across the bar to sit with them.

Chauncey watched as they fell deeper into conversation. He saw Louis's hand rest lightly on the knee of one of the men. It had initially been laid there ostensibly to emphasise a point. Chauncey smiled as more pressure was applied. He watched the soldier become more animated. He looked at the clock and noticed that last drinks were due to be called any moment. 'Does she let you lot stay after hours?' he asked Colin.

'No more than five minutes,' Colin slurred. 'She's very strict about that. It's the licence, y'see,' he said superfluously. 'Police watching an' that. But there's time for one more,' he added, proffering his glass hopefully.

'I think it's time we skedaddled,' said Chauncey. 'Here's another tenner to be gettin' on with. You've been a good lad, so far.'

'Good-night, Colin. Good night, sir,' Auntie sang out as Chauncey supported his unsteady sidekick out of the bar, taking care to conceal himself as much as he could. But Louis was concentrating on the two soldiers. As they passed through the double doors the laughter in the bar and Auntie's final 'If you can't be good, Colin, be careful' rang after them.

In the street they passed Sir Martyn Milman's Rolls with Tony asleep over the wheel. Chauncey made for the Grand. Colin staggered towards his room in far-off Knowle, in a street behind the dog track.

Pleased with the way his night's work had started, Chauncey reached the Grand and hurried upstairs. Smiling broadly, he passed the door to Martyn Milman's suite and noticed the 'Do Not Disturb' sign on the door handle. You'll be lucky, he thought. Entering his own more modest room almost opposite, he made sure that the door stood very slightly ajar. Then he took his address book from his case and began methodically to compile a list of telephone numbers on a single sheet of paper.

Chauncey had not embarked on his 'Wicked Men' series without a number of discreet enquiries. Alerted by the home secretary's call for a new drive against male vice, he had taken the trouble to enquire further into Sir David Maxwell Fyffe's intentions.

His first step was to seek an interview with the new commissioner of Scotland Yard, Sir John Nott-Bower, who had been extraordinarily open. 'Got a tip from the FBI,' he barked. 'Homosexuals, hopeless security risks. My duty to weed 'em out. I sent Cole, one of my commanders, across to the States. Gave him three months to suss out what they were up to. Now he's back we're going to swing into action. Flush the buggers out. For too many years the police have turned a blind eye to this sort of thing. Let 'em go unless there was a definite complaint from an innocent party. Do you realise the Yard have been sitting on the names of scores of perverts, some of 'em in high positions, even world famous, and did damn all. Got to stop. That Burgess and Maclean business put the lid on it. Lit the blue touch-paper. They were well known to have pervert associates. Somebody has to go behind bars. Make an example.'

'Is this just a London problem?' Chauncey asked with every appearance of naivety.

'By God no! Country's riddled with it. I am enlisting the support of local police throughout England. We have to step up the number of arrests.'

'If I can be of any humble assistance, Sir John.'

'How, Mr Martin?'

'Pool information, sir. I already have a very substantial dossier on the London scene. My editor's very hot on it. I'm about to look into the rest of the country.'

'Where are you starting?'

'Probably Bristol.'

'Excellent man there. First-rate chief constable. Let him know before you go down there.' Sir John handed over the name and promised to alert him. 'Glad to have you on our side, Martin. Very important to have the press with us. Be careful, man. Not too much of that entrapment business. We don't want the *Manchester Guardian* and the *Statesman* kicking up a song and dance. Got to catch the blighters fair and square.'

Chauncey went to Bristol soon afterwards and found the chief constable most amenable. He even introduced him to a senior detective who had special responsibility for rooting out the men who had suddenly become so great a threat to the nation.

Detective Superintendent Coldstream's career had not prospered on his expulsion from Clevedon College. However, after several false starts, he eventually found his natural home in the police force and was now, a few years off retirement, relishing the new responsibility he had been given. His homosexuality had evaporated as he escaped the confines of a single-sex school; but it left him with a vindictive attitude to those he could persecute. Already a couple of his better-looking young officers had gained commendation for entrapping men in some of the city's urinals.

'When d'you reckon to come back to Bristol, Chauncey?' Coldstream asked. After their introduction, they had gone off to have a drink and compare notes.

'Can't say exactly,' Chauncey said. 'I thought I might kill two birds with one stone. I don't know if you saw my piece in the *Digest* about that old rogue Max Milman, the veteran actor?'

'Indeed I did,' said Coldstream. 'I was at school with his bloody son. The little blighter got me expelled.'

'No!' said Chauncey, sensing another rich nugget of information. 'What for?'

'It's a long time ago.' Simon Coldstream pretended to find it hard to remember. 'It was either gambling, you know, pitch and toss, something like that: or maybe it was smoking. Yes, that's it! Smoking behind the bike sheds. Can you believe it? Blakiston, the housemaster, was red-hot against the weed. Stupid bastard! He's Bishop of Gloucester now.'

It was a quarter to eleven when Chauncey Martin dialled the Detective Superintendent's home number from his room at the Grand. After an initial snort of anger at being disturbed, Coldstream rapidly became fascinated by the information the old reporter gave him.

Chauncey put down the phone and tiptoed to the door. He could hear what sounded promisingly like a disturbance at the bottom of the stairwell. He opened the door a little wider and heard Louis Armbruster ordering room service from the night porter.

'For God's sake, man! Cut us some sandwiches. Anything! My friends are starving. And send up a bottle of scotch and a bottle of champagne. Sir Martyn Milman's suite, you idiot. Come on, guys. Tony, you'd better hang on in the car. The boys have to get back to barracks before roll-call.'

Chauncey heard Tony protest that he was sure Sir Martyn was asleep.

Louis overruled him. 'Don't be a stupid cunt, Tony,' he slurred. 'I'm bringing him a present. Everybody likes a present. You like a present, don't you, night porter? Here's a tenner. Now get the sandwiches.'

Hauling the two soldiers up the stairs, Louis made for the suite. Chauncey Martin silently closed his door and knelt before the keyhole. After a lot of stage giggles and hushings, he saw the lower halves of three dishevelled figures in the hotel corridor. Two of them, the soldiers, slid to the floor. Louis's cashmere-clad back stayed upright as he wrestled with the lock.

'Do not disturb!' he giggled as he cast the warning card to the ground.

Finally the key turned in the lock and Chauncey saw him haul the two soldiers into the suite. Quickly making for the phone, Chauncey dialled Coldstream again. The answer was immediate.

'They're in,' he whispered urgently. 'Pissed as newts. I doubt if they can get it up; but I'm willing to bet they're going to try. He's kept on the Rolls to take them back to barracks in the morning. Don't let the chauffeur see you.'

'I'll be right over.'

'He's sent for room service,' Chauncey warned.

'Does your window overlook the street?'

'Of course. Sir's got the quiet side.'

'We'll be outside. Two cars and a jeep,' the Superintendent instructed. 'Give me a wave when you reckon it's time. I'm signing off now, *Mister Appleby*. Good hunting!'

Chauncey opened his window and looked down on to the dark road below. The pavement glistened from the recent shower. Keeping one ear cocked for action in the corridor, he waited for the little caravan to pull up behind the stationary Rolls. He could just see Tony's head, his chauffeur's cap removed. He was asleep over the wheel.

Chauncey had to wait only five minutes before two large black cars and an army jeep slid quietly up the slight incline and came to a halt twenty yards behind the Rolls.

He turned his undivided attention to the corridor outside his room. Just as he was beginning to despair of room service and to wonder if the night porter was ignoring both Louis's order and his tip, he heard a man's steady footsteps on the stairs. He took up his position again at the keyhole and watched as the uniformed figure stopped, balanced his tray in one hand and knocked firmly with the other. In a few seconds the door opened and behind the man he saw Louis's bare legs and the hem of a short silk dressing-gown. Louis took the tray and, as the porter moved away, kicked the door shut. A few seconds later the door opened again. With a sinking heart Chauncey wondered if his plan had misfired. He was relieved to see Louis scrabbling on his knees to pick up the discarded 'Do Not Disturb' sign. The choreographer replaced it and closed the door. Chauncey listened as the key turned in the lock.

He waited fifteen minutes before summoning Coldstream.

In a matter of moments a posse of plainclothes policemen in raincoats and trilby hats and two large uniformed military police-men were hammering on the door of the suite. After a moment of panic inside, the door was unlocked and Louis Armbruster, his toupée askew, was thrust back into the sitting-room. The two soldiers cowered naked behind armchairs. One clutched his pants before him. The other wrestled with his inside out shirt. Bottles, glasses and the remains of sandwiches were strewn across the floor. In the doorway leading to one of the bedrooms stood Sir Martyn Milman, bleary eyed, his hair awry, rubbing sleep from his eyes, clutching a dressing-gown around his naked body.

'What the hell's going on?' was all he managed to say.

'Are you Sir Martyn Milman?' demanded Superintendent Cold-stream.

'Yes,' said Martyn, not recognising his erstwhile lover whom he had neither seen nor thought of for over twenty years.

'Your name?' Coldstream barked at Louis.

'Armbruster.'

'Who are these men?' Coldstream pointed at the two panic-stricken soldiers. 'Come on, Sir Martyn, who are they?'

'I . . . I don't know. I have never seen them before.'

Coldstream circled Martyn, looking at the remains of the feast scattered over the carpet. 'You don't know! Hiding anyone else, are we?' he snarled.

'No, of course not.'

'Search the place,' Coldstream snapped at the other two policemen.

'Shouldn't you have a warrant?'

'I don't think so, Sir Martyn. Not with what we've found already in your front room.'

The soldiers were giving their names, ranks and numbers to the two MPs.

Coldstream allowed himself a steely smile. 'I arrest you, Martyn Milman, for offences of gross indecency . . .' The litany continued as the others were similarly charged.

Martyn's shocked mind could recall only the number of times he had heard the caution in innumerable plays and films and the warning that anything he said might be taken down and used in evidence against him.

'I must get in touch with my lawyer,' he said.

'That can wait, Milman. He won't be in his office at this time of night, will he?'

'I have his home number.'

Coldstream ignored him. 'Get them off to Larkhill,' he said to the MPs, nodding at the dishevelled soldiers. 'I'll take statements in the morning.'

As the youths staggered shamefaced into their clothes, Louis rallied. 'What is this? You can't do this to me. I am an American citizen.'

'Shut up,' said Coldstream, 'or I'll add resisting arrest to the charges.'

As the two soldiers were hustled away Coldstream crossed the room to Martyn. 'You're in a pretty bad position, you know,' he said. 'I'm amazed to find you mixed up with this rubbish. Don't you think you'd feel better if you made a clean breast of it?'

Martyn sat on the arm of a chair. 'I am not "mixed up" in this. I had taken a sleeping draught and I was in bed. I have a vitally important day at the theatre tomorrow. I was trying to get some sleep. I was succeeding until I heard this incredible noise. I got out of bed. I opened my bedroom door and I saw you and this hideous mess.'

'Put some clothes on,' said Coldstream. 'And you,' he spoke to Louis, 'you're both coming to the station. You'll be there overnight. You will be charged tomorrow.'

'I insist on telephoning my solicitor.'

Reluctantly, Coldstream agreed and while Martyn telephoned

the three rooms were pulled apart. Louis hurried into a suit and sat, bemused and already hung-over, on the side of his bed.

'May I go to the bathroom?' asked Martyn when he had established that his solicitor, who had hardly taken in the enormity of the incident, promised to drive immediately to Bristol.

'Don't do anything silly,' said Coldstream as Martyn washed his hands, threw water over his face and saw his drawn likeness in the mirror looking remarkably like a criminal's identity photograph. He shuddered at the prospect before him.

'Oh, Milman,' said the policeman, 'I didn't introduce myself. 'Detective Superintendent Simon Coldstream.'

Martyn froze. The only thing he could think of was Oscar Wilde's reaction when he heard that Edward Carson was to prosecute him. 'No doubt,' he said, paraphrasing, 'you will pursue your case with all the vigour of an old friend.'

Martyn

Martyn had been allowed to ring Harry Harmon from the station. To Harry fell the melancholy task of driving to Chewton Mendip in the early hours to break the news to Maude. He found Tony still asleep in the Rolls unaware of the events of the night. With Maude in the car and Tony at the wheel he had returned to the children's digs to tell them.

'How can we hush it up?' Maude despaired.

'Why don't you try telling Vi Redding?' asked Darcy, no fan of his father's publicist.

'Shut up!' said Maude, with rare asperity.

There was a family conference in Martyn's suite, now hoovered and tidied. The news was broken to Zelda, who, still unaware, had called on Martyn to question whether one of her costumes was quite right. Tony remembered the parents and shot off to Clifton to bring in Max and Amanda.

'That American bugger's at the bottom of it,' Max kept repeating, not recognising his *double entendre* as the Rolls purred down Whiteladies Road, round the Tramway Circle and up to the Grand. 'Never trusted that bastard.'

'Martyn's over forty, darling,' said Amanda levelly. 'He is not a child to be led astray.'

Chauncey's call had not reached Fleet Street in time for the west country editions. The rumours which ballooned as the company checked into the theatre were wilder than the reality. They encompassed murder, suicide and, worst of all to the junior members of the company, shutting down the show.

It fell to Harry to address the cast. He asked the stage crew, who had worked through the night, to take a break. He stood on the edge of the stage, a tiny harassed figure in a neat grey suit, wondering which piece of bad news to dole out first. He had made a list of headings at which he glanced nervously; but he found when he started to speak that they swam before his eyes. He abandoned the paper. He decided to explain first about the set, adding the good news that the missing pieces of machinery had been located in London and were being rushed to Bristol. Discounting other rumours and imagining the worst was over, those who knew no better cheered. Gravely silencing them, Harry went on to say that there had been a terrible incident at the hotel. It was, he emphasised, certainly a mistake, a misunderstanding; but at that moment Sir Martyn and Mr Armbruster were under arrest.

The youngest members of the company sat silent, uncomprehending. The Pensioners indulged in a variety of reactions, some wailing, one screamed, others sobbed. When he had re-established some order Harry called for calm and a break until lunch. He announced that at two o'clock they would reconvene at the Colston Hall for a first band call. He led the family out through the front of the house where cars were waiting and took them in a solemn caravan to the magistrates' court. There they would show solidarity when the two men were charged.

By now the news was everywhere and a pack of reporters and photographers began to descend on Bristol. Martyn and Louis, drawn and unshaven, were brought up before the magistrates, charged with acts of gross indecency and formally remanded for seven days. The magistrates' court, dark and solemn, smelling of dust and leather, was an incongruous setting for the handsome, well-dressed Milman clan. They sat, backs stiff, while the two accused pleaded not guilty, and Harry Harmon stood bail. There was no sign of their alleged partners in indecency.

The crowd outside the court had grown even larger by the time they emerged. Maude was on Martyn's arm; Louis followed with Imogen; Darcy and Lysander with their grandparents.

A short, fat woman in country tweeds spat at the window of the Rolls as Martyn and Maude drove off.

Martyn made his peace with Maude in the car. She suggested

that she move into the Grand. He warmly agreed. In his confused panic he was encouraged by Harry's news that the problems of the set might be overcome. He was amazed to find himself coldly in command as he outlined his plans to the family in the hotel suite.

'I have pleaded not guilty,' he told them, 'and I am not guilty.' He ignored the question of Louis's guilt. 'There is some possibility that this prosecution is motivated by spite. I intend to fight it on the evidence. It will not make it easier that we are setting out on a great theatrical enterprise. However, I do not intend to let that enterprise suffer. We are already behind with the show. Badly behind. I want you as far as you possibly can to put this business from your minds. This is my cross. Do not speak to the press. Say as little as you can to the police if they wish to question you. Above all keep your heads up with the company. The birth of a musical is always an anxious time. No one knows that better than my family. Let us lead by example.'

Maude embraced him and Max, who had been silent, shook him by the hand.

'Well said, my boy,' he muttered, placing his other hand on Martyn's shoulder. 'Don't know what it's all about, but we're with you.'

From his vantage point across the corridor Chauncey Martin watched as another tray of sandwiches was delivered to the door.

At the Colston Hall the company assembled promptly at two o'clock. The orchestra, under the musical director Carl Shelton, had set their instruments up on the concert platform. The cast, who would not normally be admitted to the first band call, slouched in the stalls. With the theatre not ready and the future of the show in such jeopardy they clung together, whispering about the disastrous events of the last twelve hours. When Martyn led the phalanx of Milmans into the hall there was a loud spatter of applause. Standing erect at the conductor's podium, he reassured them that the events of the night must be put aside. He urged them to think only of the play and gave Shelton instructions to strike up the orchestra.

No moment in musical theatre is as exciting as the first band call. Not even a first night. Musicals are about music and the first revelation of a score filled in by ravishing orchestrations, after weeks during which its themes have been thumped out and endlessly repeated by a vigorous piano player, is an unforgettable experience. Usually the first call with the orchestra alone is a fiddling business as tempi are corrected, wrong notes put right and copying errors discovered. Somehow, miraculously, little needed to be changed. Freda August passed round the parts to the members of the orchestra. Song followed song and the playing gained in inspiration as the score unfolded. The effect on the actors and singers was wonderful. Smiles spread over tense faces. Boys who had sat stiffly allowed their arms to cradle the girls who lounged next to them. Principals hummed quietly along. Hope crept back into the company.

Martyn took the opportunity to slip away to the Hippodrome with Harry to check on the set. Things looked better. Two key pieces of the intricate machinery had been located and rushed to Bristol. An exhausted Tom Tanqueray proudly demonstrated the ease with which his screens and panels moved in and out of position. Chairs and sofas slid across the vast stage. Aloft, the great staircase was in position ready to be lowered at the appropriate moment.

In the wings, ASMs stacked props on carefully labelled trestle tables. Two quick-change rooms were set up. Dressing-rooms were allocated.

'We've lost a day, maybe two,' calculated Martyn as he planned the new timetable with Harry and Caswell. 'If they focus tonight and we light tomorrow we should be able to stagger the tech on Wednesday. That's bound to take all day.'

'So we could have the dress on Thursday and open one day late on Friday,' said Harry.

'The harder we work them the more it will take their minds off . . . off other things,' said Martyn, almost to himself. 'If we could open on Thursday as planned it would do wonders for morale.'

'And we wouldn't be passing up a fully paid house,' Harry interjected. 'But how do we do that?'

'We'll run the dress at two in the afternoon and open at seven thirty.' Martyn decided. 'They'll be fired up by the dress. The adrenalin will flow. They'll give it their best shot. Let's go for it.'

On Thursday the dress rehearsal started half an hour late but the first act played smoothly to the hour and a quarter length expected. The actors conserved themselves, aware that their big test would come that same evening. They took a leisurely half-hour break before resuming. In the second act there were a couple of minor complications with the set but a halt was called and the problems were sorted out with cool deliberation. Just after five the curtain fell on the Milmans' duet of reconciliation – 'A New Life Is Beginning' – and Martyn summoned the company to arrange their calls. First the dancers raced down the stage in a line, bowing, curtseying and retreating gracefully to part for the next group. They were the singers who played butlers, footmen and maidservants. They too stepped aside to admit the Pensioners who bowed and curtseyed to one another in pairs. Adrian Arbuthnot was delighted to find that he had been given a solo call. Then came the three young Milmans: Darcy and Lysander handing forward a radiant Imogen as they swept down. At a somewhat slower tempo Max and Amanda made a royal progress, taking their time and nodding to the company as they advanced. Max held Amanda's hand for her deep curtsey as he made his low bow to the stalls. Maude took a solo call, followed by Zelda who just had time to don another extravagant gown in the quick-change room in the wings.

Martyn had offered Zelda the final call but she flatly refused. It was his show and she was astute enough to know that there would be no more dramatic final entrance than that of the author, director, composer, star . . . and accused.

As Martyn came on stage, she led the company in their applause, kissed him affectionately on the cheek and then released him to Maude, who did the same. Zelda and a line of Milmans filled the forestage and, taking their lead from Martyn, applauded conductor and orchestra and then bowed and curtseyed out front as Caswell gave the signal for the curtain to fall.

Martyn turned to address the company. 'I'm not going to say much,' he said. 'I'm proud of you all. It hasn't been easy but you've kept your heads in extremely difficult circumstances. You are all giving the performances I dared to hope you might. If I may make one personal point, it has been my great joy today to see my mother and father reunited on stage doing their best. I hope we can team them together many more times in the years ahead.'

In Society!

At the Hippodrome the police held back the crowd, which was experiencing the rare excitement of a West End first night in the west country. It was a bright spring evening and all Bristol and a generous number of Londoners made their way to the theatre. Kurt Kornfeld and Mae Madely had shared a compartment in the train and paid their calls backstage together. Mae collected her ticket from Lysander and Hanna embraced Kurt. But not everyone who made the journey wished the project well. What might have been a discreet out-of-town opening attended by one or two theatre enthusiasts had now attracted gossip columnists, photographers and rival managers anxious to see if Harry Harmon had fallen on his face.

A long line of those waiting to claim their tickets snaked out of the doors and on to the pavements which ringed the Tramway Centre. A couple of journalists were quizzing the queue for their impressions. A photographer shot flashes whenever he saw a familiar face.

It was almost time to call the half. The concentrating fear of that first performance had reached the company and established a firm presence backstage. The cast reacted in different ways. Vocal exercises echoed around the dressing-rooms. Amanda, in hers, was holding her arms high above her head and wriggling her fingers. 'It helps to make my hands look white on stage,' she explained to Grace, who was dressing both her and Maude. 'I got it from Olga Nethersole.'

Max was fast asleep, having left instructions to be woken at the half.

Maude had called for several vases and with studied concentration was arranging flowers from the bouquets she had received.

Adela Skelton was shouting at her dresser who, having suffered for over thirty years, took it in her stride and said simply 'Yes'm' to every insult. She could not understand why Adela was working up so much nervous energy for such a small role.

The Milman children, too young and inexperienced to feel more than heady excitement, rushed in and out of each other's dressing-rooms, showing off costumes and reading out telegrams and letters of best wishes.

In Zelda's quarters Braden Jefferson sat with the star while she opened her vast pile of transatlantic cables, and gently massaged her shoulders and repeated little jokes which had become a game between them over the years they had worked together. 'How's Darcy?' asked Zelda, who knew what had passed between them.

'He's all right,' said Braden. 'He knows about older men. He warned me not to fall in love with him.' They both laughed.

Martyn took the most drastic diversionary action. He summoned his solicitor who had spent the last three days preparing his case. The lawyer revealed the reason why the two soldiers had not been charged. In long interrogations, first with the military police and then with Superintendent Coldstream, they had been questioned separately, and told that the other had squealed. Their kit had been searched and compromising letters written by a number of other men had been found. Both had been accused of gross indecency, and both had confessed. Then they had been told they would not be prosecuted for any of the offences – if they turned Queen's evidence against Martyn and Louis.

'But I didn't see the little bastards until the police banged on the door,' reasoned Martyn.

'That is not, I understand, what the prosecution will allege,' said Wells, a young lawyer who, alone among the high-powered theatrical solicitors, specialised in criminal law.

'You mean they're going for Sir Martyn and me on the same charges?' demanded Louis.

'It would appear so, Mr Armbruster. I cannot condone their action. They have gone to extreme lengths to force the confessions from these young men. They have, in the course of so doing,

287

uncovered evidence of the soldiers' offences with other male persons. Yet they are not pursuing these others. They prefer to offer the soldiers a free pardon if they help them to secure a conviction against the two of you. There is such a firmness of purpose, such a directness about this attack, that I suspect it is driven by policy or by malice or both. I have no idea why.'

'Oh, I have,' said Martyn. 'It's Coldstream. We were at school together. He holds me responsible for his expulsion.' He told them the story of the school play.

'Christ,' said Louis, 'who'd have thought you could get a fuck out of Shakespeare?'

'I've arranged for us to see counsel in the morning, Sir Martyn.' Wells politely ignored Louis's interjection. 'Khaki Roberts is available. He has just had a great success in a similar case and he has very kindly agreed to come down to Bristol overnight. Indeed, I have secured him a seat for your first performance. We're in the stalls.'

Martyn turned back to the dressing-room mirror where he continued to make up his face. 'Thank you, Wells. I realise this is not your usual line of business. I'm most grateful. Enjoy the show,' he said. 'I'll see you both afterwards.'

After Wells had left the room, Louis bent over Martyn's back so that both their faces were framed in the mirror. 'I'm sorry, Martyn,' he said, 'I really am.'

'Me too, Louis,' Martyn turned and looked up to place a forgiving kiss on the choreographer's cheek. 'I think this ends it,' he said. 'Thank you for the good times.'

'I guess so,' said Armbruster. '*Merde* for tonight – I must go and *merde* my dancers.'

Martyn rested his head in his hands, looked into the mirror and then, picking up a make-up stick, concentrated on Sir Robert Chiltern.

Backstage, the excitement was barely contained. The crew scurried about testing lighting, sound and the complicated machinery. In the front of house the usherettes were on parade. Any moment now the crowds would be admitted. Behind the heavy red curtains an electrician stood on a vast metal ladder replacing a gel.

Hanna led Kurt through the pass door into the stalls and confirmed the position of their seats. The empty house had changed its character. The temporary steps to the stage had gone. So had the vast lighting desk which for the last three days had straddled two rows of the stalls in the centre. The detritus of costume material, coffee cups, food wrappers and the tangle of wires and cables which made the aisles an obstacle course, had disappeared. As Hanna and Kurt approached the doors leading to the foyer, these were thrown open and the first group of ticket-holders, massed in readiness, besieged the programme-sellers and flooded the aisles.

Excited expectation always pervades a theatre at the first public performance of a musical. This audience, its anticipation gilded by the court case, was more keen than most to file to its place. It would probably be less demanding, less inclined to criticism. Simply by handing over tickets, taking seats and being there, it had had its money's worth.

Hanna and Kurt worked their way through the throng. They smiled at Harry Harmon who was greeting his London colleagues, and joined Mae Madely, who broke away quickly from an older man to whom she had been talking.

Chauncey walked off into the stalls. On his way he nodded briefly to a man who was shepherding his wife to a seat. Detective Superintendent Coldstream had changed his mind and was looking forward to the play.

'Who was that?' asked Hanna.

'Some journalist,' said Mae.

'Pigs,' said Kurt, loyally.

The house lights dimmed. Carl Shelton slipped on to his podium to a spatter of applause and raised his arms. The overture began, its medley of lyrical ballad themes and up-tempo numbers setting heads nodding and feet tapping. Hanna clutched Kurt's hand, prayed silently for the success of the play and wondered if it was too self-serving a request to be heard and granted. The house lights went out as the polite applause rippled. The great red curtains rose and parted, snagged back to reveal Tom Tanqueray's Rotten Row screens moving smoothly in counterpoint to Louis Armbruster's spirited choreography. The changing screens enabled the action to encompass turn of the century Mayfair as it moved in and out of the Row and the grand houses which looked down upon it, climaxing in the reception at the Chilterns' home for which the great staircase was lowered. Perhaps there was too much movement. Martyn's wittier lyrics did not stir the audience to laughter. Hanna grasped Kurt's hand tighter.

Solid applause greeted all the songs. The house drew on its sense of privilege. Martyn and Maude were well received. Zelda's entrance was rapturously acclaimed. A legend remained a legend and she acquitted herself well. The Milman children enjoyed themselves and the enjoyment communicated itself to the audience. Enough people had read of Max's raffish career to relish his appearance, and he and Amanda made the most of their lines and played up with an overdose of courtly behaviour to one another. Adrian Arbuthnot stopped the show with his silly-ass number which he had sensibly insisted on performing quite still.

The first act finished with a great crash in the percussion section. Martyn had ended it not on a song but on a dramatic turn of the plot as he swept from the drawing-room and Lady Chiltern threw herself sobbing on to a *chaise-longue*. The drums thundered out and, as he slammed the door, the great red curtains swept down and together.

Kurt and Hanna were out of their seats and up the aisles immediately. They divided by a pre-arranged plan. At every Milman first night they followed this course. Their own fortunes were so bound up with the Milmans that they mingled with the audience at the interval to gather as much information as they could about how the punters were reacting.

'Do you think he's guilty?'

'He doesn't look worried.'

'I call it cheek. Singing and dancing after that!'

'I wonder what his wife thinks about it?'

'And with the whole family down here!'

'What about his father and mother?'

'He looks a sweet old gentleman.'

'Apparently he was a bit of a goer – but it was girls with him, dear.'

When they met outside, Hanna was dismayed. 'All they want

to talk about is the court case,' she whispered. 'What did you hear, Kurt?'

'Just the same.'

Mae Madely joined them. She had registered the same buzz, but had her own comments to add. 'It's a bit busy,' she said. 'There's some good stuff there; but I'm not getting a lot of it. And it's ten minutes too long.'

'Isn't Amanda great?' said Billy Little.

'She's lovely,' Hanna agreed loyally. 'I didn't know she could sing so beautifully. But the audience isn't interested. They are all talking about Sir Martyn and this stupid case.'

The second act proceeded smoothly enough although once again it did not quite catch fire. Louis's energetic dances were not chiming with the elegance of Wilde's dialogue or the stately romantic ballads with which Martyn had supplied his singers.

As the curtain fell on the Chilterns' reunion and a flurry of dance, sympathetic applause burst from the stalls and was picked up by the rest of the house. In the pit Carl Shelton raised his baton. He held the downbeat for the affectionate tableau as the tabs rose again. Martyn embraced Maude and gently brushed a tear from her eye. The irony was not lost upon the audience.

Chauncey Martin made a note on his pad.

The calls began as rehearsed – eager chorus dancers and singers springing on with the wide smiles of youngsters who know they have cleared the first hurdle. The ovation swelled as the young Milmans ran gaily from the wings. Applause settled into an appreciative, emphatic hand clap as Amanda and Max made their less exuberant entrance. Maude was warmly received. Zelda swept on in the extravagant creation she had hastily donned in the quick-change room. Turning centre stage, first smiling up at the gallery then sweeping the circle with her violet eyes, she prepared to walk down. Suddenly a crack echoed through the theatre. She stood, immobile for a moment, an expression of horror across her face. As she began to crumple Max leapt to her side to support her.

'My leg . . .' she cried as he held her.

Martyn, watching in dismay at the side of the stage from which he was due to appear, rushed on.

The applause faded into confusion. Ignoring the cheers that had scrappily resumed on his entrance, he swept Zelda up in his arms and carried her across to the prompt corner.

'Bring it in!' he yelled to the stage manager. The chorus parted to let him through to the wings and to Zelda's dressing-room where he laid her on a couch. The great curtain swept down leaving the audience buzzing with excitement. They had come for a non-theatrical, theatrical excitement. They had got it.

Zelda fought to collect herself. 'My ankle, my leg,' she breathed. 'I heard it crack. I must have caught it in one of those damn tram lines. We rehearsed the show with them in mind, but I forgot about the calls. My fault, Martyn. I'm so sorry, my darling. This is all you need!'

The onslaught on the pass door nearly caused another fracture. Outside Zelda's dressing-room Brad stood guard allowing no one to enter until the doctor who had been in the audience announced himself without the traditional invitation. In the crush to get backstage a fight nearly ensued. Hanna, Kurt, Max and Billy Little were elbowed aside by an elderly gentleman clutching a note pad.

Chauncey Martin made a dash towards Zelda's dressing-room. Unfortunately for him, he was met by the one person in the company who recognised him.

Max's huge hand grasped his collar and turned him around on his feet. 'Where d'you think you're going, scum?' enquired the old actor. 'Don't tell me. You're goin' this way.' So saying, Max frog-marched him down the corridor, past the stage door Cerberus, Ronald, who was trying to make sense of families, friends and fans.

Seeing a convenient step, Max kicked Chauncey down it and pursued him, launching out with his vigorous old legs until the journalist panted round the corner with the breathless threat, 'I'll get you for this, Milman.'

Max hastened back to a scatter of uncomprehending applause from the stage door supplicants and, making for his dressing-room, collided with Hanna. 'Hey! Hey! Little lady, go a bit slower!'

'Oh, Mr Milman. It's so terrible! She's broken her leg. Miss

Zelda! She cannot play! We do not know for how long!' Hanna threw herself into Max's comforting embrace. He patted her head and rubbed her back paternally.

'I hear Martyn has engaged an excellent understudy,' he said gently, 'a very glamorous continental enchantress.'

Hanna made her way up to her dressing-room at the top of the theatre. It was bare, cold and empty. She looked round the darkened room which was only illuminated by the street lights opposite. A beam caught the red-covered script of *In Society!*. It was well thumbed. She switched on the unshaded light, took her overcoat off a peg and pulled it around her shoulders. Then she sat at her dressing-table and began to turn the pages. She mouthed her lines to herself, gaining a little confidence as she found that they were coming back to her. She was encouraged to find that she could pick up her cues. When she reached her songs, the melodies were lodged securely in her brain. Part of her began to want to go on the next night as Mrs Cheveley.

As she sat there remembering lines she had never spoken aloud and imagining moves she had never made, there was a sharp knocking on the door.

'Are you in there, Hanna?' Robert Caswell, the stage manager, entered and Hanna looked up from her script. 'You're going to be on tomorrow,' he said. 'I'd better take you through the moves.'

'The scenes I can do, I think,' said Hanna. 'The songs too I think I know; but those dances. Never have I done these dance steps.'

'Louis's assistant Wendy is downstairs. She's ready to run through them with you.'

'But it took Miss Fane four weeks to learn them.'

'Ah,' said the stage manager, 'that was because Louis was building them around her – inventing them. Half the time was the creative process. It's much easier now it's all been set.'

'Set for her,' Hanna pointed out doubtfully. 'MGM style. Me, I was never a dancer like that.'

'Let's give it a go,' the stage manager coaxed. 'Let's make a start.'

Hanna worked through the early hours impressing the small

293

crew with her acting and her singing but invariably ending in tears as she lost her way in the dance routines.

At four in the morning, exhausted, she trudged back to her digs wondering if Kurt would be asleep on the sofa. She opened the door and peered in, reluctant to switch on the light lest she awaken him. The dawn glow fell across the empty piece of furniture. Hanna shrugged, banished her disappointment with a smile, imagined him with Imogen and climbed wearily into bed.

Next morning the dancers and Hanna were called for eleven o'clock. Once again she began her battle with Louis's choreography. However, this time Wendy's apparently inexhaustible patience was replaced by Louis's short fuse. As Freda August thumped out the music Hanna tried again and again to master the intricate numbers. The four boys with whom she performed most of the routines gently guided and pushed her into position as best they could. Every now and again Louis would take the stage and demonstrate gracefully just how easy the challenge was. Each time he left Hanna more confused and nervous.

Finally he turned on her. 'Fat German cow!' he yelled. 'What the fuck made you think you could go on the stage? You're a klutz! A fucking hopeless klutz! Why did Hitler let you get away?' He turned to see Martyn, who had just hurried into the stalls after a breakfast meeting with his lawyers.

'Louis!' he said icily, 'come down here.' He stood at the foot of the temporary set of steps which gave access to the stage. 'For Christ sake, man, the poor woman's got to go on tonight.'

'She's ruining my routines.'

'She won't learn them any quicker if you shout at her.'

'She isn't thinking. I only shouted at her once. And I did it with humour . . .'

Martyn had had an uneasy morning with Wells, his solicitor, and Khaki Roberts, his famous counsel. Roberts was a stocky, bull-like figure. His purple jowls dangled over his collar. Half of Martyn's mind was imagining him as raw material for the next time he played a barrister, the other half attended to the advice he was offering.

'They appear to be determined to make an example of you, Sir Martyn,' said Roberts. 'From the police evidence it may be easier for them to get a conviction with Mr Armbruster – but your scalp is the one they want for publicity. I cannot but see this as a political trial. I shall fight it as vigorously as I can for you.'

'Can you speculate on the outcome?'

'I would rather not, Sir Martyn. We can only do our best. That I assure you I will do.'

'Thank you, Mr Roberts.'

'And may I congratulate you on last night? An excellent show. How is the poor young woman's ankle?'

'Broken I fear. In more than one place. No one can be sure when she will return to the cast. Or, indeed, if she will return.'

'Dear me, dear me,' said Roberts. 'When troubles come . . . I must return to London.' He started to pack his papers into his briefcase. 'We should get the noon train, I think, Mr Wells.'

'Easily, Mr Roberts.'

'Then I shall see you on Monday, Sir Martyn. I trust the understudy gives a good account of herself.'

'You'd better get Wendy to sort out her steps,' said Louis. 'I don't have the patience for the old cow.'

'If that's how you feel,' said Martyn. He watched as Louis strode moodily up the aisle and slammed out through the foyer into the street. Then he turned and retraced his steps to the stage. 'I hear you're doing wonders, Hanna,' he said. 'Word perfect and note perfect, my spies tell me. Now, Wendy, we've got to get these routines sorted out.'

'I'm so sorry, Martyn . . .' Hanna began to apologise.

Martyn cut her short. 'We've got another audience in tonight. We've got to give a show. It won't be quite the same show as last night. I'm cutting your "Scandal" number with the boys. Wendy, I want you to take Hanna through her other songs and where something isn't working for her – simplify, simplify!'

'But Louis said . . .'

'Louis has other things on his mind. So have I . . .' he added.

Gowned in Zelda's sumptuous costumes, given height by the great hats which topped them off, and delivering her lines with the hint of an accent which immediately made her more sophisticated and more cosmopolitan than Zelda, Hanna was astonished at the warmth of the reception when Martyn led her forward at the end of the evening for a special call.

'Of course,' Kurt heard the woman sitting next to him say to her escort, 'of course, I never saw that Zelda Fane; but I can't believe she was any better than this woman . . .'

'If as good,' the man agreed.

In her dressing-room – she was no longer exiled to the top of the theatre – surrounded by flowers, including a massive basket from Zelda, Hanna happily held court. She was thrilled to see Kurt and Imogen together, both flushed with pride. Martyn and Maude, changed and ready to return to the hotel, added their congratulations.

'Should I now rehearse the dance with Wendy?' Hanna asked.

'I think not yet,' said Martyn. 'You did so well tonight. You gave me some ideas about the show. Just let it settle over the weekend. We'll talk about it on Monday.'

Martyn

Monday dawned cold and wet. The magistrates, local men who, to Martyn, seemed distinctly pleased by the size of the role they were playing in a case which placed them so firmly in the lime-light, puffed out their chests and assumed grave expressions. A court official, impressed in a different way, slyly slipped Martyn a document to autograph. The charge of committing indecent acts and conspiring together to commit them was read out. The two defendants reserved their defence for the higher court; but Khaki Roberts rose to suggest that the magistrates should exercise their right to hold the hearing *in camera*. Such, he suggested, was the interest in the case and so distinguished one of the accused, that the proceedings were bound to be reported in detail in the papers. This would almost certainly prejudice anyone picked as a juror at a subsequent trial.

Dismay flashed across the faces of the magistrates as they saw the depressing prospect of exercising their jurisdiction anony-mously. It took the worthies less than five minutes to announce that, as they sat as the representatives of justice, the interests of justice would be far better served if every allegation made by the crown, whether subsequently disproved or not, was trumpeted over the front page of all the papers in the land the next day.

Mr Blytheley-Chaplin QC, prosecution counsel, rose impress-ively, clasping his hands behind his back, projecting his gown into a loose hanging bustle as he began to describe the vile liaison between the two army witnesses and the accused. As he warmed to his task he withdrew his hands and gesticulated firmly, his voice urgent and fruity, throbbing with disgust as he expanded on his theme. Such was the depth of revulsion which he managed to work up, that occasionally he felt the need to pause dramatically in his oration and help himself carefully to a teaspoon of a vivid cochineal-coloured cough mixture, a bottle of which stood among the documents cluttering his desk. He made much of the celebrity of the accused and much of the obscurity of the witnesses he was about to call. He appeared reluctant even to name them lest their names soiled his lips. Eventually he spat out the words Bishop and McNab – dismissing both as 'men of the lowest possible character' and then painting a bacchanalian picture of the den of luxury into which they had been lured. Champagne and spirits, exotic sandwiches and sweetmeats, a bizarre word which he particularly relished and repeated, these were the bait which had procured them. Indecency was the object of the invitation.

Martyn, sitting in the dock and looking straight ahead, recalled his sleeping draught, the heavy slumber from which he had been awakened and the awful sight of the semi-naked trio. He could see their forms sprawled on the floor of the sitting-room of the suite as he confronted Simon Coldstream entering from the hall. He could not even remember Bishop's and McNab's faces, so quickly had they been hustled away. Now he studied them clinically as they gave evidence. Bishop was first up. His answers came out in a dull, clockwork recitation. He claimed obscene behaviour by both the accused and, when asked if the 'lavish entertainment' was the only thing which had tempted him, replied that he 'thought the older bloke might come across with a few quid'. Mr Blytheley-Chaplin prised out of McNab the information that Louis Armbruster had led them to believe that this was the case. Thus he involved Martyn in the conspiracy of which he was innocent.

Faced by the inevitability of a committal for trial, Roberts held his fire for the higher court.

The Bristol run was sold out. The production moved to Birmingham on the next stage of its progress towards London. The trial of Martyn and Louis was fixed for a date just before the West End opening. The show was to close for a week. Would it re-open with the leading man found innocent or would he have to be replaced, detained at Her Majesty's pleasure?

'I shall hope to give Her Majesty a great deal more pleasure, by appearing before her on stage,' Martyn said wryly to Harmon. 'But you'd better put out some feelers for a replacement.'

'And for Hanna?' Harry asked.

'It's a difficult one.' Martyn pondered the question. 'She's witty. She gets away with glamour in Cedric's clothes. And she finds a pathos in Mrs Cheveley which I'm sure Wilde never intended. But she can't dance. If I'm spared to open, I'd rather keep her. She might get "star overnight" rubbish in the press. On the other hand, if we have to change the leading man, it might be better to make a clean sweep.'

'I don't know how you keep going.'

'Bloody-mindedness! Forcing myself to think about the show takes my mind off the wretched case. When I do think about it I get so annoyed with myself and furious with Louis. You know the old cliché about "Doctor Theatre"? You go on stage dying and the adrenalin banishes death from your mind and, for the moment, from your body? Well, it's almost "Judge Theatre" in my case. I believe in the show and I'm damned if I'm going to let Coldstream ruin it.'

'Birmingham seems to approve of you, anyway. There was a line round the box office this morning. *Post* and *Mail* were fine.'

'Yes,' said Martyn, 'but the *Post* sensed something that's been worrying me. The rhythm of the show isn't right. We haven't bound that explosive choreography into the play. A musical must create its own world in which the artifices of song and dance become an accepted part of that world. We have just established an elegant, sedate, comfortable society and then suddenly a quite different one rushes on stage and blows a bloody great hole in it. I don't know what to do yet.'

'You can't pep up the English half,' said Harry gloomily. 'When are you going to tell Armbruster to pull back on his?'

'God knows,' Martyn paced the floor of his suite, 'he's so touchy these days. I can understand it. I wouldn't care to be faced with a jail sentence anywhere, let alone in a foreign country.' For a moment he remembered how near he had come to it in California. 'He's drinking too much. He's on a short fuse. It's kid gloves.'

'What did he think of last night? He missed the last few shows in Bristol.'

'I didn't see him. Come to think of it, he hasn't been around the theatre since we got here. Wendy handled the afternoon rehearsal when we moved in.'

'You don't think he's done a runner, do you?'

Martyn looked shocked. It was a new thought. 'Jumped bail? God no! Surely not.'

He ran to a desk and dialled Louis's number in Hollywood Road.

He let it ring for some time without an answer. Together they checked with the theatre, Louis's assistant, Billy Little and the company manager. No one knew where Louis Armbruster was.

Martyn rang Wells, his solicitor, and caught a note of surprised alarm in his voice.

'What will it do to the case if he has bolted?'

'Too early to say, Sir Martyn. I'll speak to Mr Roberts.'

'Does it count as an admission of guilt?'

'I'll speak to Mr Roberts.'

Martyn put the phone down. 'You stood bail for him, Harry,' he said apologetically.

The days went by and Louis failed to put in an appearance. Martyn and Wendy went to work on the dance sequences until they fitted seamlessly into place with the rest of the show.

Martyn's reserves of strength and clarity of purpose kept the company together. Maude turned her dressing-room into a haven for the younger members of the cast, acting as mother confessor and agony aunt. Max was on his best behaviour.

'A lot of laughter coming from your dressing-room tonight,' said Adrian Arbuthnot to Darcy one evening as they made their way to the Olympia, a restaurant in Dale End which the company had adopted.

'Ah yes,' said Darcy. 'That was the sound of Milmans closing ranks.'

A procession of senior actors was coaxed and conveyed to Birmingham and Manchester. Noel Coward, Michael Redgrave and Rex Harrison arrived, saw the show, made polite noises and left. They could hardly agree to take the role since it could not yet be offered: but Harry and Martyn were determined that what might be on offer should be inspected. Simultaneously, a selection of leading ladies was cosseted and cajoled into looking at the part Hanna was playing with such joy. Elisabeth Welch, Mary Ellis, Evelyn Laye and Pat Kirkwood were put up overnight at the Midland Hotel, given a chance to admire Cedric's dazzling wardrobe and to speculate on how much better they would look in his clothes. Martyn received them warmly in his dressing-room and entertained them over dinner with Maude and his parents. Max treated them all as *ingénues*, to their mature delight.

One night in Manchester, Max bought Hanna a drink in the stage door pub after the show.

'Thank you, Mr Milman, you are so kind,' she said.

'Not so much of the Mr Milman.' Max frowned. 'We're colleagues now. And y'know,' he added, 'you're doin' damn well as Mrs Cheveley. I hope young Martyn's been telling you so often enough.'

'Martyn is very kind. But I can't help to know that all these glamorous English ladies are coming up to cast their eyes on my part. If this awful case goes wrong I will have to go.'

'They won't have your continental sparkle.'

Hanna was reluctant to be cheered up. 'It is very critical for my son Kurt and his education that I keep this job.'

'Is he the lad who's romancin' my granddaughter?'

'They are very fond of each other.'

'He spends a fair bit on her. Where's that coming from? You?'

'We had a lucky windfall.' Hanna was evasive. 'But it is harder for young people to realise how quickly the money goes and how hard it is to replace it. It is I who must look ahead.'

'You know Zelda's definitely out?' Max asked.

'Maude told me.'

'Leg's playing up still and they've offered some sort of wheelchair role in a movie back home. Martyn told her to cut and run, so to speak. She wouldn't have been able to do the routines that bastard Armbruster devised for her and it wouldn't be her if she wasn't leaping around the stage, would it?' Max sighed. 'Pity really. Nice girl. None of the Hollywood Madam, was there?'

'She was very good to me. Not what you call an old cow at all.'

Max laughed. 'No, she ain't an old cow, Hanna, not by any means. If I'd been twenty years younger I might have fancied my chances.'

'You think you would have been successful?'

'Not really.' Max scratched his head. 'She's still with some girlfriend. God, the world's changed since I left England! There were rumours that old Tree was a bit ambidextrous but in those days that sort of thing was for chorus boys and supers, walking gentlemen, rag-tag and bob-tail.'

Hanna considered for a moment before replying. 'The only thing that hasn't changed', she said, after her pensive pause, 'is the law.'

'Too bloody right.' Max slapped his knee. 'And we've got to see it don't knacker the boy. I didn't come thousands of miles to see my son clapped in irons. We must fight.'

Martyn

The Manchester run came to an end conveniently before Martyn was due to return to Bristol for his ordeal. Louis was still missing, but the director of public prosecution was determined to proceed and make an example of the bigger fish.

The Milmans made a sombre, united return to the west country. As the trial began Martyn saw his family ranged loyally in the front seat. To his left, six more benches accommodated the public, and beside them stood the witness box. Just behind Martyn and slightly to his right sat a warder who doodled a set of abstract scrawls on a small sketch-pad. Below him sat leading counsel, Blytheley-Chaplin for the prosecution, and Khaki Roberts, backed by their juniors and various solicitors. All that Martyn could see was their gowns, their grey and white wigs, and rolls of papers secured with pink tape. Facing him across the court was the judge's dais topped by an elaborate throne-like chair, and two less impressive seats for the chaplain and the sheriff. As his eyes travelled to his right he considered the benches for the jury. Khaki Roberts's hope had been to avoid an all-male jury. His experience suggested that women jurors were likely to be more fair-minded and sympathetic in a case of this nature. They might also be more susceptible to Martyn's matinée idol charm. However, on the long list of people called for duty that day, not a single woman appeared. Plainly the officers of the crown shared Roberts's view.

The twelve men who finally constituted the jury did not look to Martyn to be particularly good or particularly true. He wondered if they appreciated how his life depended on their decision. One seemed permanently on the edge of sleep. Another was to feature a succession of eye-catching bow-ties. For the most part they looked like respectable Bristol citizens, shopkeepers, a labourer or two, perhaps a couple of professional men.

When the charges had been read out by the clerk of the court, and Martyn had pleaded not guilty, Mr Blytheley-Chaplin took a swig of the cough mixture which still accompanied him, thrust his thumbs into his lapels, and embarked on his opening address.

'Bishop and McNab,' he thundered, 'are put forward as perverts. Men of the lowest possible character. A slight on the noble service they have dishonoured. They are men who were corrupted, who apparently cheerfully accepted corruption, long before they met the defendant or his absconding co-defendant. We do not claim the defendant was a party to the initial corruption. Let us be clear. Let us be fair.' Martyn winced. 'These are witnesses whom we, in law, know as accomplices. They were willing parties to a series of unnatural acts – though, of course, these acts were committed under the seductive influence of the lavish hospitality proffered by the defendant and Armbruster. Both men, certainly the accused, a knight of the realm and a highly successful actor,' Martyn noticed that his inflection managed to make his profession sound like an accusation of guilt, 'both men infinitely their social superiors.'

Blytheley-Chaplin recounted with relish the incidents of the evening, painted a lurid picture of the inside of the Two Cabots – 'a sink of iniquity, a close harbour of vice, a breeding ground for perversion, a culling field for gross indecency' – and suggested that Martyn had despatched 'Armbruster there upon a fishing expedition, trawling for degraded souls to share in their debauched revels'.

Martyn scanned the faces of the jurors, trying to assess their reaction to the melodramatic recital. They were blank. The apparently-sleeping member kept his eyes closed throughout the tirade.

Blytheley-Chaplin then went on to describe the scene in the suite at the Grand. He placed Martyn firmly in the hotel sitting-room: 'discovered, aghast as well he might be, naked but for a silken dressing-gown, loose and ungirdled, he was caught red-handed amidst this orgy of depravity'. He then dealt momentarily with Armbruster's absence, hinting that his fleeing the country was tantamount to a confession of guilt. 'But what does it matter,' he implored the jury, 'if the organ-grinder's monkey has fled when we have the organ-grinder himself here to face his own music?'

Max turned to Amanda and whispered that he hadn't heard language like that since he toured *The Christian* in the nineties. Amanda laid a gentle hand on his to hush him, and was surprised and pleased when he grasped hers in return and held it.

Bishop was brought up first. In the magistrates' court he had been hesitant and confused. Now, in his whining voice, he made a series of glib responses, phrases from some police handbook, reiterating that 'he had been interfered with' and that they had 'all committed indecent acts together'. As Blytheley-Chaplin concluded his examination-in-chief, Martyn looked straight into Bishop's eyes hoping to catch some flicker of uncertainty, some small suggestion of doubt. He saw nothing but two dead, brown spots.

Khaki Roberts rose, clasped his hands behind his back, and looked at Bishop as though he was something he had found sticking to his boot.

'Would you turn and look at the man in the dock?' he asked. 'Is that man Sir Martyn Milman?'

'Yes, sir.'

'On that night in Sir Martyn's suite at the Grand Hotel, you were introduced into the room by Mr Louis Armbruster. Is that correct?'

'Yes, sir.'

'Were you introduced to Sir Martyn by Mr Armbruster?'

'Not so much introduced, sir. More pushed into it.'

'Pushed into it.' Roberts considered the phrase. 'Pushed into what?'

'An indecent act, sir.'

'You may or may not have been pushed into an indecent act with Mr Armbruster, but I put it to you that Sir Martyn never laid a finger on you and that he never saw you until he opened his bedroom door in answer to the commotion created by the loud knocking of the police.'

'I was definitely interfered with – by 'im.'

The eyes of the jury turned from the witness to the accused and back as though they were watching a tennis match. Max, glancing across at the press-box, flushed red with anger as he saw Chauncey Martin scribbling furiously at every lubricious detail.

Martyn realised that Bishop had been coached to tell the court what had happened between him and Louis, but to recount it as though it also described his conduct with Martyn. By a simple transference, Coldstream had enabled him to give detailed evidence in an account which did not vary or falter because it *had* happened – but not with the man in the dock. Martyn now knew that he was the victim of two witch-hunts. First there was the home secretary's crusade, calculated to allay American fears that people who could be blackmailed in high places were a security risk. Then there was Coldstream's personal vendetta.

Martyn's counsel had reckoned that Louis's absence would make it harder for the prosecution to ram home their charge of conspiracy. But his flight made Martyn more vulnerable than ever. Louis might have spoken for Martyn. Now, there was only Martyn's word against that of Bishop and McNab.

Reading the lurid newspaper reports, Hanna despaired. In her London flat there was no one to point out to her that so far only the prosecution case had been stated. She buttered her thin toast, sipped her strong, black tea, and gazed bleakly at her future.

McNab insisted that he, too, had been 'interfered with' by Martyn. He seemed petrified and frequently dabbed at his eyes; but even under Khaki Roberts's most searching cross-examination he refused to retract. Martyn gazed at McNab as he blurted out the resumé of lies. He wondered what powerful threats Coldstream could have manufactured to terrify him so.

When Coldstream himself was called to give evidence he sprang on to the stand as if he could not wait to testify. He stood straight and confident, smiling his most ingratiating smile at the judge and jury. He was evasive about how the police were summoned to the Grand. 'We were acting,' he preferred to say simply, 'on information received.' He lingered over the elaborate details of the scene on the floor of the suite when he entered it, relishing his account of the state of undress of the soldiers and Louis

Armbruster. He laid heavy emphasis on Martyn's tousled hair and open dressing-gown. 'Arising, I judged,' he said, 'from carnal frolics with the other three perverts.'

When Roberts rose to cross-examine him, he returned to the question of who had sounded the alarm. Coldstream reiterated that he was acting on information received.

'Received from whom?'

'I had a telephone call suggesting that acts of indecency were being committed.'

'Who telephoned you?'

'I hardly think the information is relevant, m'lud?' Blytheley-Chaplin intervened.

'Mr Roberts?'

'My Lord, it is my intention to show that this arrest came about as an arrangement between Detective Superintendent Coldstream and a journalist by the name of Chauncey Martin, determined to blacken my client's name. It is my contention that it became obvious that, whatever occurred between the soldiers and Mr Armbruster, Sir Martyn played no part in these proceedings. Mr Martin still required sensational copy for his Sunday newspaper and Superintendent Coldstream, who was settling an old score, was only too happy to feed him false information.'

Coldstream winced as Roberts turned to his schoolboy career at Clevedon, his expulsion and the glittering prizes denied him as a consequence. Martyn watched, fascinated, as his counsel took the witness back, again and again, to the incidents of the night of the arrest and to those so much longer ago after the last performance of *Richard III*. In an uncanny way he created the impression of a direct parallel between the two events. Martyn emerged as the victim in both cases, Coldstream the guilty party.

It was a subdued, white-faced Superintendent who left the dock.

On the fourth day of the trial Martyn took the stand. He faced the jury and tried, with some difficulty, to look twelve good men and true in the face, all at the same time. Roberts led him through an account of his previous life. He asked him for his version of the events on the evening of the arrest. He drew from him the

307

account of the crisis over the set, his anxiety about a postponed opening, his tiredness, and his decision not to go out with Louis, but to take a sleeping draught in order to be refreshed in the morning. He established a picture of a happy home life, indicating Maude and the children loyally in court, and also the presence of Martyn's reunited parents. Finally he asked Martyn directly if he was homosexual. They had talked exhaustively about this and had concluded that, in the current climate and state of the law, only one answer was possible. Martyn pronounced: 'No,' concentrating, as he said it, on the foreman of the jurors, the most solid of those solid citizens.

Mr Blytheley-Chaplin fidgeted with his ring as he rose to cross-examine, opened his mouth for his first question, changed his mind, and then took a swig at his cough mixture before launching into his attack.

'Sir Martyn,' he said in his quietest voice, 'can you suggest any reason why these two men, Bishop and McNab, should manufacture and repeat, as learned counsel has suggested, such vicious untruths about you?'

'I would have thought the reason was quite obvious,' Martyn replied levelly. 'They were required to do so by Superintendent Coldstream or the military police or both. They were saving their skins.'

'How, may I enquire, were they saving their skins by fabricating untruths about you?'

'I understand that both McNab and Bishop have been promised complete immunity from prosecution provided they give evidence against me. That constitutes a very complete salvation. Though not perhaps of their souls,' Martyn added unwisely and bit his lip in annoyance. He had not read about the trials of Oscar Wilde for nothing, and had promised himself that he would answer plainly and simply and leave point-making to his counsel.

'Ah, their souls, Sir Martyn, their immortal souls,' said Blytheley-Chaplin, wrapping his gown around him, determined to make the most of the opening. 'And *your* immortal soul, Sir Martyn, is it the soul of an invert, an invert or a pervert who seeks his sexual associates in a different walk of life to his own?'

'No,' said Martyn.

'No?' Prosecuting counsel savoured the denial. 'No – and yet you were sharing this lavish suite in the finest hotel in Bristol with a much younger, American ex-dancer,' Blytheley-Chaplin made each adjective sound more incriminating than the last, 'while your wife was exiled in a country inn?'

'It was my wife's decision to take advantage of the country air. Mr Armbruster and I were virtually co-directing my play. It was convenient for us to share the two-bedroomed suite.'

'It was convenient. And it was convenient for the younger man to roam the city searching for other perverts to gratify your lust? Very convenient?'

'I was not aware of their presence until the police arrived.'

'Even more convenient . . .'

Martyn was in the witness box for almost five hours.

'My learned friend, Mr Roberts, has suggested that you have some complaint against the conduct of the police, Sir Martyn?'

'I believe that I have reason.' Martyn saw a spasm of displeasure cross the face of the judge.

'Do you realise that the police have their duty to perform whether they are arresting Sir Martyn Milman or the Artful Dodger?' pressed Blytheley-Chaplin. 'You realise that, do you not?'

'I do.'

'And there must be no distinction whatsoever?'

'I would hope not.'

'Why should you suppose, how can you conjecture that this young soldier would invent such a wicked accusation against you?'

'I think the most likely explanation lies in words I heard spoken by Bishop before the examining magistrates.'

'Yes?'

'He said he was so terrified that he was ready to say "yes" to anything that was put to him: that he had abandoned hope and he did not know how much to say to please them.'

'Who frightened him?'

Martyn allowed himself a wintry smile. 'I wasn't there,' he said.

Bishop Blakiston was a surprise character witness for Martyn. The old cleric, grey now, wrapped round with distinction, the embodiment of muscular Christianity, was an impressive figure. He talked enthusiastically of Martyn's school career, of his distinction in the theatre and various charitable acts he had performed more recently in Blakiston's diocese of Gloucester.

Roberts then asked him about his other pupil, Simon Coldstream. As soon as the Bishop had explained that he had found it necessary to expel Coldstream from Clevedon, Blytheley-Chaplin leapt to his feet to protest. 'M'lud, it is not Superintendent Coldstream who is on trial.'

'Quite, quite,' said the judge, testily upholding the objection and turning sternly to rebuke Roberts, who obediently closed his case. Prosecuting counsel prudently decided against cross-examining the bishop. The judge adjourned the court for counsels' closing speeches on the following day.

The anxious Milmans dined together at the Grand.

'If it's between you and those swine, boy,' grunted Max, 'I know who I'd believe.'

'It's not as simple as that,' Martyn protested. 'You all know I adore Maude . . .' His wife nodded. 'But you all know that our lives together are not as simple as that. I have had to deny emphatically something which is a part of me. I have had to lie and to keep lying about a facet of my character because it is a felony. I am not ashamed of that aspect of myself and I think you have all grown to know it and accept it. In spite of all this, I have repeated this lie over some five hours of cross-examination. If there are jurors who know something, who have heard gossip, listened to rumours and know that I am lying in this respect, why should they believe me over the other accusations?'

When Blytheley-Chaplin began his closing speech the next morning he asserted that the police had only been doing their duty, and doing it particularly well. They had acted promptly on information received. Information supplied by a public-spirited citizen who had simply done *his* duty. In the press seats Chauncey smiled to himself. He would be applauded. 'My Part in Pervert's Downfall' was the headline he envisaged for the final glorious instalment of 'Wicked Men' that Sunday.

Blytheley-Chaplin went on to attack the defence – they had, he trumpeted, not only tried to smear a senior police officer who had an unblemished record, they had also thrown every stone, every calumny, every insult at two self-confessed perverts who were at last showing some signs of redemption. Unlike the accused, they had admitted their vices and sought to atone for them by making a clean breast of the vile practices of an evening when, 'seduced by sweetmeats' and 'sabotaged by expensive wines and strong liquors they had been tempted to become the play-things of the rich and famous – and they fell!'. Blytheley-Chaplin thundered out the words as if he was recalling the descent of Lucifer. Then, having reached his climax, he added a coda of sweet reasonableness.

'Members of the jury, if I have presented this case with too much ardour, too much horror, too much passion; in a word if I have *over*-presented it, I am sure that I can depend on you to stand as the guardians of justice, a bastion between the prosecution and the possibility of injustice. You will of course have the opportunity to listen to my learned friend's argument before you have the privilege of hearing his Lordship's summing up.' His thumbs came to rest in his lapels as, a picture of righteous self-satisfaction, he surveyed the jury. 'I can only submit,' he added, 'that, low and sordid as was the story these two unfortunate men had to tell, we have seen it thoroughly proved. There is only one explanation of the facts. It is the true one. And it is the one I have given you. The only crime these soldiers have committed, earning them the contumely of my learned friend, is that they have told the truth. Would that I could say the same for the defendant, Sir Martyn Milman.'

At lunchtime in the bar of an hotel on College Green the press were taking bets on the outcome of the case.

'I wouldn't underestimate Khaki,' offered a grizzled hack from the *Telegraph*, 'he can pack a punch.'

'Ruin it for you, Chauncey,' said another, 'if he doesn't go down, that is.'

'I get it either way,' Chauncey boasted. 'If he squirms off the main charge, I've got an inside on his father that's going to make 'im sit up.' His colleagues looked up, interested. 'Nuff said.' Chauncey tapped his nose with a finger.

Scotch eggs consumed and glasses drained, the parade of rain-coats returned to the court room.

Khaki Roberts pitched his case for Martyn in as low a key as he could find. 'This,' he told the jury, 'has been described as a sordid tale. Of course it is a sordid tale. Let us not mince words. It is an ugly story. If it were not for the eminence, the fame, the distinction of my client the public benches would stand empty, the press-box would hold, perhaps, one apprentice reporter. Today I see the self-styled stars of Fleet Street determined to witness the destruction of a genuine star of the theatre.

'Grave charges have been made against a unique, indeed, an enobled artist. An actor, a composer, a playwright. I suppose we ought not to be surprised that the public should queue up outside the court room in inclement conditions to be present at the declaration of his innocence of these charges – the declaration, gentlemen, that is in your hands. It is your fair-mindedness that we are hoping to feel. It may be that the gentlemen of the press would relish a denial of his innocence. That would perhaps offer them better copy. More column inches. But you are here, his Lordship is here, we are all here, to see justice done, not to accommodate the press.

'The question put to you was, "Who is telling the truth?" My friend Mr Blytheley-Chaplin has made much of the feast laid out for these sad soldiers. He has only produced their tarnished evidence that Sir Martyn was present as host, participant and promoter of such bacchanals.'

Roberts slowly and painstakingly went through every shred of evidence. 'There is no contention,' he reiterated, 'that Mr Armbruster, who has fled the country, was not involved with the sordid specimens which the prosecution has paraded before you. But Sir Martyn? Preparing for one of the great challenges of his life? Do you believe? *Can* you believe that he would risk all – on such a night – for a moment of sexual gratification with such undesirable rubbish?'

Martyn looked down from the dock at his counsel. He saw Roberts's wig bobbing up and down, its off-white horsehair looking absurdly like a cauliflower. He felt an actor's instinct to respond to the moment of high drama. He knew that he must suppress it.

Roberts, like Blytheley-Chaplin, subdued his peroration. Very quietly, he said to the jury: 'This man is in your hands. If you convict him it is on the evidence of two men who have been unable to remember a single word he has spoken. Do not be moved by sympathy. Do not be moved by pity for this great man. Do not be swayed by anything but his transparent innocence of the charges brought against him. Respond only to his honesty.'

Chauncey was surprised to see Mae Madely nursing a glass of lager in a corner of the bar of the hotel on College Green. He made his way across to her. 'Down for the verdict, darling?' he asked as he settled beside her.

'I'm down to support Lysander,' Mae replied.

'Where's Master Milman tonight, then?'

'The family are all together. I thought I'd find you here.' Mae shifted uneasily. 'I want you to drop all that business about Max being my grandfather.'

'Ho! Ho!' Chauncey chortled. 'After what the Digest has invested in you?' His attempt to sound genial failed. 'I don't think my editor would see the sense in that, Miss.'

'The Milmans have enough on their plate. I don't want to make things worse for them.'

'Fallen for young Lysander, have we? Reckon he'll look after you, do ye?' he sneered. 'I wonder what he'll say when he gets to know how you wormed your way into his life? When he hears who paid your fare from Australia and who put you up in that bedsit in Earl's Court? What's he going to think, eh?'

'Please don't print the story, Mr Martin,' Mae pleaded. 'I feel so bad about it.'

'A bit late for regrets, my dear.' Chauncey took out a pad and made a note on it. 'You should have thought of that before. It's all tied up now. My men in Melbourne have confirmed it. There's no doubt Max Milman had a fling with your grandma. They tracked down a barmaid who worked with your gran. The poor old bitch is in a home now; but she remembers it all like yesterday. It was quite a scandal. The dates definitely fit.'

'I shall deny it.'

Chauncey laughed and with his crippled arm raised his whisky glass to his lips. His rheumy eyes gazed at her over the rim. 'Sorry, darling; but I've got your letters. I've got the bills and the receipts. I've got the affidavit from Melbourne. You're going to look a very silly little adventuress.' He watched as Mae sniffled into her handkerchief. 'It's not the end of the world, girlie,' he said. 'Martyn and your mother were only half-brother and half-sister. That only makes you and Lysander almost cousins. Can't say I know the proper name for the relationship – all that twice removed rubbish, I dare say. It won't prevent you tying the knot.' He could not resist adding: 'That's if he still wants to.'

Mr Justice Ormskirk peered over his glasses and leaned forward to address the jury in so low a voice and speaking so rapidly that Max could hardly hear what he was saying. 'Wouldn't carry over the orchestra pit in a theatre,' he hissed at Amanda.

The judge was warning the jury that they might find it difficult to trust the evidence of the soldiers who had shown themselves to be spineless low-lifes. 'However,' he said, 'it would be extremely difficult in a case of this kind to launch a prosecution if it were not possible to produce this sort of witness – however despicable.' He restated the case for the prosecution, putting it, Martyn thought, rather better than Mr Blytheley-Chaplin. He went on to consider the role of the police. 'You will remember,' he said, 'that the police had a very delicate job to do. They had been apprised that acts of indecency were being performed in an exclusive luxury hotel. The temporary domicile of many respectable people. It is a tribute to the speed with which they acted, and the discretion with which they carried out their actions, that the other guests in residence were not disturbed and that the malefactors were arrested. It is for you to decide who those malefactors were. Bishop and McNab have admitted their guilt. The absconding of the defendant Armbruster may or may not be an admission of his guilt. Certainly the arresting officers surprised him *in flagrante*.

Sir Martyn Milman was also in the room. He denies that he was a party to the acts of the others. He asserts that he neither participated as a principal nor as a spectator. That is the substance of his case. To him it came as a complete surprise. You, gentlemen, have to decide if that is the truth.'

It took Mr Justice Ormskirk until the lunch adjournment to analyse the defence case, always, Martyn thought, to the credit of the prosecution. He reinforced their horror at the scene on the sitting-room floor and he took the opportunity to rubbish the suggestion that Coldstream had been harbouring a schoolboy grudge for some thirty years. 'Fanciful,' he called the notion.

At thirty-five minutes past twelve the jury retired to consider their verdict.

Wells, the solicitor, came to the cells to sit with Martyn. He was not optimistic. Trying to lighten the gloom, Martyn pointed to graffiti scrawled on the wall: 'Mister Justice Ormskirk is a constipated old bastard. He can't count. All he can say is Five, Seven, Nine years.'

'What is he going to say today?' asked Martyn.

'I don't know, Sir Martyn. But he didn't give the jury much choice, did he?'

'Are there any grounds for appeal?'

'Not that I can see. Mr Roberts reckons there was no actual misdirection in law.'

They lunched on sandwiches in the cell. Afterwards, Martyn sought out one of the warders who had previously brewed him a cup of tea. He found him pouring another. Martyn took it and sat beside him on the bench. 'My solicitor thinks I've had it,' he said.

'Oh, don't say that. You never know with juries.'

Martyn noticed that the man had stopped calling him 'sir'. It struck a new note of fear in him. He wondered if their positions would be reversed and he would be calling the warders 'sir' after the verdict had been announced. He knew that he could be sentenced for up to fifteen years.

At half past three the jury returned. Martyn was hustled up the stairs and into the dock for the last time. He looked at his family and was touched to see that they were looking steadfastly at him. He turned to watch the jury as the clerk of the court asked the foreman for the verdict. The court seemed unnaturally hushed. Then the two words he had hoped so much to hear were pronounced – twice.

'Not Guilty . . . Not Guilty.'

A cheer rang out from the public benches. A spasm of annoyance flashed across the judge's face as he called for order. He found great difficulty in saying that Martyn was free to go but finally he managed it. He could not bring himself to thank the jury.

Martyn, stepping from the dock, fell into Maude's arms.

In the press-box Chauncey Martin snapped his pencil into two pieces. The director of public prosecutions, Sir Theobald Mathew, furtively disappeared, disappointed.

As the family piled into the car, the crowd swelled around them and cheered. Maude started as she heard the uglier sound of booing. Martyn heard it too. 'Ignore it, darling,' he said as he settled her in her seat. 'It's just like a bad first night.'

'No, Dad,' Darcy interrupted, pointing to the back exit from the court. 'It's Bishop and McNab they're booing!' The two soldiers, white-faced and weeping, were being stuffed into the back of a police car. The angry crowd beat on the vehicle with rolled-up newspapers and umbrellas.

As the Milmans drove past, Martyn's abiding image of the ugly scene was Simon Coldstream's snarling face as he slapped the boot of the police car, yelled 'Get going!' to the driver, turned on his heel and re-entered the building.

Harry Harmon had not wasted his time during the week of the trial. Taking a chance on Martyn's acquittal, he installed Tanqueray's mechanised set with care and deliberation. Nothing was left to chance. The stage crew laboured through four days of building, checking and perfecting the smooth movement of the period furniture and the gliding *trompe l'œil* screens.

As soon as the news of the verdict was announced the call went out to the cast. There would be technical rehearsals through the weekend. The dress was scheduled for Monday. The opening would be as Martyn had originally planned, on Tuesday, 26 May, exactly a week before the coronation.

In the West End the bush telephone became red-hot. Adela Skelton rang everyone to complain that Martyn had still not written the little numberette for her. 'Poor boy,' she said. 'I suppose he has had rather a lot on his mind, but I know people are going to be disappointed. They will expect it. And it would certainly give the show a lift.'

Hanna, who had not gone down to Bristol, sat by her telephone and trembled when at last it rang. She was summoned to St Leonard's Terrace.

'Oh, my dear,' she said to Kurt, 'this must mean I am out, *kaputt*, finished. Back to the understudy.'

'Don't be silly, Mama. Nobody else knows the songs. They open on Tuesday.'

'Zelda, excuse me, Miss Fane. She knows them.'

'Mama, her leg is broken. She's going to do a movie in Hollywood sitting in a wheelchair. She's flying out after the opening. Relax.'

'You really think I shall play this role?'

'Of course you will. Haven't you seen the posters? It may not put you at the top like Zelda Fane, but Imo tells me that to be at the bottom but alone and in big letters, "*and* Hanna Paxmann!", is very nearly as good.

'I will take you to St Leonard's Terrace,' Kurt said firmly. 'Then you will see.'

Hanna smiled her most expansive smile. Then she threw back her head and laughed as she had not laughed for many years. 'Oh, Kurt,' she cried, when she collected herself, 'we have travelled so far and we are here still. And you want to escort me so that you can have an excuse to see Imogen. Very good. We will go.'

Grace had dusted every inch of the house, polished every wood, brass and silver surface, and filled the house in St Leonard's Terrace with flowers. She had no idea how many would be coming for supper but she was ready for an army. She stood in the dining-room and surveyed her immaculate table with pride. She strolled to the big window which looked across the cricket field. Glancing down to the roadway which stood between it and the tall house she wrinkled her nose in displeasure as she saw the small army of reporters awaiting the return of the family. An unexpected scatter of rain which whipped across them brought a smile to her face. Then she saw the Rolls advance in a stately progress along the Terrace and pull up in front of the house. Darcy leapt out first and helped his mother down. Lysander and Imogen followed them up the steps. Collecting herself, Grace raced to the door and flung it open. As she greeted Maude, she could see Martyn as the photographers and reporters converged upon him, clamouring for a statement.

'Of course,' he said, as they parted to let him through to his front door. He turned to them as he reached it and said simply: 'Gentlemen, we open on Tuesday at the New Olympic. Thank you.' He entered the house and quietly closed the door.

By the time Hanna and Kurt arrived, only a couple of reporters remained. Not rating the newcomers, they too disappeared. Max and Amanda, who had stopped off in Kinnerton Street so that she could change, were next. They were followed by Harry Harmon. Finally the small, dark, pale figure of Mae Madely crept up the steps and rang the bell. Tony opened the door. Imagining her to be a reporter, he was about to close it in her face when she said: 'I've come to see Lysander. He's expecting me.'

'Beg your pardon, Miss, what name?'

'Mae. Mae Madely.'

Lysander came running down the stairs to greet her.

'Is your grandfather here?' Mae asked.

'Yes. Everybody's here.' Smiling broadly, Lysander took her into the drawing-room and introduced her to the only two Milmans who had not met her in Bristol – Max and Amanda. 'This is Mae,' he said.

'I've met Mr Max Milman before,' said Mae, nervously. 'Back home. I don't expect you remember.'

Max looked at her closely. 'Can't say I do, young lady.' He laughed. 'You can't have been a fan. There weren't any left.'

The others, puzzled by the serious demeanour of the visitor, joined in the laughter.

'I've come to apologise, Mr Milman. I hope I've done it in time. We met in the library at Sydney. You were reading *An Ideal Husband*. You bought me lunch.'

'No,' said Max ruefully, 'you bought me lunch.' He turned to the others. 'This young woman thought I might be her grandfather. Wrong side of the blanket.'

'On the law of averages, it seems possible,' said Amanda drily.

'Goodbye Miss Mouse, hello Juliet Greco. By God, you've changed. How d'you get to know young Lysander here?'

'I'm afraid I've been very dishonest,' said Mae, turning to Lysander. 'I'm sorry – I was sure Mr Milman was my grandmother's lover in Melbourne. He said he wasn't. Then, when that awful Chauncey Martin man's story came out in Australia, I'm afraid I wrote to him.'

Maude looked aghast. Just when she thought they had cleared the last press hurdle, the threat of another Chauncey Martin exposure seemed to be hanging over them.

'He replied immediately,' continued Mae. 'He had detectives on the job. They ferreted out an old barmaid who knew Granny. She used to work at the Civil Service Club Hotel in Melbourne. Maisie Mary Hannigan was Gran's name. Gran's mother was Nancy Lola. Mr Milman told me he didn't know our family; but the detectives turned up a newspaper report. Great-grandma sued Mr Milman for not paying one pound ten and sixpence for drinks. She got five bob costs as well. And there was something about breaches of the peace in Collins Street, too.'

'When was all this, Max, you old sinner?' asked Amanda.

'Long before I met you, darling. When I was out there the first time. We were playing some dreadful American rubbish. *All is Lost*, I think it was called. That old bitch Romany French sacked me for it. Said I was a disgrace to the "emerging Australian theatre". Wouldn't let me play Romeo opposite her either. Gave it to young Tommie Kingston. Couldn't speak verse. Accent like a daft dingo. And he was a nancy. Oh,' Max paused, 'sorry, Martyn.' He returned to his story. 'Mind you, as Juliet she was old enough to be my mother. She'd have made a good Nurse if she hadn't been such a mean old cow.'

'But were you Miss Hannigan's lover?' Martyn broke in.

'Of course I was. Damn pretty girl. Lovely afternoons. I can still see that spot under the gums on the banks of the Yarra.' Max was beginning to grow sentimental.

'What happened, exactly?' Martyn insisted.

'I let her down, didn't I? The same day she told me she was pregnant Miss Romany Bloody French sacked me and packed me off on a train for Perth.' He turned to Mae. 'Never saw your gran again,' he said sadly.

'I was stupid,' Mae told the room. 'Now he hasn't got his grand climax to his awful "Wicked Men" series, Chauncey Martin's threatened to go to town on this story instead. You know the sort of stuff: "Seventy-Year-Old Sinner Refuses to Own Up to Granddaughter". It's not as sensational but he'll write it up for all it's worth.'

'I don't think it's such a bad story.' Max stroked his chin. 'The good thing about 1953 has been finding my family again. All that's happened today is that I've found a bit more of it. And this bit I didn't know about. Or wouldn't admit to.' He took Mae's hands in his and gently kissed her cheek. 'And I like what I see.'

Martyn was already on the telephone to Violet Redding. 'Get on to the *Mail*,' he said. 'Tanfield or some gossip column. We must get it in tomorrow to spike Chauncey Martin's guns. It'll be old news by the time he prints on Sunday. Don't be so down-beat, Vi,' he snapped. 'It's a romantic story. "Grand Old Man of Theatre Delighted to Discover Long-Lost Granddaughter" . . . No, no, no, Lysander and Mae are not yet engaged. They've only just met and they are both far too young.'

'Are you sure there aren't any more grandchildren lying about in Australia?' Amanda asked Max. 'If you are moving into Kinnerton Street' – Maude pricked up her ears – 'I'd like to know who their mother is when they come calling on you.'

'Amanda, old girl,' said Max sheepishly. 'I can't guarantee it. But I think I'm at an age when I can promise good behaviour from now on.'

'Not *too* good,' said Amanda. 'That would be so dull. And dull you never were!'

Finale

The opening night curtain at the New Olympic was at seven. The Strand was blocked from six and backstage the atmosphere was one of high expectancy. The dress rehearsal had gone smoothly the night before. As professionals the cast placed no faith in the old saw about a bad dress rehearsal heralding a good first performance. Telegraph boys and florists besieged the stage door. Martyn opened a telegram from Mexico. There was no salutation, no signature and no address. '*Merde*' it read. He consigned it to the wastepaper basket.

Amanda cherished one from Evadne Rivers. 'Available to take over next year – if let out – Love.' Amanda smiled and stuck it on her mirror.

Barricades were put up at the front of the theatre to give the celebrity crowd access. The photographers who had hoped to capture Martyn's disgrace a few days earlier were out in force to record his triumph. From the dressing-room windows passers-by could hear voices warming up. In the foyer Harry Harmon stood proudly shaking hands. Kurt escorted Mae who was radiant in a long dress borrowed from Imogen. Lysander had lent Kurt a dinner jacket. A cheer went up for Zelda as her car drew up under the brightly lit theatre awning. The chauffeur came rushing round to unfold her wheelchair. Braden Jefferson was on hand to help her into it and the fans' applause was redoubled as the tall, broad-shouldered figure of the Western star Keate Watershed emerged. 'I wasn't goin' to miss this one,' he had said to Martyn when he telephoned to announce his arrival.

From the moment the curtain rose, the audience enveloped *In Society!* in affection. No trace of Louis Armbruster's energetic, eye-catching routines remained to drive destructively through the witty, thoroughly English feel of the show. Immediately the audience, deeply committed though they were to the brash American shows which had been dominating the West End, realised they were listening to an authentic English voice again, and they liked what they heard. Wilde's wit and Martyn's humour chimed happily together. Martyn's duets with Maude were welcomed with heightened emotion as a result of the court case. The freshness of the children's performances came as a charming surprise to the critics. Adrian Arbuthnot duly stopped the show with his song. Amanda appeared to have lost her way for a moment in her duet with Max: but the old boy neatly turned the slip to their advantage and led her proudly into their encores. However, it was Hanna who was the revelation of the evening. Her slight accent, rigorously held in check, gave perfect expression to Martyn's sophisticated lyrics and Wilde's sharpest repartee. Cedric had completely refitted her wardrobe. Encased in the *fin-de-siècle* fashions, her head held high, her bustle twitching magisterially when she was angry, her smile ravishing when she wished to persuade or cajole, she brought off the trick of being a villainess whom everybody loved. After her final defeat, the joyful comic ensemble 'Luncheon is on the table', united the Chilterns on stage. Max and Amanda, Darcy, Lysander and Imogen proudly paraded in to luncheon.

Martyn and Maude were left alone together.

They both knew that the exchange before the reprise, inserted by Martyn just before the Bristol opening, had been the most dangerous moment of an evening which had ricocheted between joy and terror. Sir Robert Chiltern, his weakness exposed to his wife, sinks on to a chair, wrapped in thought. Martyn had not tampered with Wilde's delicate, oblique statement of forgiveness. Maude held her pause for what seemed an age and then, bending over Chiltern's chair, stretched out her hand and said simply: 'Aren't you coming in, Robert?'

Martyn looked up slowly, raking the house with his famous

wide eyes, looking for absolution. Then he took her hand. 'Gertrude,' he said, 'is it love you feel for me, or is it pity merely?'

Maude bent down to kiss him. 'It is love, Robert. Love and only love. For both of us a new life is beginning.'

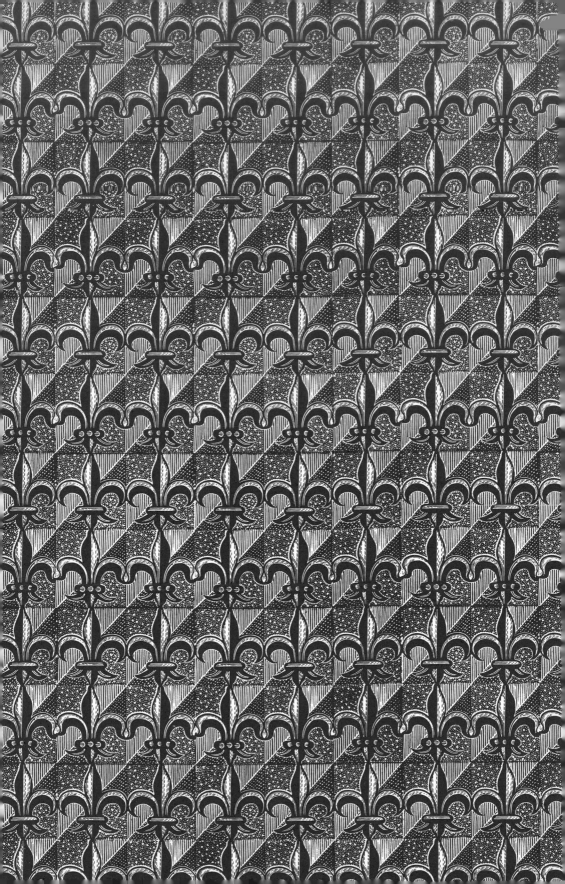